A-Z of Evergreen Trees & Shrubs

Staff for A-Z of Evergreen Trees & Shrubs (U.S.A.)
Senior Associate Editor: Theresa Lane

Contributors
Editor: Thomas Christopher
Art Director: Diane Lemonides
Editorial Assistants: Troy Dreier, Claudia Kaplan
Consulting Editor: Lizzie Boyd (U.K.)
Consultant: Dora Galitzki
Copy Editor: Sue Heinemann

READER'S DIGEST GENERAL BOOKS
Editor in Chief: John A. Pope, Jr.
General Books Editor, U.S.: Susan Wernert Lewis
Affinity Directors: Will Bradbury, Jim Dwyer, Kaari Ward
Art Director: Evelyn Bauer
Editorial Director: Jane Polley
Research Director: Laurel A. Gilbride
Group Art Editors: Robert M. Grant, Joel Musler
Copy Chief: Edward W. Atkinson
Picture Editor: Marion Bodine
Head Librarian: Jo Manning

The credits and acknowledgments that appear on page 176
are hereby made a part of this copyright page.

Originally published in partwork form.
Copyright © 1990 Eaglemoss Publications Ltd.

Based on the edition copyright © 1994
The Reader's Digest Association Limited.

Copyright © 1995 The Reader's Digest Association, Inc.
Copyright © 1995 The Reader's Digest Association (Canada) Ltd.
Copyright © 1995 Reader's Digest Association Far East Ltd.
Philippine Copyright 1995 Reader's Digest Association Far East Ltd.

Library of Congress Cataloging in Publication Data

A-Z of Evergreen Trees & Shrubs.
    p.   cm. — (Successful gardening)
  ISBN 0-89577-698-7 (hc) — ISBN 0-7621-0046-X (pbk)
  1. Ornamental trees—Encyclopedias.   2. Ornamental Shrubs —
  Encyclopedias. 3. Ornamental evergreens—Encyclopedias.
  I. Reader's Digest Association.   II. Title: A-Z of evergreen trees
  and shrubs.   III. Series.
  SB435.A225   1995
  635.9'76—dc20   94-47610

READER'S DIGEST and the Pegasus logo are registered trademarks of
The Reader's Digest Association, Inc.

Printed in the United States of America

Opposite: Low-growing heathers form a happy association with
dwarf conifers and thrive in the same conditions as rhododendrons.

Overleaf: In early summer the blue flowers of the *Ceanothus
thyrsiflorus repens* takes pride of place, yielding later to the
silver-blue spruce Picea pungens 'Kosteri" and the prostrate bright
green *Juniperus conferta*.

Pages 6-7: The constant green of an imposing conifer adds life
to a winter landscape rimmed by frost.

THE READER'S DIGEST ASSOCIATION, INC.
Pleasantville, New York / Montreal

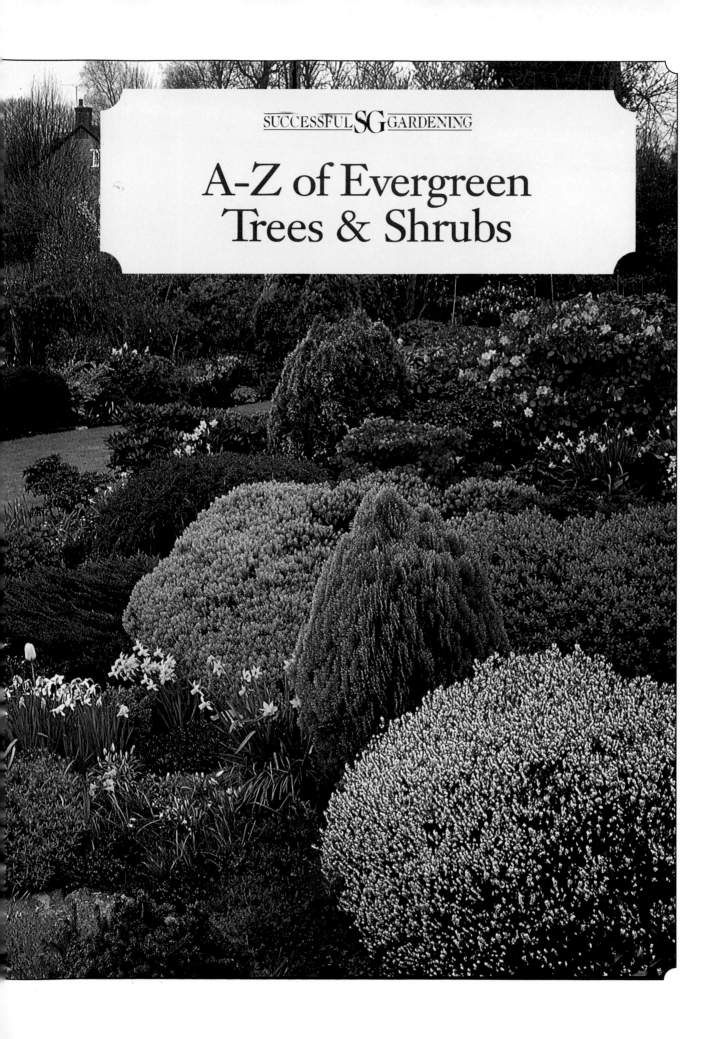

A-Z of Evergreen
Trees & Shrubs

CONTENTS

Special Features

A–Z of Evergreen Trees

A–Z of Evergreen Shrubs

Conifer plantings in a group A silver-blue spruce dominates a grouping of prostrate, pyramid, and dome-shaped conifers.

A–Z of Evergreen Trees

Most evergreen trees are conifers, native to the Northern Hemisphere. Although the huge forest conifers are unsuitable for most gardens, hundreds of cultivars have been bred from them that do not reach the overwhelming proportions of their wild ancestors. However, even nursery-bred conifers can outgrow a garden if the cultivar is poorly chosen to match the available spot — always consider the eventual height and spread when making a choice. The magnificent Atlas cedar, for example, should be planted only in very large gardens, but the related deodar cedar makes a splendid specimen tree for average gardens.

The spruces, pines, and cypresses all have spectacular cultivars with foliage in different colors and textures, from bunches of stiff needles to soft and feathery leaf sprays. Their habits are equally diverse: some produce tiers of symmetrical branches, while others form perfect cones or pyramids, slender columns, or broad, wide-spreading heads. Junipers are among the most accommodating conifers, suitable for small gardens. Their cultivars range from slender pillars to narrow pyramids and have green, gray, blue, or golden foliage. All bear small fleshy cones that look like berries.

Although there are only a few broad-leaved evergreen trees, they include the magnificent magnolias and live oaks of the South, the bright-berried hollies, and the graceful and aromatic eucalyptuses from Australia, which have proved superbly adapted to southern California and Arizona.

Grow evergreen trees in small groups where space allows, or in spectacular isolation as specimen plants, positioned so that their outlines and foliage can be admired and enjoyed throughout the year.

To help you determine if a particular tree will thrive in your area, we've given you zones that correspond to the plant hardiness map on page 176.

CHOOSING CONIFERS

Conifers — hardy, easy to grow, and colorful the year round — are among the most versatile of garden plants.

Conifers grow across the United States, flourishing in climates too extreme — too wet, cold, or dry — for most broad-leaved trees. In form, conifers range from tall and straight forest trees to dwarfs that creep across a rocky mountain face. But all conifers have needlelike foliage and the ability to bear seed-holding woody cones.

These plants offer the gardener an astonishing range of shapes, sizes, colors, and growth rates — making it difficult to choose just one conifer for your garden. Take care to match the plant to the spot. Majestic conifers, such as the Atlas cedar, the Douglas fir, or the blue spruce are suitable only for large gardens and park landscapes. Fast-growing conifers, like the eastern white pine and the Leyland cypress, are ideal for hedging and screening but do not work as ornamental specimens in average-size gardens.

Most conifers are evergreens, the exceptions being the larches, the bald cypress, and the dawn redwood, all of which shed their needles in fall. Evergreen conifers typically are hardy and long-lived, need little care once established, and add a sense of maturity to even a new garden. They contrast well with flowering plants and deciduous and broad-leaved evergreen trees and shrubs, and in winter provide the bulk of color in the garden.

Garden conifers

For the average-size garden it's sensible to select slow-growing conifers with limited spread. Choose columnar and pyramid-shaped types in preference to tall and wide-spreading ones. Numerous cultivars have been bred from the species, and there are conifers to suit gardens of every size and situation. Some conifers are genuinely dwarf, never exceeding 2 ft (60 cm) in height and spread. Others that are labeled dwarf may grow to medium-size trees but take decades to do so.

Dwarf conifers are especially useful for small gardens, since a whole range of colors, foliage, and

---

▼ **Conifer planting** The diversity of form, foliage, texture, color, and scale is given full expression in a group planting of mature conifers.

▲ **Conifer hedges** The western red cedar *(Thuja plicata)* is excellent for hedging. Its bright, glossy green foliage is pleasantly aromatic and responds well to clipping. It thrives in sun or shade and on alkaline soil.

▼ **Eastern white pine** Though the natural form of the eastern white pine *(Pinus strobus)* can reach 150 ft (45 m) high, it offers a number of fine compact cultivars, such as 'Pendula,' a picturesque dwarf form with gnarled, drooping branches.

forms can fit in a limited space. They are also suitable for window boxes, and the low-growing, wide-spreading types often make ideal ground covers. Dwarf conifers of all descriptions are perfect for a rock garden.

Garden centers and retail nurseries sell conifers, but the selection can be limited. However, specialized conifer nurseries offer hundreds of species and cultivars from which to choose.

Soil and site
Most conifers prefer a sunny, open site, but yews *(Taxus)* will grow in shade, and some yellow-foliaged conifers need light shade to prevent sun scorch. All conifers need good drainage. Neutral soil is ideal, but certain junipers *(Juniperus)*, pines *(Pinus)*, arborvitaes *(Thuja)*, and yews *(Taxus)* tolerate alkaline soil, and some pines and firs *(Abies)* prefer acid soil. The richer the soil, the faster the growth rate; so poor soil can be an advantage. Avoid frost pockets, as spring frosts can kill young growth. While some junipers, chamaecyparises, yews, and arborvitaes are used as windbreaks, other conifers need shelter from drying winds.

Using conifers
Conifers, particularly dwarf forms, have strong characters and should be selected and sited with care. Before choosing, consider what you want from each plant and where each species will perform best in the garden.

Year-round interest Conifers offer an array of year-round color in the garden. Foliage ranges from pale to rich yellow through pale, bright, and deep green to gray, silver-blue, and bronze.

Some conifers have variegated foliage or leaf undersides in a contrasting color. In others, juvenile and adult foliage differ or color changes dramatically in winter.

Cones vary considerably. Some are borne upright on the branches, others droop down; some are squat or barrel-shaped, others long and narrow, while still others, such as those of junipers *(Juniperus)*, resemble fleshy berries.

Beds and borders Dwarf conifers are often associated with heaths and heathers. They also mix well with low-growing hebes, cotoneasters, and brooms. They make lovely neighbors for spring

▲ **Colorado blue spruce** The 'Glauca' (blue) cultivar of the Colorado spruce *(Picea pungens)* is a superb selection for creating a focal point. This slow-growing, medium-size tree takes many years to reach maturity. Its horizontal branches are densely clothed with blue foliage. The color appears even more intense against a background of dark green trees.

▲▶ **Golden juniper** Superb as a ground cover, *Juniperus communis* 'Depressa Aurea' grows only 1 ft (30 cm) high but spreads its slender branches to 4 ft (1.2 m). The branches are packed with sprays of foliage that turn from butter-yellow in spring to golden in summer and bronze in winter. It glows most brightly in full sun.

▶ **Lawson cypress** A container-grown *Chamaecyparis lawsoniana* exerts a calming influence on the riotous colors of summer bedding plants. Conical in shape, with broad fanlike leaf sprays, it will thrive in this half barrel for several years and can then be transplanted into a garden bed.

bulbs and low-growing summer-flowering plants, such as shrubby cinquefoil and dianthus. Slow-growing, narrowly columnar conifers are ideal in large mixed borders, adding height and contrast to deciduous shrubs and herbaceous perennials.

Conifers as focal points Upright conifers, such as Rocky Mountain juniper (*Juniperus scopulorum* 'Skyrocket') make striking focal points above low-growing plants. The same is true for conifers shaped like pyramids, cones, globes, ovals, and domes. Weeping standards and irregular, picturesque forms have more impact as isolated specimen plants.

The perfect symmetry of upright shrubby or pyramidal conifers is ideal for adding formality to a garden. A pair of identical conifers flanking a front door or garden gate creates a welcoming impression, and the trees keep their form without clipping.

Conifer hedges Tall and fast-growing conifers, such as Leyland cypress (× *Cupressocyparis leylandii*) and false cypress *(Chamaecyparis lawsoniana),* are used for screening and shelterbelts. Even when kept in check by regular trimming, they will make a tall hedge. Use dwarf conifers for the compact hedge that edges a bed: a row of the globular dwarf pine (*Pinus mugo* 'Mops'), for example, or the conical golden false cypress (*Chamaecyparis lawsoniana* 'Minima Aurea') will make an elegant boundary between different garden areas.

Large conifer hedges and windbreaks cast shade and block the rain on their windward side as well as provide shelter, but their roots compete with nearby ornamental plants for moisture and nutrients. Dwarf conifer hedges cause no such problems, but they are more expensive; not only is the cost of each dwarf conifer high, but they must be planted close together for a solid effect.

Rock gardens For landscapes in miniature, dwarf conifers provide excellent scaled-down versions of windswept mountain trees. Weeping forms can cascade over rocks, and prostrate types can hug the ground in the company of sedums, sempervivums, and saxifrages. Slender columns of common juniper (*Juniperus communis* 'Compressa') or feathery globes of dwarf Japanese cedar

▲ **Flower-covered yew** Japanese yew *(Taxus cuspidata)* and Anglojap yew *(T. x media)* are frequently used for hedges. Here a yew hedge plays host to the bright red flowers of a climbing nasturtium.

◄ **Japanese spirals** Junipers respond well to close clipping and artistic topiary. Years of training and pruning have created an arresting focal point from the erect-growing, bright green *Juniperus chinensis* 'Kaizuka.'

(*Cryptomeria japonica* cultivars) add proportionate height.

Conifers as ground cover Provided you are prepared to weed by hand for the first 2 or 3 years, prostrate conifers make excellent ground covers, smothering weeds and hiding all traces of soil. They are a sensible alternative to lawns on sloping ground, as well as on steep or uneven banks where mowing is difficult and where soil erosion might occur.

Prostrate junipers, with their tidy, dense growth, are suitable ground-cover plants; *Juniperus* × *media* and *J. sabina* cultivars tolerate light shade. The creeping juniper *(J. horizontalis)* is ideal for ground cover, especially the blue-needled cultivars 'Wiltonii,' 'Blue Chip,' and 'Bar Harbor.'

Window boxes and containers The truly miniature conifers are ideal for container gardening. Upright forms that barely grow 1½ ft (45 cm) tall, such as the tiny *Juniperus communis* 'Compressa,' or slow-growing mounded forms such as the deodar cedar (*Cedrus deodara* 'Pygmaea') which grows ½ in (1.25 cm) in a year, make excellent companions for primroses and trailing ivy in a window box or for choice specimens in a trough garden.

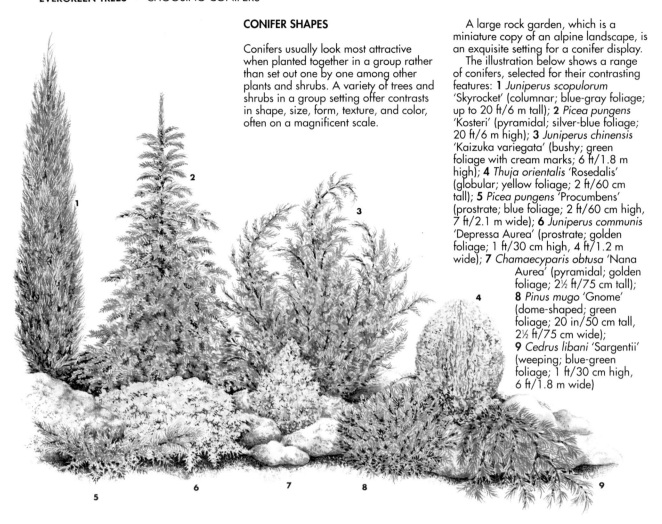

CONIFER SHAPES

Conifers usually look most attractive when planted together in a group rather than set out one by one among other plants and shrubs. A variety of trees and shrubs in a group setting offer contrasts in shape, size, form, texture, and color, often on a magnificent scale.

A large rock garden, which is a miniature copy of an alpine landscape, is an exquisite setting for a conifer display.

The illustration below shows a range of conifers, selected for their contrasting features: **1** *Juniperus scopulorum* 'Skyrocket' (columnar; blue-gray foliage; up to 20 ft/6 m tall); **2** *Picea pungens* 'Kosteri' (pyramidal; silver-blue foliage; 20 ft/6 m high); **3** *Juniperus chinensis* 'Kaizuka variegata' (bushy; green foliage with cream marks; 6 ft/1.8 m high); **4** *Thuja orientalis* 'Rosedalis' (globular; yellow foliage; 2 ft/60 cm tall); **5** *Picea pungens* 'Procumbens' (prostrate; blue foliage; 2 ft/60 cm high, 7 ft/2.1 m wide); **6** *Juniperus communis* 'Depressa Aurea' (prostrate; golden foliage; 1 ft/30 cm high, 4 ft/1.2 m wide); **7** *Chamaecyparis obtusa* 'Nana Aurea' (pyramidal; golden foliage; 2½ ft/75 cm tall); **8** *Pinus mugo* 'Gnome' (dome-shaped; green foliage; 20 in/50 cm tall, 2½ ft/75 cm wide); **9** *Cedrus libani* 'Sargentii' (weeping; blue-green foliage; 1 ft/30 cm high, 6 ft/1.8 m wide)

▶ **Dwarf Colorado spruce** Sharp blue needles are crowded along the branches of the dwarf *Picea pungens* 'Procumbens.' Rarely more than 2 ft (60 cm) high but eventually spreading to 7 ft (2.1 m), it forms the centerpiece in a group of shrubby conifers. Its silver-blue hues are accentuated by purple irises.

▼ **A clutch of conifers** Cones, pyramids, domes, and wide-spreading mounds are just a few of the shapes presented by conifers, which thrive in each other's company and blend happily with low-growing heathers.

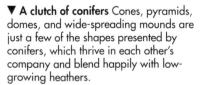

▲ **Fall colors** Golden conifers add shafts of light to a fall garden. They retain their brightness long after the deciduous shrubs have shed their vivid foliage.

▶ **Cedar of Lebanon** The slow-growing, graceful *Cedrus libani* 'Nana' droops its feathery foliage over a rug of heathers. It rarely exceeds 5 ft (1.5 m) in height but becomes flat-topped with age.

▼ **Sculptural juniper** Prostrate *Juniperus sabina* 'Tamariscifolia' drapes its horizontal green-blue branches over low stone walls and sunny banks, spreading almost indefinitely.

THE ART OF TOPIARY

**Through topiary, evergreen trees and shrubs are sculpted
into geometric designs or whimsical shapes to
enhance both modest and elaborate gardens.**

Topiary has a chameleon-like quality, changing its appearance to suit its surroundings. Roman nobles, Italian Renaissance royalty, and later the owners of America's great estates filled their gardens with topiary, but this art form is equally at home in modest modern-day settings.

Depending on its size, shape, and symbolism, topiary work can add dignity and style to a garden or display a sense of humor, and it often reveals a great deal about the owner's personality.

An obelisk or ball of greenery seen against neoclassical architecture, for example, reinforces its formal backdrop. In a small country garden, that same topiary serves as a pleasant contrast to the informality of the plants.

A tall, crenellated topiary hedge extending as far as the eye can see is a sign of wealth, as maintenance can be costly. In a suburban garden a scaled-down crenellated boundary hedge indicates tidiness, skill, patience, and a pride in gardening.

Choosing the plants

Topiary plants need a rigid woody framework; training and pruning are pointless if the branches hang limply or die back to ground level each fall. They should also have a dense (or potentially dense) growth habit so that the form fills out convincingly, and the plants should respond well to regular pruning.

Small leaves are best, since close clipping of large leaves, such as those of laurel, takes time to do attractively and looks sloppy if done in a hurry. The texture of large leaves, even from a distance, makes "reading" a geometric shape difficult, unless the topiary is very large.

Topiary plants are often evergreen or semievergreen, so they retain their shape and beauty throughout the year. Linden, hornbeam, hawthorn, and willow can also be pruned into ornamental shapes, such as interlaced arches lining a walkway. Such deciduous trees naturally grow thick and dense, and even when leafless, they appear solid.

Select suitable plants that grow reasonably quickly but not so fast that they exhaust themselves in a few years.

In spite of these requirements, there are many topiary plants from which to choose. Boxwood (*Buxus sempervirens*) and dwarf edging boxwood (*B. s.* 'Suffruticosa') are popular; other suitable broad-leaved evergreens include bay (*Laurus*), firethorn (*Pyracantha*), and holly (*Ilex*). Yew (*Taxus*) is the best conifer for topiary, especially for hedging; juniper (*Juniperus*) and cypress (*Cupressus*) are good options. Popular semievergreen shrubs are privet (*Ligustrum*) and evergreen honeysuckle (*Lonicera*).

Gold- or silver-leaved cultivars are stunning for topiary, especially when seen against a dark background. They are, however, often slower-growing than their all-green counterparts, and very strong variegation can distract from the overall clarity of form.

Ready-made topiary

Topiary adds individuality to a garden and creates a link, however lighthearted, with the past. A piece of topiary, even if bought fully trained, takes some of the rawness away from a new garden, in the same way that planting a large semimature tree does.

Topiary's main drawback is that it requires an ongoing commitment; it takes at least 5 years to train a small specimen, and

◀ **Bird sculptures** With its dense foliage, yew responds well to clipping, but creating topiary figures like these birds demands skill, patience, and artistic ability. It takes about 5 years to establish such impressive examples, but thereafter maintenance is simple.

even trained specimens need regular maintenance. If you are enthusiastic about topiary but contemplating a move, grow topiary plants in containers so that they can be easily transported.

Already-trained topiary comes in various sizes, often in geometric shapes or as lollipop-like boxwood *(Buxus)* or bay laurel *(laurus)* "standards." Because they take so long to train, ready-made topiary specimens can be very expensive. Another reason, apart from cost, for not opting for ready-made topiary is the greater personal satisfaction experienced every time you look at a perfectly shaped shrub that you started from a cutting or tiny rooted sprig. In either case, whether you spend time or money to create

---

◄ **Architectural designs** Deceptively simple, large-scale topiary pieces shaped as an archway, a horseshoe, and a lofty column create a formal elegance and a sense of tranquillity.

▼ **Cottage garden charm** This topiary "cottage," whose door is actually a garden's front gate, took 10 years to fashion from a yew hedge. A large wire frame hidden in the foliage marks where it must be clipped back annually.

▲ **Oriental topiary** Low-growing boxwood has been meticulously pruned into a string of Chinese characters. An annual trim preserves their shapes.

▼ **Visual art** A bold example of topiary in yew, complete with facial expression, demonstrates an alternative to formal geometric shapes.

▲ **Animal shapes** Some popular topiary designs, trained and pruned over wire frames, include peacocks, goats, pigs, and elephants.

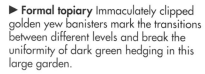

▶ **Formal topiary** Immaculately clipped golden yew banisters mark the transitions between different levels and break the uniformity of dark green hedging in this large garden.

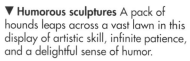

▼ **Humorous sculptures** A pack of hounds leaps across a vast lawn in this display of artistic skill, infinite patience, and a delightful sense of humor.

topiary, the expense will keep it rare and ensure that your specimens will stand out as unusual.

Types of topiary
Topiary work can be divided into two main types: architectural and sculptural.

Architectural topiary is often linear, in the form of hedges or edging, ranging in size from 1 ft (30 cm) to well above 6 ft (1.8 m). It can mark boundaries, extend the lines of the house into the garden, create interior garden "walls" to divide a large plot into smaller compartments, or neatly define beds, borders, and paths.

Large-scale architectural topiary can lead the eye to a lovely view or it can frame a small landscape scene. It can hide eyesores or unwanted views of a neighbor's home. You can also use architectural topiary to create three-dimensional garden buildings — cottages, castles, or whimsical structures of greenery.

Large-scale architectural topiary can take the form of a maze, with geometric hedges arranged in an intricate pattern that poses a puzzling challenge to all who enter. A related kind of garden feature is parterre, a carefully crafted pattern of low, clipped hedges that are interwoven to form a "knot," an arabesque, or other geometric pattern.

Sculptural topiary is used in the same way as garden sculptures made of stone: as freestanding, three-dimensional, garden ornaments and focal points. Sculptural topiary can enhance the main entrance to a garden or house, distinguishing it from less important gates or doors. Pairs of container-grown topiary plants can decorate a flight of steps for a sense of grandeur. Like architectural topiary, sculptural topiary ranges in size from little round bushes 8 in (20 cm) wide to large pieces 10 ft (3 m) or more high.

Architectural and sculptural topiary may also be combined. A crenellated topiary hedge can be topped at regular intervals by topiary sculptures, such as balls, animals, or cubes. Halfway between architectural and sculptural topiary are huge hedges, often yew *(Taxus)*, clipped into fluid abstract bulges and curves, resembling modern sculpture.

Formal topiary
In a sense, all topiary is formal, since plants are trained and pruned to form shapes they would not develop naturally. Geometric topiary, however, conveys more formal overtones than topiary in the shape of animals. Leafy ducks and cats, for example, signify a friendly character.

▲ **Evergreen colonnade** Topiary can richly enhance a planting design. This carefully trained and trimmed row of x *Cupressocyparis leylandii* provides an elegant see-through division between shrubbery and a flower border.

Much depends on symbolism and scale. A row of topiary peacocks across a grand lawn seems impressively formal, but a single peacock may seem quaint; likewise a single pyramid or sphere strikes a different note from a pattern using such objects.

Ideas for topiary
Simple geometric shapes, such as cubes, balls, cones, and pyramids, are easier to create than complex ones, which are likely to require special wire frames. You can prune geometric shapes starting at ground (or pot) level or fashion "lollipops" on standard or half-standard stems.

A more challenging approach is to stack two or more geometric shapes over each other on a straight trunk, as if stringing beads on a vertical necklace. A topiary cone, spiral, or pyramid can be topped with a topiary ball or cube. You can also trim a large topiary cone or pyramid to form two or three separate tiers, with gaps between, revealing the bare central trunk.

◀ **Topiary circus** A far cry from the formality of columns and obelisks, this tiny front yard is a showplace for the topiarist's sense of fun. Here, a horse and rider, a lion, and a baby elephant adorn the tall plinth of close-clipped hedge, turning a bit of suburbia into a circus.

▼ **Privet wizardry** Simple forms of topiary can be as arresting as complicated designs. Here, the ordinary privet (*Ligustrum ovalifolium*) and its golden cultivar 'Aureum' have been cleverly intertwined and clipped into roundels, thus creating a fascinating focal point by the waterside.

A topiary cube, ball, or cone can be topped by a topiary bird, or you can create pedestals — basically elongated cubes — of topiary and place a geometric shape or animal on top.

Tapering topiary obelisks can alternate with fruit trees or ornamental trees or simply line both sides of a driveway. To stop people from constantly taking shortcuts across a lawn, a small topiary hedge can be as effective as a fence and more ornamental.

You can spell out your name or the street number of your house in dwarf boxwood (*buxus*) topiary. Mounding the ground up to form an angled plane makes the topiary easier to "read."

In ancient Roman times high topiary hedges were clipped into a series of niches in which sculptures were displayed. Instead of sculptures, consider placing standard roses, fuchsias, or colorful annuals in the niches. Topiary alcoves holding a seat or bench also have classical origins but are still attractive today. Topiary walls over 3 ft (90 cm) high create a windbreak and introduce a sense of privacy. A topiary alcove large enough to hold a table and chairs is equally enchanting.

On a more modest scale, topiary in a large pot can conceal a utility cover or turn a tree stump into an attraction.

Cheating at topiary

You can achieve the effect of topiary with far less work by choosing dwarf conifer cultivars with

naturally geometric shapes, such as balls, columns, or cones. Besides giving you a head start on shaping, the use of dwarf forms reduces the clipping required for upkeep. If you want an instant ball shape, try *Cryptomeria japonica* 'Compressa,' a perfectly round miniature Japanese cedar; *Picea abies* 'Gregoryana,' a mounded miniature spruce; or the slow-growing cultivar *P. a.* 'Echiniformis.'

For columns, consider *Juniperus communis* 'Compressa,' a slender dwarf juniper, or the narrow blue-gray conifer *J. scopulorum* 'Skyrocket.' Conifers ideal for a conical shape include the golden dwarf false cypress (*Chamaecyparis lawsoniana* 'Aurea Densa') and the blue dwarf Oriental arborvitae (*Thuja orientalis* 'Blue Cone').

These dwarf conifers are effective in multiples and grown in containers. Maintain their shape by trimming any sprigs or shoots that break the shape in spring and early summer.

Abies

fir

Abies pinsapo, foliage

Abies pinsapo

- ❑ Height at 25 years 15-36 ft (4.5-11 m)
- ❑ Mature height 15-100 ft (4.5-30 m)
- ❑ Spread 6-35 ft (1.8-10.5 m)
- ❑ Moist, acid soil
- ❑ Hardy zones 3-7, depending on species
- ❑ Features: needlelike foliage; oval cones

Majestic firs are suitable for background planting, screening, or as specimen trees. Best adapted to cool, moist climates, firs flourish in the northern half of our country. A few species such as *Abies fraseri* grow well in the southeastern highlands; some do well at higher elevations in the Southwest. Its tiered branches form a conical shape with needlelike dark to gray-green leaves, which are often white underneath. The narrow, oval, erect cones, 2-4 in (5-10 cm) long, are borne on the upper branches of mature trees.

Popular species

Abies balsamea (balsam fir), a slow-growing tree, grows 45-75 ft (13.5-23 m) high and 20-25 ft (6-7.5 m) wide. The tree forms a symmetrical, narrow cone when young but is more rugged as it ages. Its dark green needles are banded with silver underneath. The cones are dark violet when young. It is hardy in zones 3-6.

Abies bracteata (bristlecone fir) grows quickly up to 30 ft (9 m) high and 15 ft (4.5 m) wide. It forms a pyramid with drooping lower branches, dark green needles banded with silver underneath, and bristly cones. Its tolerance of heat and drought makes it suitable for the Southwest. It is hardy to zone 7.

Abies concolor (white fir), hardy in zones 3-7, is 30-50 ft (9-15 m) high and 15-30 ft (4.5-9 m) wide. It has gray bark, gray-green leaves, and pale green cones with a purplish bloom. 'Candicans' (silver-white) is a cultivar.

Abies koreana (Korean fir) grows slowly to 15-30 ft (4.5-9 m) high and 6-12 ft (1.8-3.7 m) wide. This species is grown for its pink, green, or crimson flowers in late spring. It has sparse dark green leaves that are white underneath. Even young trees bear blue-green cones. It is hardy in zones 6-7. 'Compact Dwarf,' a neat, spreading cultivar, doesn't bear cones.

Abies lasiocarpa arizonica (Arizona fir), up to 33 ft (10 m) high and 12 ft (3.7 m) wide, is hardy in zones 5-7. It has gray corky bark, silvery-blue leaves, and brown cones. 'Compacta' is a cultivar.

Abies nordmanniana (Nordmann fir) grows 40-60 ft (12-18 m) high and 12-18 ft (3.7-5.5 m) wide. Glossy green needles with silvery undersides crown the branches. The brown cones are 6 in (15 cm) long. It is hardy in zones 5-7.

Abies pinsapo (Spanish fir), up to 20 ft (6 m) high and 8 ft (2.4 m) wide at 25 years, can reach 80 ft (24 m) high. It bears dark green leaves and purple-brown cones. This fir tolerates alkaline soils and is hardy to zone 6.

Abies veitchii is a fast-growing tree from 50-75 ft (15-23 m) tall and 25-35 ft (7.5-10.5 m) wide. It has a broad conical shape with dense green leaves. The mature tree bears small bluish-purple cones. It is hardy in zones 3-6.

Cultivation

Transplant firs in early spring as young burlapped specimens under 3 ft (90 cm) tall. They like full sun or light shade and do best in well-drained, moisture-retentive,

Abies lasiocarpa arizonica 'Compacta'

Abies koreana, cones

but slightly acid soils. *A. pinsapo* can tolerate dry and alkaline soil.

Mulch with shredded bark or pine needles; feed in late fall or early spring with a fertilizer created for acid-loving woody plants.
Pruning No pruning is required, except to retain a single trunk. If the leading shoot forks, cut the shoot farthest from the main axis flush with the main stem.
Pests/diseases Spruce budworm destroys buds; woolly aphids suck sap, making tufts of waxy white wool. Canker makes sunken areas on trunks and kills branches.

Abies koreana

Abies concolor

Abies lasiocarpa arizonica

Acacia

mimosa, silver wattle

Acacia dealbata

- ❏ Height at 25 years 20 ft (6 m)
- ❏ Mature height 30 ft (9 m)
- ❏ Spread 5 ft (1.5 m)
- ❏ Well-drained soil
- ❏ Hardy zones 8-10
- ❏ Features: broad-leaved foliage; flowers

Known in their native Australia as wattle trees, acacias flourish only in dry, warm climates; because they are notably drought and heat tolerant, they are one of the most valuable groups of plants for southern California and Arizona. One species, *Acacia dealbata*, will survive most winters in zone 8 if grown in the shelter of a warm, sunny wall.

Fast-growing trees or tall, multistemmed shrubs, acacias may produce feathery, much-divided leaves; broad, leathery leaves; or even flattened leafstalks that replace the foliage entirely. Many produce fragrant yellow flowers in late winter or spring.

Cultivation

In frost-free regions, plant young pot-grown specimens in early fall. Acacias need sun and shelter from winds and will grow in any well-drained soil; they are extremely drought tolerant.
Pruning If you remove the leaders when acacias are young, they form shrubs; if you leave the leaders and remove lower branches, they form trees.
Pests/diseases Trouble free.

Araucaria

monkey-puzzle tree

Araucaria araucana

- ❏ Height at 25 years 30 ft (9 m)
- ❏ Mature height 65 ft (20 m) or more
- ❏ Spread 10 ft (3 m)
- ❏ Rich, moist soil
- ❏ Hardy to zone 7 on sheltered site
- ❏ Features: foliage

An odd but striking specimen tree from Chile and Argentina, the slow-growing monkey-puzzle tree (*Araucaria araucana*) has stiff, ropelike branches. A young tree, which may take up to 10 years to reach a height of only 4 ft (1.2 m), grows in a broad columnar shape, becoming domed with age.

Suitable only for large gardens, the monkey-puzzle tree was popular with Victorian gardeners. It is notable for its symmetrical tiers of branches, which sometimes sweep upward, sometimes downward. The leathery, needlelike dark green leaves are rigid, with spines at the tips. They are set closely along the branches and point upward; it's said that a monkey can climb up but not down the tree — hence the name.

Monkey-puzzle trees are either male or female. Male trees bear clusters of banana-shaped catkins, which shed pollen in early summer before turning brown. Mature female trees bear globular cones, 6 in (15 cm) or more long, on the upper branches; they are covered with golden spines

Araucaria araucana, foliage

and take three years to mature before breaking up and expelling large seeds.

Cultivation

The monkey-puzzle tree thrives in moist but well-drained, slightly acid, loamy soil. The tree is highly wind resistant. Plant young container-grown specimen trees in midfall in the South and in early spring farther north.
Pruning None required.
Pests/diseases None serious.

ARBORVITAE — see *Thuja*

Arbutus

strawberry tree, madrone

Arbutus x andrachnoides

Arbutus unedo, flowers

Arbutus unedo, fruits

- ❑ Height at 25 years 12-25 ft (3.7-7.5 m)
- ❑ Mature height 20-75 ft (6-23 m)
- ❑ Spread 7-20 ft (2.1-6 m)
- ❑ Well-drained, acid soil
- ❑ Hardy zones 7-9
- ❑ Features: flowers; fruits; bark

Arbutus species are some of the loveliest evergreen trees for the garden. Their dark green oval leaves are decorated in spring or fall with sprays of white or pink urn-shaped flowers. The red or orange strawberry-like fruits are edible, though tasteless. The bark is attractive — the smooth top layer often peels, exposing new bark. See also page 62.

Popular species

Arbutus andrachne grows up to 20 ft (6 m) high and 15 ft (4.5 m) wide. It has smooth cinnamon-red bark and leathery dark green leaves, which are sometimes shallowly toothed. Sprays of white flowers appear in early spring to midspring, followed by orange-red fruits. The species is sensitive to frost when young, but if nursed along with winter protection and kept in a sheltered spot, it can survive as a mature tree as far north as zone 7.

Arbutus × andrachnoides, syn. *A. × hybrida*, reaching 12 ft (3.7 m) high and 7 ft (2.1 m) wide, has cinnamon-red bark and shallowly toothed, dark green leaves. Sprays of 3 in (7.5 cm) long ivory-white flowers appear in late fall or early spring to midspring. It can bear red fruits. The species is hardy in zones 7-9 and tolerates some alkalinity in the soil.

Arbutus menziesii (madrone) is up to 75 ft (23 m) high and nearly as wide in its native Pacific Northwest. The smooth reddish-brown bark peels away to reveal the young green bark beneath. The glossy dark green leaves are sometimes shallowly toothed. Upright sprays of white flowers appear in late spring and are followed by round orange-yellow fruits. The tree is hardy to zone 7.

Arbutus unedo can grow into a gnarled tree up to 40 ft (12 m) tall but is more typically 15 ft (4.5 m) high and 10 ft (3 m) wide. It has deep brown, rough and shredding bark, which is red underneath, and shiny toothed leaves. The drooping white or pink flower clusters appear in fall, often at the same time as the orange-red fruits. It is hardy in zones 7-9.

Cultivation

Using well-drained loam, plant in fall in the South or in spring in zone 7; *A. × andrachnoides* and *A. unedo* tolerate some alkalinity. *A. menziesii* is best transplanted when a seedling less than 1½ ft (45 cm) tall. All species prefer full sun and a sheltered site.

Pruning Cut back straggly shoots in midspring.

Pests/diseases Leaf spot shows as small brown spots.

CEDAR — see *Cedrus*

Cedrus
cedar

Cedrus deodara, cones

Cedrus atlantica 'Pendula'

Cedrus deodara (young tree)

❏ Height at 25 years 10-40 ft (3-12 m)
❏ Mature height 40-70 ft (12-21m)
❏ Spread 30-50 ft (9-15 m) or more
❏ Any well-drained soil
❏ Hardy zones 6-9, depending on species
❏ Features: beautiful specimen trees; handsome foliage

The long-lived cedars serve as magnificent and aromatic specimen trees for large lawns. The young tree is usually conical but may lose its lower branches later, revealing a large, smooth, dark gray trunk and becoming broad and flat-topped. The species are too large for most gardens, but several compact, slow-growing, or dwarf cultivars are available — including weeping trees — for smaller gardens.

The slender needlelike leaves are carried in tufts arranged spirally along the branches. They grow in shades of green, gray-green, or golden yellow and range from 1-2 in (2.5-5 cm) long. Male flowers stud the branches with a display of bright yellow in fall and shed clouds of golden pollen. Mature trees carry upright, barrel-shaped cones; these cones can grow up to 5 in (13 cm) long on the upper branches.

Popular species
Cedrus atlantica (Atlas cedar) is a fast-growing species from the Atlas Mountains of North Africa. It commonly grows to a height of 40-60 ft (12-18 m) with a spread of 30-40 ft (9-12 m). The tree has dark green foliage and horizontal branches that reach slightly upward when young. The cones are up to 4 in (10 cm) long. Cultivars include 'Aurea' (golden yellow foliage), 'Fastigiata' (narrow; upright; gray-blue foliage), 'Glauca' (blue cedar; silver-blue foliage), 'Glauca Pendula' (weeping form of 'Glauca'), and 'Pendula' (slow-growing when young; weeping branches; green to gray-green foliage). It is hardy in zones 6-9.
Cedrus deodara (deodar cedar), from the western Himalayas, commonly reaches a height of 40-70 ft (12-21 m) with an almost equal spread. It has gracefully drooping branches and blue-gray young leaves that mature to dark green. Cultivars include 'Albospica' (young shoots have cream-white tips), 'Aurea' (to 10 ft/3 m high, 6 ft/1.8 m wide; grows slowly; golden young foliage in spring; matures to greenish-yellow), 'Aurea Pendula' (weeping form of 'Aurea'), 'Pendula' (top-grafted

tree, reaching up to 3 ft/90 cm high; wide-spreading pendulous branches), and 'Pygmaea' (slow-growing dwarf cultivar; forms a small mound; blue-green foliage; suitable for a rock garden or in a trough garden). This species is hardy in zones 7-8.
Cedrus libani (cedar of Lebanon), from Syria and Turkey, is a fairly slow-growing tree that usually reaches 40-60 ft (12-18 m) high and 30-50 ft (9-15 m) wide. Its large, horizontal branches form a cone shape when young, though when mature, the tree has a tiered, flat-topped appearance. The leaves are dark green or banded with silver-blue. Cones are produced only on extremely

Chamaecyparis
false cypress

Chamaecyparis obtusa 'Crippsii'

❏ Height at 25 years 12-30 ft (3.7-9 m)
❏ Mature height 30-75 ft (9-23 m)
❏ Spread 3-12 ft (1-3.7 m); 10-30 ft (3-9 m) at maturity
❏ Any well-drained soil
❏ Hardy zones 5-8, depending on species
❏ Features: form; foliage color

Cedrus libani 'Nana'

old trees. Dwarf and weeping cultivars suitable for small gardens include 'Aurea Prostrata' (slow-growing; almost prostrate; yellow foliage), 'Comte de Dijon' (slow-growing; of conical habit; densely clothed branches; up to 5 ft/1.5 m high and wide); 'Nana' (compact conical shrub; slow-growing; eventually reaches 5 ft/1.5 m high and wide), and 'Sargentii' (slow-growing; blue-green foliage; weeping if the short trunk is staked, otherwise prostrate; suitable for a rock garden).

Cultivation
Cedars do best in any reasonably moist and fertile, well-drained soil. Plant container-grown specimens that are between 1-1½ ft (30-45 cm) high with a single, well-developed leading shoot in early fall or spring. For the first few years apply a fertilizer that is formulated for trees and shrubs in early spring.

Cedrus deodara and its cultivars do best in a lightly sheltered site when growing in the northern end of their range.
Pruning Prune to maintain a single leader. On older trees, remove lower branches when they begin to deteriorate, cutting them

off flush with the bole from late winter to midspring.
Pests/diseases Cedars may be killed by various root-rot fungi.

These fine specimen trees offer a vast range of form and color. They are excellent for screening, hedging, or background planting in almost any situation.

The tiny leaves are borne in flattened sprays or plumes and come in shades of green, blue-green, gray-green, and golden yellow. A false cypress tree may be open or dense and form a cone, pyramid, or pillar shape.

For shrubby and dwarf forms of false cypress, see pages 76-79.

Popular species
Chamaecyparis lawsoniana (Lawson cypress), a fast-growing conical tree from California and Oregon, grows 40-60 ft (12-18 m) high and 20-30 ft (6-9 m) wide. It has drooping branches with fan-like sprays of dark green leaves with white marks beneath. Clusters of red male flowers appear in midspring. Cultivars are more popular for garden planting than the species. These include 'Allumii' (30 ft/9 m high and 8 ft/2.4 m wide; columnar; blue-gray foliage), 'Columnaris' (narrow column; 15 ft/4.5 m high, 3 ft/90 cm

Cedrus atlantica 'Glauca'

Chamaecyparis lawsoniana 'Lutea'

wide; pale gray foliage), 'Fletcheri' (grows slowly; columnar; up to 12 ft/3.7 m or more high, 5 ft/1.5 m wide; several main stems; gray-green foliage, bronze in winter), 'Lane' (20 ft/6 m high, 8 ft/2.4 m wide; columnar; bright golden, feathery foliage), 'Lutea' (24 ft/7.3 m high, 8 ft/2.4 m wide; columnar; golden foliage), 'Stewartii' (25 ft/7.5 m high, 10 ft/3 m wide; golden yellow foliage), 'Triumph of Boskoop' (40 ft/12 m high, 10 ft/3 m wide; vigorous; dense conical habit; gray-blue foliage), 'Winston Churchill' (up to 25 ft/7.5 m high, 8 ft/2.4 m wide; broad column; rich gold foliage), and 'Wisselii' (up to 30 ft/9 m high, 8 ft/2.4 m wide; slender column; blue-green foliage). This species is hardy in zones 6-8.

Chamaecyparis noonotkatensis (Nootka cypress), from the Pacific Northwest, is a conical tree, growing 30-45 ft (9-13.5 m) tall and 10-15 ft (3-4.5 m) wide. It has drooping branches and flattened sprays of dark green foliage, which smells pungent when crushed. The cultivar 'Pendula' has upcurved branches with drooping branchlets. This species is hardy in zones 5-7.

Chamaecyparis obtusa (Hinoki cypress), a Japanese tree, reaches a height of 25 ft (7.5 m) and a spread of 10 ft (3 m) in 25 years; it may finally grow up to 50-75 ft (15-23 m) tall. It has upward-sweeping branches and flattened sprays of bright green leaves with

Chamaecyparis nootkatensis 'Pendula'

silvery undersides. 'Crippsii' is a pyramid-shaped, slow-growing cultivar up to 15 ft (4.5 m) high and 8 ft (2.4 m) wide, with young golden foliage that turns dark green. It is hardy in zones 5-8.

Chamaecyparis pisifera (Sawara cypress), a conical Japanese tree, reaches up to 20 ft (6 m) high and 8 ft (2.4 m) wide at 25 years, with an eventual height of 50-70 ft (15-21 m). This tree has horizontal sprays of bright green foliage with silver lines beneath. The older trees may lose their lower branches. Cultivars, more commonly seen than the species, include 'Filifera' (15 ft/4.5 m high, 10 ft/3 m wide; pyramid shape; threadlike dark gray-green foliage), 'Filifera Aurea' (like 'Filifera' but slow-growing; golden foliage), 'Plumosa' (25 ft/7.5 m high, 10 ft/3 m wide; pale green, fluffy foliage), and 'Squarrosa' (30 ft/9 m high, 20 ft/6 m wide;

broad and conical; upswept blue-gray foliage). The species is hardy in zones 5-8.

Cultivation
False cypresses thrive in any ordinary well-drained but moisture-retentive garden soil in full sun or light shade. Golden cultivars show the best color in full sun. The best time to plant balled-and-burlapped or container-grown trees is in midfall in the South and midspring in the North.

Pruning Rarely necessary, except to maintain a single leading shoot if forking occurs. Long branches that spoil the shape should be cut back.

Pests/diseases Root-rot fungi may attack Lawson cypress.

Cryptomeria

Japanese cedar

Cryptomeria japonica 'Elegans'

- ❏ Height at 25 years 20-40 ft (6-12 m)
- ❏ Mature height 50-60 ft (15-18 m)
- ❏ Spread 15-16 ft (4.5-4.9 m); 20-30 ft (6-9 m) at maturity
- ❏ Moist but well-drained, acid soil
- ❏ Hardy zones 6 to northern zone 9
- ❏ Features: elegant form; attractive foliage

An excellent specimen tree, the Japanese cedar *(Cryptomeria japonica)* forms a neat cone when young, spreading into a more open form as it ages. Mature trees have soft, stringy, orange-brown shredding bark and decorative sprays of tiny, round brown cones at the end of their shoots. The tiny dark green or blue-green leaves are awl-shaped.

The species is a large, fast-growing tree up to 40 ft (12 m) high and 16 ft (4.9 m) wide after 25 years. Smaller, slower-growing cultivars include 'Elegans' (just 15 ft/4.5 m high, 12 ft/3.7 m wide; feathery blue-green foliage, bronze-red in winter) and 'Lobbii' (30 ft/9 m high, 15 ft/4.5 m wide; longer branchlets; rich green).

For dwarf and shrubby cultivars, see pages 87-88.

Cultivation

Plant in slightly acid, deep, moist but well-drained soil. This species prefers a sunny site that is protected from the wind.

Plant young container-grown trees, up to 2 ft (60 cm) high, in early fall to midfall in the South or in midspring in the North.

Top-dress the area over the roots annually in early spring with a fertilizer formulated for evergreen trees and shrubs. Keep young plants moist and clear of any weeds.

Pruning Prune only to maintain a single leader.

Pests/diseases Leaf spot and leaf blight may cause dieback, especially in the Southeast.

× Cupressocyparis

Leyland cypress

× *Cupressocyparis leylandii*

- ❏ Height at 25 years 60 ft (18 m)
- ❏ Mature height up to 100 ft (30 m)
- ❏ Spread a fifth or an eighth of height
- ❏ Any well-drained soil
- ❏ Hardy zones 7-9
- ❏ Features: fast-growing; tolerates windswept sites

The graceful Leyland cypress *(× Cupressocyparis leylandii)*, a popular choice for hedging and screening, is one of the fastest-growing conifers. This species is a cross between *Cupressus macrocarpa* and *Chamaecyparis nootkatensis*. Growing at an annual rate of 5 ft (1.5 m) when young, this cypress can easily grow 60 ft (18 m) high and 15 ft (4.5 m) wide within 25 years. The species can eventually achieve a height of 100 ft (30 m), though with frequent pruning it can be kept much smaller and trimmed into a formal shape.

As a specimen tree, the Leyland cypress rapidly forms a dense, tall column. It is extremely vigorous, making it well suited for use as a windbreak or tall boundary hedge at the perimeter of the yard. Because it can adapt to acid and alkaline soils and is tolerant of salt spray, heat, and humidity, this is perhaps the finest conifer for the Southeast.

The dense foliage of scalelike leaves is held in flattened or irregular, slightly drooping sprays and is blue-green in the species. Mature trees bear small cones.

Available cultivars include 'Castlewellan' (plumelike young foliage that is golden yellow, maturing to bronze-green; slower-

Cupressus

cypress

× *Cupressocyparis leylandii*
'Castlewellan'

Cupressus macrocarpa

Cupressus lusitanica

growing than green forms; suitable for hedging), 'Haggerston Gray' (dark gray-green foliage in irregular sprays; it rarely cones), 'Leighton Green' (tall columnar tree; widely planted for screening; rich green foliage; bears cones often and plentifully), 'Naylor's Blue' (narrow column; gray-green foliage, bluish gray in winter), 'Robinson's Gold' (compact; broad column; golden foliage, bronze in spring), and 'Silver Dust' (very similar to 'Leighton Green' but foliage differs — it's strongly speckled with creamy white).

Cultivation
Plant container-grown trees in mid- to late spring in any ordinary well-drained soil that allows deep rooting and in sun. These conifers tolerate both alkaline and acid soils and coastal exposure but require full sun. Specimens that reach a mature height on shallow soil may blow over in a high wind. If planting young trees for hedging, space them about 1½-2 ft (45-60 cm) apart.
Pruning Clip established hedges and screens annually in late spring. Avoid cutting into old growth, or dieback will occur.
Pests/diseases None serious.

❏ Height 20-50 ft (6-15 m)
❏ Spread 2½-20 ft (75-600 cm)
❏ Any well-drained soil
❏ Hardy zones 7-9
❏ Features: decorative specimen

Cypresses may form a pyramid or cone, densely clothed with sprays of scaly leaves in shades of deep green to blue-green or gold. For dwarf cypresses, see page 88.

Popular species and cultivars
Cupressus arizonica (Arizona cypress), a conical tree that grows 30-40 ft (9-12 m) tall and 15-20 ft (4.5-6 m) wide, flourishes in hot, dry conditions and full sun. Its blistered purple bark peels off to reveal yellow patches. The blue-gray leaves often have white spots. The profuse male flowers are yellow. The cultivar 'Gareei' has silver-blue foliage. This

Cupressus arizonica, cones

species is hardy in zones 7-9.
Cupressus lusitanica (Mexican cypress), up to 50 ft (15 m) high, is a graceful tree with gray-green foliage on drooping branchlets. Hardy only to zone 8, it is a good conifer for the Southwest.
Cupressus macrocarpa (Monterey cypress) from coastal California is a fast-growing columnar species up to 50 ft (15 m) high and 12 ft (3.7 m) wide. It becomes flat-topped and open with age. The foliage is a rich dark green. This species is hardy in zones 7-9 but doesn't tolerate the humidity of the Southeast and is prone to disease outside its natural range.
Cupressus sempervirens 'Stricta' (Italian cypress) forms a narrow dark green column up to 25 ft (7.5 m) high and 2½ ft (75 cm) wide. It is hardy in zones 7-9.

Cultivation
Plant container-grown trees in early fall or midspring in any well-drained soil in sun.
Pruning Prune to maintain a single leader in spring.
Pests/diseases *C. macrocarpa* is prone to coryneum canker fungus, mostly outside coastal areas.

CYPRESS — see *Chamaecyparis,* × *Cupressocyparis,* and *Cupressus*
DEODAR CEDAR — see *Cedrus*
DOUGLAS FIR — see *Pseudotsuga*

Eucalyptus

eucalyptus, gum tree

Eucalyptus globulus

Eucalyptus dalrympleana

❏ Height at 25 years 10-165 ft (3-50 m)
❏ Mature height 10-200 ft (3-60 m)
❏ Spread 10-50 ft (3-15 m)
❏ Well-drained but moisture-retentive soil
❏ Hardy zones 7-10, depending on species
❏ Features: graceful form; interesting foliage and bark

There are hundreds of different species of *Eucalyptus,* and the vast number of trees in this genus grow in an enormous range of sizes. With a few exceptions, eucalyptuses are natives of Australia and Tasmania. They have naturalized in California, however, and in many regions they are one of the most common trees.

Renowned for their outstanding aromatic foliage and patterned bark, these trees thrive in heat and drought and provide some of the finest shade trees for California and Arizona. Although fast-growing, eucalyptuses are commonly long-lived.

The juvenile leaves, which grow on wood up to 3 years old, are usually round or oval; they may differ from the adult leaves, which are oval or lance-shaped. The leaves range in color from glistening silvery-white to gray or pale to dark green. Unpruned trees will flower when they reach 4 to 6 years old. The fluffy flowers are white, rose, or red and produce a sweet scent.

Popular species

Eucalyptus coccifera (Tasmanian snow gum, Mount Wellington peppermint) grows 25 ft (7.5 m) high and 10 ft (3 m) wide. Its bark peels away in long strips, revealing white patches underneath. The juvenile leaves are gray; the 2½ in (6.25 cm) long, peppermint-scented adult leaves are silver-gray. This species flowers in early summer and is hardy to zone 8.

Eucalyptus dalrympleana (mountain gum) can grow 100 ft (30 m) high and 25 ft (7.5 m) or more wide. Its bark is a patchwork of cream, brown, and pink. The oval juvenile leaves are dark green or blue-green; the pendulous, light green adult leaves are up to 9 in (23 cm) long and 1 in (2.5 cm) wide. The tree flowers in fall and is hardy to zone 8.

Eucalyptus erythronema (red-flowered mallee) makes a small, bushy tree 10-25 ft (3-7.5 m) tall, with narrow, dull green leaves and smooth bark in patches of pink, white, tan, and green. The 1 in (2.5 cm) wide flowers range from pink to deep red. Hardy to the warmer parts of zone 8, this is an excellent tree for irrigated desert plantings.

Eucalyptus globulus (blue gum) makes a towering tree, growing up to 150-200 ft (45-60 m) tall. The rounded juvenile foliage, which persists into the second and third year, clasps the stems and is silvery-gray in color. The adult leaves are narrowly lance-shaped, blue-green, and grow to 10 in (25 cm) long. The bark is smooth and bluish white when newly exposed. Creamy white to yellow flowers appear in late winter to early spring. This tree is hardy to zone 8 and needs deep soil. It makes an ideal windbreak or background tree but is too big and too messy (it strews the ground with debris) for growing in highly cultivated areas.

Eucalyptus niphophila

Eucalyptus parvifolia, bark

Eucalyptus perriniana (round-leaved snow gum) grows 15-30 ft (4.5-9 m) tall if left unpruned; it is best kept compact with shears and saw. Its bark is gray, blotched with brown. The silvery juvenile leaves join at their bases to make disks that are pierced at the center by the stem; the leaves remain on the shoots long after they have died and spin in the wind. This species bears small white flowers in summer. It is hardy to zone 8 and, when kept cut back, makes a fine gray plant for a border.

Eucalyptus pulverulenta (silver mountain gum) makes a sprawling tree 15-30 ft (4.5-9 m) high, with attractive white and pale

Eucalyptus gunnii (cider gum) reaches a height of 40-75 ft (12-23 m), making a dense, upright tree. The juvenile leaves are silver-blue and round; the adult foliage is lance-shaped, smooth, and green. Excellent as a shade tree, windbreak, or screen, the cider gum bears small cream-white flowers in late spring. It is marginally hardy in zone 7.

Eucalyptus niphophila (snow gum), reaching up to 20 ft (6 m) high and wide, typically forms a picturesque crooked trunk. Its ornamental peeling bark is mottled green, gray, cream, and brown-red. The sparse juvenile foliage is pale green, and the 4 in (10 cm) long adult leaves are lance-shaped and silvery blue. Clusters of white flowers appear in early summer. This species, one of the hardiest of the genus, is capable of thriving in the warmer parts of zone 7.

Eucalyptus parvifolia (small-leaved gum), 30 ft (9 m) high and 20 ft (6 m) wide, thrives on dry, alkaline soil. It has small, narrow, blue-green juvenile and adult leaves. It flowers in midsummer and is hardy to zone 8.

Eucalyptus pauciflora, syn. **E. coriacea**, is known as the ghost gum. It makes a spreading tree 40 ft (12 m) high and wide, with a white trunk and branches and narrow gray-green leaves. Unlike many eucalyptuses, this species is not very messy and makes a fine lawn tree. Hardy through zone 7, it will survive temperatures as low as 0°F (-18°C).

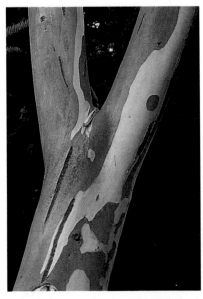

Eucalyptus niphophila, bark

Eucalyptus gunnii

Eucalyptus gunnii, juvenile foliage

Eucalyptus perriniana, adult foliage

brown peeling bark. The silver-gray, stem-hugging, oval juvenile leaves, which are good for making wreaths, are similar to the adult leaves. The flowers appear in spring. It is hardy to zone 9 or the warmer parts of zone 8.

Eucalyptus sideroxylon (red iron-bark) is a variable tree that grows 20-80 ft (6-24 m) tall, depending on the cultivar. Consult with the nursery to choose a specimen with the growth habit you desire: tall and slender or short and spreading, dense or open, even weeping. The rugged bark is nearly black, and the foliage is slender and blue-green, turning bronze in winter. From fall to late spring, this species bears fluffy pink to crimson flowers. It is generally hardy to zone 8.

Cultivation
Select vigorous, compact trees; container-grown stock is good, but check to make sure the roots are not cramped and circling the soil ball, a condition that will stunt the tree's growth. Plant the tree in a sunny site from fall to spring. Water regularly for the first year or two as the young tree roots, but avoid overwatering thereafter; occasional deep irrigations during dry spells are all that is necessary.

Pruning Avoid pruning from May to October in regions where the eucalyptus longhorn beetle is a problem. Unchecked, most eucalyptus species rapidly form tall, narrow trees, but the trees can be pruned to almost any size and shape. To create a round-topped tree, cut out the tip of a young specimen in early summer; this will encourage the growth of new side shoots.

For species where the juvenile foliage is preferred, cut the main stems back almost to the ground annually in spring, just as growth begins to appear.

Pests/diseases Eucalyptus long-horn beetle attacks stressed trees in California and causes dieback or the death of the plant.

Eucalyptus coccifera, bark

FALSE CYPRESS —
see *Chamaecyparis*
FIR — see *Abies*
FIR, DOUGLAS —
see *Psuedotsuga*
GUM TREE — see *Eucalyptus*
HEMLOCK — see *Tsuga*
HOLLY — see *Ilex*

Ilex

holly

Ilex opaca

Ilex aquifolium, yellow-berried form

Ilex aquifolium, species form

❏ Height at 25 years 5-25 ft (1.5-7.5 m)
❏ Mature height 10-50 ft (3-15 m)
❏ Spread 5-20 ft (1.5-6 m)
❏ Ordinary soil
❏ Hardy zones 6-9, depending on species
❏ Features: foliage; berries

Grown for its glossy evergreen foliage and brilliant red or yellow berries, the holly tree provides interest throughout the year. The leaves are often spiny and many forms have interesting variegations. *Ilex* is excellent as a specimen tree and is a good choice for hedging and screens.

In growth habit, hollies vary from shrubs (see pp.118-119) to tall and dense trees, although they grow slowly. In most species, male and female flowers are borne on separate trees; for a female to produce berries, a male must be planted nearby.

Popular species

Ilex aquifolium (English holly), up to 25 ft (7.5 m) high and 15 ft (4.5 m) wide, has dark green spiny leaves and red berries. Cultivars offer variegated leaves, weeping forms, and yellow berries. It is hardy in zones 6-9.

Ilex opaca (American holly) grows up to 40-50 ft (12-15 m) high and 18-40 ft (5.5-12 m) wide, though a height of 15-30 ft (4.5-9 m) is more common. It is hardy in zones 5-9. The large spiny, elliptical leaves are dark yellow-green to lustrous green. Red berries appear in fall and persist into winter. Hundreds of cultivars offer variegated foliage, yellow and orange fruits, and compact forms.

Ilex vomitoria (cassina, yaupon) is hardy from zones 7-10. It forms an irregularly branched small tree up to 15-20 ft (4.5-6 m) tall with a somewhat lesser spread. It has ovate, slightly toothed leaves and bears an abundance of scarlet berries, which persist through the winter. It tolerates humid heat, making it ideal for the Deep South; its tolerance for alkaline soils makes it useful in many areas in the West. 'Pendula,' a weeping form, is a fine cultivar.

Cultivation

Plant in midfall or early spring to midspring in sun or partial shade. Hollies prefer moist but well-drained, loamy, slightly acid soil.

Pruning Clip to shape after new growth hardens.

Pests/diseases Leaf spot and holly leaf miner may disfigure foliage; canker may cause dieback of branches. Scale insects and spider mites may also infest hollies.

JAPANESE CEDAR — see *Cryptomeria*

Ilex aquifolium, variegated weeping form

Juniperus

juniper

Juniperus chinensis 'Aurea'

Juniperus scopulorum 'Blue Heaven'

Juniperus recurva coxii

- ❑ Height at 25 years 10-20 ft (3-6 m)
- ❑ Mature height 15-50 ft (4.5-15 m)
- ❑ Spread 1-20 ft (30-600 cm)
- ❑ Any well-drained soil
- ❑ Hardy zones 2-9, depending on species
- ❑ Features: attractive shape and foliage; berrylike cones

Junipers thrive in most soils and situations, including dry and alkaline soils. They range in form from creeping and prostrate types (see pp.121-123) to narrow, pillar-shaped trees or broad pyramids. They are ideal in rock gardens.

Junipers have two types of foliage: prickly, awl-shaped juvenile leaves and scalelike adult leaves. Some species have both types of foliage at the same time, but most have only juvenile foliage.

The black or blue fleshy cones resemble hard, knobbed berries.

Popular species

Juniperus chinensis (Chinese juniper) is a conical and bushy tree up to 15 ft (4.5 m) high and 4 ft (1.2 m) wide. It bears dull green adult and bluish-green juvenile foliage. Male trees bear yellow flowers; females bear bright blue-black fruits. The species has been superseded by its popular cultivars, including 'Aurea' (Young's golden juniper; male; grows slowly; columnar; to 10 ft/3 m high, 4 ft/1.2 m wide; golden foliage), 'Keteleeri' (narrow; 15 ft/4.5 m high, 3 ft/1 m wide; vivid green adult leaves; profuse fruits), and 'Stricta' (slow-growing; conical; to 20 ft/6 m high, 4 ft/1.2 m wide; blue-gray juvenile foliage). This species is hardy in zones 3-9.

Juniperus communis (common juniper) is a small tree or large shrub with aromatic juvenile foliage. It grows wild worldwide, including North America. The true species is rarely seen in gardens. A popular cultivar is 'Hibernica' (syn. 'Stricta;' Irish juniper; narrow column; to 12 ft/3.7 m high, 2½ ft/75 cm wide, gray-blue foliage). It is hardy in zones 2-7.

Juniperus recurva (drooping juniper) is a small conical tree or shrub, up to 15 ft (4.5 m) high and 8 ft (2.4 m) wide. It has gray-green adult foliage and drooping branchlets. A good garden type is *J. recurva coxii* (coffin juniper; to 20 ft/6 m high, 6 ft/1.8 m wide; longer, more pendulous branches; sage-green leaves). This species is hardy to zone 8.

Juniperus rigida (needle juniper) is a wide-branched, pyramid-shaped tree, up to 20 ft (6 m) high and 8 ft (2.4 m) wide. The slender, pendent branches have yellow-green juvenile foliage, bronze in winter. It is hardy to zone 6.

Juniperus scopulorum (Rocky Mountain juniper) is a conical cypresslike tree, sometimes with several trunks. Up to 40 ft (12 m) high and 15 ft (4.5 m) wide, it has light green to blue-green adult leaves. Cultivars include 'Blue

Juniperus scopulorum 'Skyrocket'

Heaven' (narrow; bright silver-blue foliage), 'Gray Gleam' (pyramidal; slow-growing; silver-gray foliage), 'Pathfinder' (narrow, conical; bluish gray foliage), and 'Skyrocket' (narrow column; up to 20 ft/6 m high, 1 ft/30 cm wide; blue-gray foliage). This species is hardy in zones 3-7.

Juniperus virginiana (eastern red cedar) is up to 50 ft (15 m) high and 20 ft (6 m) wide. The

Juniperus virginiana

Juniperus communis 'Hibernica'

pointed adult leaves are dark green. The tree also bears some grayish juvenile foliage. Cultivars include 'Burkii' (narrow pyramid; steel-blue foliage, bronze-purple in winter), 'Canaertii' (conical; bright green foliage; shiny blue fruits), and 'Pendula' (20 ft/6 m high, 8 ft/2.4 m wide; drooping branchlets; green foliage). This species is hardy in zones 2-9.

Cultivation
In midspring plant container-grown or balled-and-burlapped stock in ordinary well-drained garden soil; choose a sunny spot.
Pruning Cut back straggly shoots to the main stem.
Pests/diseases Twig blight may kill branches or, rarely, entire trees. Mites, scale insects, bagworms, and webworms may infest junipers. Cedar-apple rust causes 1 in (2.5 cm) galls to form on leaves; galls sprout orange hornlike projections in spring.

LEYLAND CYPRESS — see × *Cupressocyparis*
MADRONE — see *Arbutus*

Magnolia

magnolia

Magnolia delavayi

- ❏ Height at 25 years 10-30 ft (3-9 m)
- ❏ Mature height 35-80 ft (10.5-24 m)
- ❏ Spread 10-50 ft (3-15 m]
- ❏ Well-drained, loamy soil
- ❏ Hardy zones 7-9
- ❏ Features: flowers; attractive leaves

Magnolia grandiflora 'Exoniensis'

Magnolia grandiflora, flower

Evergreen magnolias are one of the glories of southern gardens, where they grow into mighty trees, though at the northern edge of their range they are of more modest dimensions. These trees do best in a sunny, sheltered spot; in zone 7 a courtyard or the south side of a building is best.

The exquisite chalice-shaped flowers open in late spring, but the trees are imposing at any time of year, with their large, glossy evergreen leaves.

Tree magnolias that have been propagated from seed may not flower before they reach maturity, but most cultivars are grafted and flower at an earlier age.

Popular species

Magnolia delavayi, a bushy and alkaline-tolerant species from China, can eventually reach a height of 35 ft (10.5 m) with a spread of 30 ft (9 m) under ideal, sheltered conditions. It bears huge leathery leaves that grow up to 1 ft (30 cm) long; they are mat gray-green above and bluish-white underneath. The creamy white flowers, which can grow as much as 8 in (20 cm) wide, usually appear in late spring or early summer. These flowers have a spicy fragrance, but each bloom lasts only a couple of days. The species is hardy to zone 9.

Magnolia grandiflora (bull bay) is native to the Southeast. It is an alkaline-tolerant tree that reaches a height of 60-80 ft (18-24 m) with a 30-50 ft (9-15 m) spread. Densely pyramidal in form, with lower branches that sweep the ground, it has thick, leathery, glossy rich green leaves with red-brown felting beneath. It bears huge bowl-shaped flowers, up to 10 in (25 cm) wide, in late spring and intermittently into fall; they are creamy white and fleshy, with a rich, spicy fragrance. Cultivars that flower when young include 'Edith Bogue' (tight pyramidal form; narrow, dark green leaves; exceptionally cold hardy), 'Exoniensis' ('Exmouth' or 'Lanceolata'; 10 in/25 cm long, glossy, soft green leaves; large, exceptionally fragrant flowers), and 'Victoria' (lustrous foliage with felted brown undersides; exceptionally cold hardy; a favorite in the Pacific Northwest). This species is hardy in zones 7-9.

Cultivation

Plant balled-and-burlapped or container-grown specimens in winter in the South or in early spring elsewhere. Evergreen magnolias need moist but well-drained loamy soil and tolerate alkalinity. At the northern edge of their ranges they are best grown in sheltered sites, such as in a sunny courtyard, or espaliered against a south-facing wall. Top-dress with organic matter each year in spring and give a protective winter mulch to young trees for the first couple of years until they are well established.

Pruning No pruning is necessary. However, on espaliered specimens, remove forward-facing shoots from the base in spring. On mature trees set in open ground, prune back the lower branches flush with the trunk to create a shade tree.

Pests/diseases Botrytis may appear as a brown-gray coating on frost-damaged shoots, causing dieback. Leaf spot can afflict foliage; canker can cause dieback. Magnolias are also subject to root-rot fungi. These trees are mostly trouble free in the South.

Picea

spruce

Picea engelmannii

Picea abies, cones

Picea orientalis, cones

- ❏ Height at 25 years 15-60 ft (4.5-18 m)
- ❏ Mature height 30-115 ft (9-35 m)
- ❏ Spread 8-30 ft (2.4-9 m)
- ❏ Deep, moist, ideally acid soil
- ❏ Hardy zones 2-7, depending on species
- ❏ Features: graceful, symetrical form; range of foliage color; cones

Spruces grow with natural grace in conical or pyramid-shaped form and with dense foliage in a wide range of colors.

The branches grow in neat whorls with needlelike leaves, ranging from dark green to gray, blue-gray, silver, and yellow. The trees produce woody-scaled cones.

Spruces make ideal specimen trees and are good for screens and shelterbelts in large gardens. Slow-growing and dwarf cultivars are best for restricted areas, rock gardens, and trough gardens.

Popular species

Picea abies (Norway spruce), syn. *P. excelsa*, up to 40-60 ft (12-18 m) high and 15-30 ft (4.5-9 m) wide at 25 years, slowly grows to 115 ft (35 m). It has glossy, dark green leaves and bears 6 in (15 cm) long cones. It is hardy in zones 2-7. Cultivars include 'Acrocona' (to 15 ft/4.5 m high; branches droop; large cones) and 'Pyramidalis' (narrow; 30 ft/9 m high, 4 ft/1.2 m wide). Dwarf forms include 'Clanbrassiliana (3 ft/90 cm high and wide), 'Echiniformis' (prickly; slow-growing), 'Gregoryana' (pale branchlets; 2 ft/60cm high), and 'Nidiformis' (1 ft/30 cm high and 3 ft/90 cm wide; flat-topped).

Picea brewerana (Brewer spruce) reaches 20 ft (6 m) high and 8 ft (2.4 m) wide at 25 years and can grow up to 50 ft (15 m) high. This beautiful slow-growing species has spreading branches with pendent, curtainlike branchlets and dark gray-green leaves. The pointed cones are purple-brown when ripe. It is hardy to zone 6.

Picea engelmannii (Engelmann spruce), up to 40-50 ft (12-15 m) tall with a spread of 20-25 ft (6-7.5 m), forms a dense pyramid with bluish-green foliage. It is hardy in zones 2-6.

Picea glauca (white spruce), from Canada and the northeastern United States, is a conical tree up to 40-60 ft (12-18 m) tall and 10-20 ft (3-6 m) wide. The foliage is gray-green. 'Caerulea' has silvery leaves; 'Echiniformis' is 2 ft/60 cm high, clothed with blue-gray and green foliage. This species is hardy in zones 2-6.

Picea omorika

Picea orientalis 'Aurea'

Picea abies

Picea pungens 'Hoopsii'

Picea brewerana, flowers

Picea brewerana

Picea abies 'Acrocona,' cones

Picea likiangensis, from western China, is up to 30 ft (9 m) high and 18 ft (5.5 m) wide at 25 years, eventually reaching 65 ft (20 m) high. This broad, conical tree with slightly upswept branches has pale blue-green foliage and red flowers. The cones are red when young. It is hardy to zone 8.
Picea omorika (Serbian spruce), an alkaline-tolerant, narrow tree, grows up to 50-60 ft (15-18 m) tall and 15-20 ft (4.5-6 m) wide. It has glossy dark green leaves and deep purple cones. Its cultivar 'Nana' grows slowly to 3 ft (90 cm), with bright green foliage. This species is hardy in zones 5-7.

Picea orientalis (oriental spruce), up to 50-60 ft (15-18 m) and 20-30 ft (6-9 m) wide at 25 years, eventually grows to 100 ft (30 m) or more. It is a broad, dense tree with glossy dark green foliage. Cultivars include 'Aurea' (slow-growing; yellow young growth turns green) and 'Pendula' (slow-growing; weeping branches). This species is hardy in zones 5-7.
Picea pungens (Colorado spruce), a pyramid-shaped tree with cylindrical cones, is 20-60 ft (6-18 m) high and 6-20 ft (1.8-6 m) wide. It is hardy in zones 2-7. Cultivars include 'Glauca' (blue foliage), 'Hoopsii' (gray-blue leaves) 'Kosteri' (intense silver-blue leaves), and 'Pendula' (gray-blue foliage). Dwarf forms include 'Globosa' (silvery-blue foliage) and 'Procumbens' (blue foliage).
Picea smithiana (Himalayan weeping spruce), up to 33 ft (10 m) high and 10 ft (3 m) wide at 25 years, eventually reaches 100 ft (30 m) or more. This imposing specimen tree has horizontal branches with pendent, curtainlike branchlets and glossy dark green foliage. The purple cones are up to 6 in (15 cm) long. This species is hardy to zone 6.

Cultivation
Spruces thrive in deep, moist, preferably acid soil. Plant young trees 2-3 ft (60-90 cm) tall in early fall or early spring in sun or partial shade. On heavy soils, delay planting until spring.
Pruning Prune only to maintain a single leader.
Pests/diseases Spruce gall aphids cause 1 in (2.5 cm) long conelike galls to form on twigs. Aphids cause yellowing foliage, while canker leads to the dieback of branches from the bottom of the tree upward on Norway and Colorado spruces. Spruce spider mites cause premature needle drop. Rust shows as whitish blisters on the lower leaf surfaces, causing the yellowing and premature drop of needles.

PINE — see *Pinus*
PINE, UMBRELLA —
see *Pinus* and *Sciadopitys*

Pinus

pine

Pinus ayacahuite

Pinus parviflora, cones

Pinus nigra maritima, bark

- ❏ Height at 25 years 6-50 ft (1.8-15 m)
- ❏ Mature height 8-80 ft (2.4-24 m)
- ❏ Spread 10-50 ft (3-15 m)
- ❏ Well-drained acid or alkaline soil, depending on species
- ❏ Hardy zones 2-9, depending on species
- ❏ Features: graceful form; cones

The majestic symmetry of pine trees is best viewed on a large, open lawn. Most pines are broad cone shapes, making ideal windbreaks or screens. Lower branches drop off as the trees age and become rounded or flat-topped.

Needlelike, 1-10 in (2.5-25 cm) long leaves are held in clusters of two, three, or five and range from green to blue, silver, and yellow. The woody cones are short and wide or long and banana-shaped.

Most pines are slow-growing but can reach a height of 30-50 ft (9-15 m) in the garden. Dwarf and shrubby types are suitable for rock gardens (see pp.145-146).

Popular species

Pinus aristata (bristlecone pine), native to the southwestern states, is a very slow-growing tree up to 8-20 ft (2.4-6 m) high; a 15-year-old plant stands only 4 ft (1.2 m) tall. The gray-green leaves are carried in bunches; the cones are bristly. It is hardy in zones 5-7.

Pinus ayacahuite (Mexican white pine) is up to 40 ft (12 m) high and 30 ft (9 m) wide. It has a narrow crown and broad base and bears long blue-green leaves. The banana-shaped cones reach 15 in (38 cm) long. It is hardy to zone 7.

Pinus bungeana (lacebark pine), from China, is a slow-growing species that reaches a height of 30-50 ft (9-15 m) and a spread of 20-35 ft (6-10.5 m). It has dark green leaves; the bark peels off to reveal yellow, green, and brown patches. It is hardy in zones 5-8.

Pinus cembra (Swiss stone pine) grows up to 30-40 ft (9-12 m) high and 15-25 ft (4.5-7.5 m) wide.

This species is slow-growing and of conical form, with dense blue-green leaves held in groups of three. It is hardy in zones 5-7.

Pinus montezumae (rough-barked Mexican pine) grows 20 ft (6 m) high and 10 ft (3 m) wide. It has a broad crown, fissured bark, and 10 in (25 cm) long gray-blue leaves. It is hardy to zone 6.

Pinus nigra (Austrian pine) reaches 50-60 ft (15-18 m) tall and 20-40 ft (6-12 m) wide. It grows well in alkaline soils in city and seaside sites. It has stiff, almost black leaves and broad yellow cones, ripening to brown. The variety *maritima* (Corsican pine) has gray-green foliage. The species is hardy in zones 5-7.

Pinus parviflora (Japanese white pine) reaches a height of 25-50 ft (7.5-15 m) with a similar spread. This species has a wide-spreading crown, purple bark, and bunches

43

Pinus wallichiana, cones

Pinus patula

Pinus sylvestris 'Fastigiata'

of twisted blue-gray leaves with silvery inner surfaces. It bears clusters of oval, upright cones and is hardy in zones 5-7.

Pinus patula (Mexican yellow pine), well adapted to the Southwest, is hardy to zone 8. It grows 25-50 ft (7.5-15 m) high, 15-30 ft (4.5-9 m) wide. Bright green foliage is held in drooping clusters as long as 1 ft (30 cm). The pine does not tolerate alkaline soil.

Pinus pinea (umbrella pine, stone pine) reaches 20-50 ft (6-15 m) high and 12-30 ft (3.7-9 m) wide. Shaped like an umbrella, it has stiff gray-green leaves and glossy

Pinus montezumae

Pinus wallichiana

Pinus sylvestris 'Aurea'

Pinus pinea

winter) and 'Fastigiata' (narrow column; up to 25 ft/7.5 m high, 3 ft/90 cm wide). This species is hardy in zones 2-8.

Pinus thunbergiana (Japanese black pine) ranges in height from 20-80 ft (6-24 m) and in spread from 20-40 ft (6-12 m). It has twisted, spreading branches, black bark, and rich green foliage. Tolerant of salt spray, it is an outstanding tree for seaside planting. It is hardy in zones 6-8.

Pinus wallichiana (Himalayan white pine), up to 50 ft (15 m) high and 30 ft (9 m) wide, has drooping blue-green leaves up to 10 in (25 cm) long. It is conical when young but develops a broad-headed crown with age. This pine is hardy in zones 6-7.

Cultivation
Pines need full sun and well-drained soil. When established, most tolerate some drought; *P. nigra* tolerates polluted air as well.

In fall or spring plant young, balled-and-burlapped trees.

Pruning Prune to maintain a single leader; to restrict growth in hedges or screens, cut back "candles" of new growth by ½ in (1.25 cm) in spring.

Pests/diseases Aphids feed on stems and foliage, making tufts of waxy white wool. The larvae of pine-tip moths kill young growth; sawfly larvae devour needles. Cenangium twig blight causes needles to brown and kills branches. Fungal cankers cause dieback of branches; fungal rusts form galls or spindle-shaped swellings on trunks or branches of young trees, stunting or killing them.

oval cones bearing edible seeds (pine nuts). It flourishes on sandy soils and by the sea but is hardy only to zone 8.

Pinus strobus (eastern white pine) grows to 50-80 ft (15-24 m) high and 20-40 ft (6-12 m) wide. Young trees make a pyramid of soft-looking blue-green needles; older trees adopt a craggier form. 'Pendula' is a dwarf weeping cultivar. The fast-growing species is hardy in zones 3-8.

Pinus sylvestris (Scots pine) grows to 30-60 ft (9-18 m) high and 30-40 ft (9-12 m) wide. The young tree has a pyramid shape; it often takes on an attractive gnarled appearance as it ages. Popular cultivars include 'Aurea' (15 ft /4.5 m high, 8 ft/2.4 m wide; yellowish young foliage, golden in

Podocarpus

podocarpus

Podocarpus macrophyllus

Podocarpus nivalis

- ❑ Height at 25 years 3-20 ft (90-600 cm)
- ❑ Mature height up to 40 ft (12 m)
- ❑ Spread 3-10 ft (90-300 cm)
- ❑ Moist but well-drained soil
- ❑ Hardy zones 8-10, southern zone 7 in sheltered sites
- ❑ Features: foliage; fleshy fruits

Podocarpus trees are related to the yews *(Taxus)* and resemble them in appearance, although they are much less cold hardy. In the lower South they form substantial trees; at the northern edge of their range they are more shrubby in form.

These are slow-growing trees, with soft needlelike foliage studded with fleshy fruits.

Popular species

Podocarpus andinus (plum fir) grows extremely slowly, reaching 18 ft (5.5 m) after 25 years, with a spread of 10 ft (3 m). This tree has bright green foliage, which is bluish-green underneath. The fruits resemble small black plums. This species thrives on good alkaline soil. It is hardy to zone 8.

Podocarpus gracilior (African fern pine) is an elegant small tree, growing up to 20 ft (6 m) high and 10 ft (3 m) wide in mild, frost-free gardens. The drooping branches are densely clothed with gray-green adult foliage interspersed with glossy dark green juvenile leaves. It is not hardy north of zone 10.

Podocarpus macrophyllus (southern yew) is one of the hardier species. It can grow up to 15 ft (4.5 m) high and 3 ft (90 cm) wide in 25 years and will eventually reach 40 ft (12 m) high. It is an excellent specimen and tub tree, with attractive dark green leaves set in spiral clusters along the branches. It dislikes alkaline soils but thrives in seaside conditions. The species is hardy in zones 8-10 and can survive in sheltered spots in southern zone 7.

Podocarpus nivalis, from New Zealand, is a low-growing species that seldom grows taller than 3 ft (90 cm); however, it can spread up to 6 ft (1.8 m), making it a good candidate for ground cover. The branches are crowded with leathery olive-green foliage. This species is hardy to zone 9 and does well on alkaline soil.

Cultivation

Plant container-grown specimens in fall or spring. They do best in moist but well-drained, loamy soil, either acid or alkaline — with the exception of *P. macrophyllus,* which prefers neutral or acid soil. A sunny, sheltered site is ideal for this genus.

Pruning None required, but you can cut back straggly shoots to the base in spring.

Pests/diseases Trouble free.

Pseudotsuga
Douglas fir

Pseudotsuga menziesii

- ❏ Height at 25 years 30-80 ft (9-24 m)
- ❏ Mature height 200 ft (60 m) or more in the wild
- ❏ Spread 15-20 ft (4.5-6 m)
- ❏ Any good, moist soil
- ❏ Hardy zones 4-6
- ❏ Features: imposing tree; cones

Synonyms for the Douglas fir *(Pseudotsuga menziesii)* include *P. taxifolia* and *Abies douglasii*. But it is neither a hemlock *(Tsuga)* nor a true fir *(Abies)*. This distinctive conifer with a stately habit is suitable only for large gardens and screening, though smaller and more slow-growing cultivars are available.

The Douglas fir has a broad columnar shape, 30 ft (9 m) or more high and 20 ft (6 m) wide, with soft, aromatic foliage, dark green above and silvery beneath. Mature trees bear pendent brown cones and have resin-blistered trunks. An ornamental cultivar is 'Fletcheri' (8 ft/2.4 m high; blue-green foliage). The variety *glauca* is alkaline tolerant; it grows slowly to 35 ft (10.5 m) high and 10 ft (3 m) wide, with blue-gray foliage.

Cultivation
Plant balled-and-burlapped trees in early spring in good, deep, well-drained but moisture-retentive soil in a sunny spot. This tree prefers a moist atmosphere.
Pruning None essential; prune out competing leading shoots.
Pests/diseases Aphids feed on the foliage and stems of young trees; cankers can cause the death of branches or the whole tree.

Quercus
oak

Quercus virginiana

- ❏ Height at 25 years 20-40 ft (6-12 m)
- ❏ Mature height up to 90 ft (27 m)
- ❏ Spread commonly 20-40 ft (6-12 m); up to 100 ft (30 m)
- ❏ Any ordinary garden soil
- ❏ Hardy zones 7-10, depending on species
- ❏ Features: foliage; attractive form

The magnificent evergreen oaks are trees of warm-weather regions, making them suitable only for the South and the southern Pacific Coast. They cannot tolerate cold winters, but in a hospitable area many are extremely long-lived trees. The southern live oak *(Querus virginiana)* may last 300 years, and a mature specimen is as imposing as its northern, deciduous relatives. Others, such as the holly oak *(Querus ilex)* from the Mediterranean region, withstand shearing well and are useful for formal effects.

Popular species
Quercus agrifolia (California live oak), a round-headed tree with hollylike foliage, can reach a height and spread of 90 ft (27 m). Hardy only to zone 9, it is useful mainly in coastal California.
Quercus chrysolepis (canyon live oak), another California native, is hardy to zone 7 in dry climates. It is a spreading tree with pendulous branches, and can reach a height of 60 ft (18 m).
Quercus ilex (holly or holm oak) grows up to 20 ft (6 m) high and

Quercus suber

Sciadopitys

umbrella pine

Sciadopitys verticillata

❑ Height at 25 years 15-20 ft (4.5-6 m)
❑ Mature height 25-30 ft (7.5-9 m)
❑ Spread 15 ft (4.5 m)
❑ Moist, neutral to acid soil
❑ Hardy zones 5-8
❑ Features: form; foliage

The umbrella pine (*Sciadopitys verticillata*) is a hardy conifer from Japan. Pyramidal in shape, it makes a choice specimen tree for a lawn and grows extremely slowly — after 50 years it reaches a maximum height of 30 ft (9 m). It takes its common name, "umbrella pine," from the arrangement of the soft, needlelike dark green leaves, which are densely grouped on the branchlets like the spokes of an umbrella.

The bark on the trunk peels away to reveal new reddish bark beneath. Mature trees bear erect, oval cones 3-5 in (7.5-13 cm) long; they ripen in the second year from green to brown.

Cultivation

Plant young trees in early fall or early spring to midspring. They thrive in neutral to acid, moist soils and dislike hot, dry situations and air pollution. A site in sun or light shade and sheltered from strong winds is ideal.

Pruning None required, but reduce competing leading shoots to the strongest at any time of year.

Pests/diseases Relatively trouble free. Scale insects may infest stems. Yellowing of the foliage occurs on poorly drained soil; it may indicate a need for fertilization.

SPRUCE — see *Picea*
STRAWBERRY TREE — see *Arbutus*

Quercus ilex

wide at 25 years and may eventually reach a height of 60 ft (18 m). It makes a majestic tree with deeply furrowed bark and a round-headed crown. Hardy to zone 9, this species is highly wind resistant and excellent for coastal gardens. It responds well to pruning and can be grown as a tall hedge or windbreak.

Quercus suber (cork oak) is a round-headed tree that grows up to 25 ft (7.5 m) high and almost equally as wide. Its thick and spongy bark is the source of cork, hence the name cork oak. The species thrives in dry, gravelly soil and grows well in California and the Southeast. It is hardy to southern zone 7.

Quercus virginiana (southern live oak) forms a massive, widespreading tree that can reach a height of 40-80 ft (12-24 m) with a spread of 60-100 ft (18-30 m). This is not a tree for a small garden, but it is a wonderful specimen for a park or large lawn. The species is hardy in zones 8-10.

Cultivation

Evergreen oaks thrive in any ordinary well-drained garden soil; they prefer an open site in full sun, though oaks tolerate partial shade. They do well in deep, alkaline soil. Plant in midfall to late fall or early spring to midspring. During the first few years, apply an annual mulch of well-rotted organic matter in spring.

Pruning In mid- to late spring prune as little as possible and merely to direct growth. Trim established hedges of *Q. ilex* in midspring; clip again, if necessary, in early fall.

Pests/diseases Various caterpillars feed on the leaves, and rootrot fungi may kill the trees in regions where it is prevalent in the soil. Powdery mildew spreads a white growth over the undersides of the leaves, and many species of insects and mites may disfigure the foliage with galls.

Taxus
yew

Taxus baccata 'Fastigiata Aurea'

❑ Height at 25 years 12-15 ft (3.7-4.5 m)
❑ Mature height up to 60 ft (18 m)
❑ Spread 2-40 ft (.6-12 m)
❑ Any well-drained soil
❑ Hardy zones 5-7
❑ Features: dense foliage; colorful fruits; good hedging plant

Yews have dense foliage that makes them desirable for hedges, screens, and foundation plantings. The spreading cultivars are ideal for covering a bank or for massed effects. Yews tolerate severe pruning and shearing, making them suitable for topiary. Because they grow slowly, yew hedges need only an annual trim.

For shrubby and dwarf yews, see pages 169-170.

Popular species
Taxus baccata (English yew) grows 30-60 ft (9-18 m) high and 15-25 ft (4.5-7.5 m) wide. The multitrunk tree has almost horizontal branches covered with red and brown scaly bark. Feathery, needlelike leaves are dark green. Male and female flowers are borne on separate trees. Pale yellow male flowers are carried in clusters on the previous year's shoots. The barely visible, single green female flowers are followed by fleshy, cup-shaped red fruits. All parts of the tree are poisonous. It's hardy only in zones 6-7.

The cultivar 'Fastigiata Aurea' (golden Irish yew) is a columnar

Taxus cuspidata, foliage

tree with golden foliage to 12 ft (3.7 m) high and 2 ft (60 cm) wide; 'Standishii' is similar to the Irish yew, but smaller.
Taxus cuspidata (Japanese yew) reaches 10-40 ft (3-12 m) high with an equal or greater spread. It has dark, lustrous green foliage and peeling reddish-brown bark. This species grows in zones 5-7.
Taxus × media (Anglojap yew) has a broad pyramid shape. It grows 2-20 ft (60-600 cm) tall and is hardy in zones 5-7. Maintain it as a shrub by pruning or train it as a tree. Outstanding cultivars include 'Brownii,' a dense and rounded specimen 9 ft (2.7 m) tall and 12 ft (3.7 m) wide, and 'Hicksii,' a columnar form.

Cultivation
Plant balled-and-burlapped trees in fall or spring in fertile, moist but well-drained soil.

For hedges, set 15 in (38 cm) high plants 15-18 in (38-45 cm) apart. Cut back leading shoots to promote bushy growth.
Pruning Cut back any sprouts and suckers at any time. Trim hedges into shape in early spring.
Pests/diseases Scale insects can encrust the stems. White, wax-covered Taxus mealybugs infest trunks and branches; black vine weevils feed on foliage at night and attack roots, causing dieback and death of the plant. Root-rot fungi can cause decline and death.

Thuja
thuja, arborvitae

Thuja plicata 'Aurea'

❑ Height at 25 years 15-40 ft (4.5-12 m)
❑ Mature height 20-70 ft (6-21 m)
❑ Spread 2½-25 ft (75-750 cm)
❑ Any garden soil, preferably moist
❑ Hardy zones 2-9
❑ Features: form and color; aromatic foliage

Thujas include not only fast-growing species suitable for large gardens, windbreaks, and hedging, but also slow-growing specimen trees and shrubby and dwarf types for rock gardens (see p.171). The scalelike leaves, borne in soft fanlike sprays, are usually aromatic when crushed; the upright cones are small, with the tips of the scales curving outward.

Popular species
Thuja occidentalis is a columnar tree ideal for screening. This slow-growing tree reaches 30 ft (9 m) high and 15 ft (4.5 ft) wide in 25 years; but it eventually grows to about 60 ft (18 m). The dull green, apple-scented leaves often turn bronze in winter. This species is hardy in zones 2-8. Cultivars include 'Elegantissima' (narrow pyramid; golden yellow new growth, maturing to yellow-green), 'Fastigiata' (narrow conical shape), and 'Spiralis' (narrow

Trachycarpus
windmill palm

Trachycarpus fortunei, foliage

Thuja occidentalis 'Elegantissima'

column; up to 20 ft/6 m high and 2½ ft/75 cm wide; rich dark green foliage in spiraling sprays).

Thuja orientalis (Oriental arborvitae), syn. *Platycladus orientalis*, a large shrub or small tree that is hardy in zones 6-9, is conical or columnar when young and becomes gaunt with age. It grows up to 18-25 ft (5.5-7.5 m) high and 10-15 ft (3-4.5 m) wide. Its midgreen foliage turns bronze in winter. The cultivar 'Blue Cone' has blue foliage; 'Elegantissima' has golden yellow foliage, turning green in winter.

Thuja plicata (western red cedar) is a fast-growing, long-lived tree good for hedging and screening. It grows 40 ft (12 m) high and 12 ft (3.7 m) wide in 25 years; it can eventually reach 70 ft (21 m) or more. The tree has peeling light brown bark, a fluted trunk, and shiny, rich green aromatic foliage. The species is hardy in zones 6-7. Cultivars include 'Aurea' (rich gold foliage), 'Fastigiata' (columnar; dense branches), and 'Zebrina' (yellow-banded foliage).

Cultivation
Thujas will grow in any garden soil but thrive in deep, moist but well-drained soil. Plant balled-and-burlapped trees or container-grown specimens in full sun in the fall or early spring.

For hedges, space 1½ ft (45 cm) high plants at intervals of 1½-2 ft (45-60 cm). Cut back the growing tips for bushy growth.

Pruning None required. Clip hedges prior to growth in spring.
Pests/diseases Few problems.

- ❏ Height at 25 years 8-10 ft (2.4-3 m)
- ❏ Mature height 40 ft (12 m)
- ❏ Spread 6-8 ft (1.8-2.4 m)
- ❏ Any well-drained soil
- ❏ Hardy southern zones 8-9
- ❏ Features: interesting foliage

The windmill palm (*Trachycarpus fortunei*, syn. *Chamaerops excelsa* and *C. fortunei*), an exotic-looking tree, is ideal for southern and southwestern gardens. Its fanlike leaves rise from sharply toothed stalks, 3 ft (90 cm) long, above a thick, rough trunk scarred by old leaf bases and fibers.

The midgreen leaves measure about 3 ft (90 cm) wide; they last for years before being replaced by new foliage. When they fall off, they leave scars on the trunk. Mature trees in mild, sheltered gardens can produce small yellow flowers in dense sprays up to 2 ft (60 cm) long. The early-summer flowers are sometimes followed by small, globular blue-black fruits.

The windmill palm makes a fine specimen tree for smaller gardens, where it looks best planted in the middle of a lawn.

Cultivation
Plant young container-grown specimens in spring in ordinary well-drained soil. Choose a sunny or lightly shaded spot sheltered from cold winter winds and from frost pockets.
Pruning Remove wind-damaged leaves flush with the trunk.
Pests/diseases Trouble free.

Trachycarpus fortunei

Tsuga
hemlock

Tsuga canadensis, foliage and cones

❏ Height at 25 years 10-50 ft (3-15 m)
❏ Mature height 50-75 ft (15-23 m)
❏ Spread 6-35 ft (1.8-10.5 m)
❏ Moist, acid soil
❏ Hardy zones 3-7
❏ Features: graceful form

For gardeners with deep, moist soil, the genus *Tsuga* provides a range of specimen trees grown for their graceful form, with sweeping branches and drooping or gently arching branchlets.

These trees have needlelike leaves in shades ranging from midgreen to dark green, often with white bands beneath. The small cones, 1 in (2.5 cm) long, droop from the tips of the shoots.

Hemlock trees are suitable for large gardens and for hedging. Dwarf types (see p.172) are more desirable for small gardens.

Popular species
Tsuga canadensis (Canadian hemlock), from eastern North America, grows 40-70 ft (12-21 m) tall and 25-35 ft (7.5-10.5 m) wide. It has a broad crown above a trunk with rough, ridged, gray-brown bark. The leaves are dark green with white-marked undersides twisted upward. This species tolerates alkaline soil. 'Fremdii' is a slow-growing cultivar with a broad, conical shape.
Tsuga caroliniana (Carolina hemlock), a native of the southeastern states, is more open in

Tsuga mertensiana

form and less feathery in appearance than *T. canadensis*. It bears yellowish-green, white-banded foliage and is hardy in zones 5-7.
Tsuga diversifolia (northern Japanese hemlock) grows slowly, up to 35-60 ft (10.5-18 m) tall. It has horizontal branches and often more than one trunk. The bark is orange-brown; the leaves are a glistening deep green. It is hardy in zones 6-7.
Tsuga heterophylla (western hemlock) is a conical, slender tree up to 50 ft (15 m) high and 20 ft (6 m) wide. Its dense dark green foliage hangs from branches that sweep slightly upward. It has dark brown furrowed bark, a fluted trunk, and profuse cones. Best adapted to the Pacific Northwest, it is hardy to zone 6.
Tsuga mertensiana grows slowly to a height of 25 ft (7.5 m) and a spread of 6 ft (1.8 m). The gray-blue leaves grow spirally around the shoots; the purple cones are

up to 3 in (7.5 cm) long. The dark red-brown bark is rough and scaly. Hardy to zone 6, it does not thrive outside the Northwest.

Cultivation
Hemlocks thrive in deep, moist, acid soils, although *T. canadensis* tolerates alkaline soil. Plant balled-and-burlapped trees in fall or spring in a partially shaded spot sheltered from the wind. Hemlocks do not tolerate air pollution or salt spray.
Pruning Clip established hedges in early summer.
Pests/diseases Mites and scale insects can be a problem; the adelgid may eliminate *T. canadensis* from its natural range.

UMBRELLA PINE — see *Pinus* and *Sciadopitys*
WATTLE, SILVER — see *Acacia*
WINDMILL PALM — see *Trachycarpus*
YEW — see *Taxus*

Woodland shrubs Rhododendrons and azaleas come into their full glory in late spring.

A–Z of Evergreen Shrubs

Evergreens make a special contribution to landscape design through their year-round colorful foliage. Green plants in a winter garden suggest a comforting assurance that spring will return; during the growing season, the sober evergreen foliages temper the vivid displays of seasonal flowers. Actually, "evergreen" is a slight misnomer, since the color of the foliage on these plants ranges from green to gray, silver, blue, or purple-black — and all of these colors may be splashed or edged with markings and variegations of yellow, pink, or white.

Foliage, plant size, and hardiness usually govern the choice of evergreen shrubs. Most are flowering plants, such as camellias and daphnes; however, the spectacular seasonal display of their flowers is brief compared with the year-round show of leaf color, shape, and texture.

The ornamental character of an evergreen also influences selection. Some shrubs, such as Portugal laurels and aucubas, are good as a background for flowering plants. Others are ideal for hedging and screening along property lines or as internal dividers between different garden areas; good examples include spiny green holly, flowering escallonia, dwarf boxwood, and sweet lavender. Still other evergreens, like the strawberry tree, the colorful pieris, or the yucca, demand a position of prominence, as specimen plants on their own or in groups. Prostrate shrubs, such as cotoneaster, heather, or bright-berried pernettya, cover the ground with evergreen carpets. On a different plane there are evergreen climbers, such as passionflower, potato vine, and ivy, to clamber up walls and fences.

Few evergreens are as versatile as the shrubby conifers. There are hundreds of cultivars, all differing widely in shape, size, foliage color, and growth habit. Tall and medium-size conifers serve the same purposes as broad-leaved evergreen shrubs, while dwarf and miniature types are tailor-made for rock gardens.

To help you determine if a particular evergreen will thrive in your area, we've given you zones that correspond to the plant hardiness map on page 176.

BROAD-LEAVED EVERGREENS

**Evergreen shrubs and trees bring permanent color
and life to a garden and also generously add
magnificent flowers and brilliant berries.**

Among garden plants, the broad-leaved evergreens (trees, shrubs, and climbers) work hardest to earn their keep. You'll find that in late fall, winter, and early spring, broad-leaved evergreens furnish green and variegated color while deciduous shrubs are dormant. During the growing season, these evergreens provide the perfect backdrop for colorful, but transitory, perennials and annuals.

An evergreen plant keeps its foliage all year. Although evergreens do shed old leaves and replace them with young ones, they do this gradually — never all at once, as deciduous trees and shrubs do. Broad-leaved evergreens have flat leaves, which range in size from the tiny ones of *Lonicera nitida* to the enormous

ones of some of the rhododendrons, which may measure 2½ ft (75 cm) or more in length.

Though many broad-leaved evergreens have round, oval, or elliptical leaves, not all do. Some, such as yucca, have long, sword-like leaves; others, such as fatsia, have fan-shaped or palmate leaves. Many broad-leaved evergreens are green, but there are also numerous cultivars with gray, silver, gold, or variegated leaves.

The category excludes conifers, most of which are evergreen but have thin, needlelike leaves.

Trees and shrubs

Evergreen trees are especially valuable for the mass of year-round foliage they provide. The largest broad-leaved evergreen

trees in North America are warm-climate species, such as the live oaks *(Querus)* and the southern magnolia. Given enough time and space, these make magnificent trees, though they are too large for smaller gardens. Northerners who want to make a statement and Southerners with smaller properties must content themselves with the wide range of smaller evergreen trees and larger evergreen shrubs, such as the hollies. Fortunately, there are hollies for almost every climate, and they may be maintained as shrubbery or hedges or, through judicious pruning, trained into trees.

For mild, sheltered gardens (zones 8-9), there are the delightful mimosas *(Acacia)*, clothed with fernlike silver-gray or bright green leaves and, in spring or summer, a glorious mass of sweet-scented yellow blossoms. There is also the hardier, picturesque strawberry tree *(Arbutus unedo)*, which combines evergreen foliage with attractive red bark, flowers that resemble lilies-of-the-valley, and bright red fruits. Other options are the different species and cultivars of eucalyptus, graceful trees with aromatic gray to blue leaves and silvery bark.

Most broad-leaved evergreens are shrubs grown as specimen plants, included in mixed borders, or pruned as hedges. There are hundreds of species and cultivars, including bay laurel *(laurus),* boxwood *(buxus),* camellia, mahonia, pyracantha, skimmia, and many berberis, cotoneasters, and viburnums. Sizes range from the huge Portugal laurels to low-growing, spreading *Cotoneaster congestus* and *Gaultheria procumbens.*

There are plain green and variegated forms of many broad-leaved evergreen shrubs, and

◄ **Shade lover** One of the best broad-leaved evergreens for shaded urban gardens, *Aucuba japonica* also thrives in industrial landscapes. The cultivar 'Picturata' is boldly splashed with yellow.

▲ **Berry color** The low, wide-spreading branches of *Cotoneaster horizontalis* are laden with bright red berries in fall. In mild winters the shrub is semievergreen; spells of hard frost cause it to drop its tiny leaves.

◄ **Variegated holly** Tolerant of close clipping, hollies (especially the variegated types) make admirable specimen trees. They can be trained as standards with clear trunks or grown as multistemmed shrubs or hedging plants.

they serve different purposes in the garden. For example, the all-green forms of Japanese laurel (*Aucuba japonica* 'Crassifolia,' and 'Nana') are visually more restful than the yellow-spotted form (*A. japonica* 'Variegata'). And though the gold- or silver-variegated forms of *elaeagnus* are strikingly colorful, the cool green-gray foliage of *E. × ebbingei* can make a welcome change.

Evergreen climbers

Ivy, the most common evergreen climber, comes in a wide range of all-green cultivars, including the bright green, frilly-edged leaves of *Hedera helix* 'Green Ripple' and the large-leaved 'Hibernica.' In addition there are numerous attractive variegated forms, such

▲ **Algerian ivy** As the common name implies, this species (*Hedera canariensis*) originated in North Africa. It is an ideal plant for the South (zones 9-10). A vigorous climber, it will soon cover a wall or a bed if sheltered from hot sun and strong, drying winds.

▼ **Dwarf rhododendrons** Gardeners with alkaline soil must forgo the pleasure of ordinary rhododendrons. But they can have the glorious flowers and handsome foliage by cultivating compact cultivars, such as this 'Baden Baden,' in tubs of peat-enriched potting soil.

▲ **Dependable firethorn** Among the most popular of broad-leaved evergreens for training up a wall, the scarlet firethorn (*Pyracantha coccinea*) is hardy to zone 6. The foliage is handsome year-round, but the moment of glory comes when bright berries appear in fall.

as the cream-marbled *H. colchica* 'Dentata Variegata' and the gold-centered *H. helix* 'Goldheart.'

The beautiful *Clematis* genus includes *C. armandii*, with large leaves and creamy white flowers, and *C. cirrhosa*, with greenish-yellow winter flowers and silky seed heads. Both need sun and shelter in order to flourish; *C. cirrhosa* is hardy through zone 9. Other climbers that require a sheltered spot include the primrose jasmine *(Jasminum mesnyi)* and the potato vine *(Solanum)*.

Flowers, berries, and fruits

Some of the showiest blooms (rhododendrons and magnolias, for example) are produced by broad-leaved evergreens, all of which flower. Others, including boxwood *(Buxus)* and privet *(Ligustrum)*, have only modest flowers; these evergreens are grown solely for their foliage.

In milder climates (zones 8 and south) many broad-leaved evergreens flower in winter, when their color is especially welcome. Camellia, daphne, garrya, *Viburnum tinus*, mahonia, and sarcococca are winter flowering under such circumstances, as are some of the evergreen clematises.

Some evergreens, including aucuba, gaultheria, holly *(Ilex)*, pernettya, pyracantha, and skimmia, produce handsome berries or other fruits, often in late fall and winter. For fruits to form, you may have to plant male and female forms in close proximity.

Using evergreens

Flowers and fruit are a welcome bonus, but year-round greenery is the main advantage of broad-leaved evergreens. Many are shade tolerant and especially useful in urban gardens and under trees. They include aucuba, boxwood *(Buxus)*, camellia, daphne, elaeagnus, fatsia, gaultheria, holly, honeysuckle *(Lonicera)*, ivy *(Hedera)*, laurel *(Laurus)*, leucothoe, mahonia, osmanthus, pachysandra, periwinkle *(Vinca)*, rhododendron, sarcococca, skimmia, and some viburnums.

As a seasonal bonus, a few broad-leaved evergreens turn red or crimson in winter; these include several of the *Hedera helix* cultivars and the mahonias. Others, such as photinia and pieris, have bright red young spring growth as colorful as any flower.

▲ **Persian ivy** Larger leaved than the familiar English ivy and coarser in texture, the fast-growing Persian ivy *(Hedera colchica)* is hardy in zones 6–9. It makes an ideal climber for walls, fences, and banks and works just as well as a large-scale ground cover. The cultivar 'Dentata Variegata' is bright green with wide margins of creamy yellow maturing to near-white.

◄ **Windmill palm** In areas with only occasional, mild frosts (zone 9 and south), the windmill palm *(Trachycarpus fortunei)* makes a spectacular focal point in a sheltered border. The leaf fans measure as much as 5 ft (1.5 m) in width. The trunk is black, usually thicker at the top than the bottom and covered with hairy-looking fibers.

Broad-leaved evergreens, as well as many conifers, make ideal boundary hedges, as they usually have a dense growth habit and remain clothed in foliage all year. For the same reason, they are also useful for camouflaging or concealing unattractive views.

For good specimen plants or focal points, chose broad-leaved evergreens with dramatic foliage or growth habits; a holly *(Ilex)* in the center of a lawn, for example, or a yucca in the center of a border. Others, such as fatsia, camellia, and ivy *(Hedera),* are ideal in pots. All provide a background for lighter-leaved plants and bright flowers; most can be used to fill in gaps in shady corners, where few other plants could survive.

Caring for evergreens

Broad-leaved evergreens grown as hedges need regular pruning to keep them dense and, in the case of hedges such as escallonia, to encourage the production of flowering wood. They also benefit from annual fertilization and a moisture-retentive mulch.

Like other plants, broad-leaved evergreens vary in tolerance to cold and heat. As a result, your choices should be guided by your

▲**Winter cheer** The glorious *Camellia japonica* may flower right through the winter in zone 8 and southward, unfolding its brilliant blooms even in the shade of a north-facing wall. Hundreds of cultivars are available with single, double, or peonylike blooms in a range of pastel and vibrant colors.

climate. Admirers of boxwood, for example, should stick to Korean box *(Buxus microphylla koreana),* which is hardy to zone 5, while Southerners should look to *B. m. japonica,* which is more tolerant of heat and humidity.

Within their hardiness range, many evergreens, such as aucuba, tolerate most growing conditions; but a few, such as fremontodendron, can be temperamental, demanding extra attention. Success depends on choosing the right plant for the right spot.

◀ **Tropical touches** The glossy green leaves of *Fatsia japonica* lend a tropical air to a shrub border. With its year-round greenery and dramatic fall display of creamy white flowers, it is ideal for shaded urban gardens.

◀ **Winter sunshine** The glossy-leaved mahonias are particularly valued for their winter flowers. Species such as *Mahonia bealei* open their sprays of fragrant lemon-yellow blooms as early as mid-January in zone 8; by late spring *M. bealei* is laden with berries of robin's-egg blue. With time this species may reach a height of 10 ft (3 m).

▼ **Winter clematises** To most people, clematises are deciduous vines that bear large, brightly colored flowers in summertime. But the genus also includes evergreen species, such as *Clematis armandii*, which bears its fragrant white flowers in early spring, and *C. cirrhosa* (pictured here), which may bloom even in late winter along the warmer parts of the Pacific Coast and in other mild climates.

Abelia

abelia

Abelia × grandiflora

- Height 3-6 ft (1-1.8 m)
- Spread 3-6 ft (1-1.8 m)
- Flowers late spring to early fall
- Ordinary garden soil
- Sunny, sheltered site
- Hardy zones 6-9

Evergreen abelias are prized for their long-lasting bloom (late spring into fall) and handsome glossy foliage. They bear an abundance of drooping clusters of tubular flowers whose red sepals remain attractive for several weeks after the petals have fallen. The small, broad, ovate leaves are bronze-green in spring, dark green in summer, and bronze in fall. These easily grown shrubs are evergreen in the South, semi-evergreen elsewhere.

Popular species
Abelia floribunda is hardy only through zone 8 and requires the protection of a sunny, sheltered wall. It grows 6 ft (1.8 m) high with a similar spread. From late spring until well into summer, the branches are clothed with brilliant rose-pink flower clusters.
Abelia × grandiflora has a spreading habit; it is 3-6 ft (1-1.8 m) wide and high. The slightly fragrant pink-and-white flowers appear from late spring until frost. It is hardy in zones 6-9.

Cultivation
Plant in early fall or midspring in ordinary garden soil in a sunny, sheltered spot.

Regular pruning is unnecessary, although you can thin overgrown shoots after they flower to encourage new growth. In spring cut out frost-damaged shoots from the base.

Propagation In midsummer, take 3-4 in (7.5-10 cm) long cuttings of the current season's wood. Root in a cold frame, and plant out the following spring.

Pests/diseases None serious.

Abutilon

flowering maple

Abutilon vitifolium, white form

- Height 8-20 ft (2.4-6 m)
- Spread 8-10 ft (2.4-3 m)
- Flowers late spring to midfall
- Any well-drained soil
- Sunny, sheltered site
- Hardy zones 9-11

Although most gardeners can enjoy these South American shrubs only as greenhouse or indoor plants, they do flourish outdoors at the southern edge of the continental United States, along the Pacific Coast, and in Hawaii. Farther north, abutilons may be grown in tubs and displayed outside in the summertime, then overwintered indoors. In zone 9 they do best when espaliered informally against a sunny wall.

Popular species
Abutilon megapotamicum has conspicuous drooping yellow-and-red tubular flowers from late spring to early fall. It is a slender-stemmed, spreading shrub, growing 8-10 ft (2.4-3 m) high and wide. It has bright green, oval, toothed leaves.
Abutilon vitifolium, syn. *Corynabutilon vitifolium*, is the hardier species, surviving in regions of occasional mild frosts. It grows into a tall shrub or small tree, to 20 ft (6 m) tall, and bears clusters of mauve or lavender-blue to white mallowlike flowers from late spring to midfall.

Cultivation
Plant abutilons in late spring in ordinary moist but well-drained soil (and against a sheltered, sunny wall in zone 9). These plants

Abutilon megapotamicum

dislike extreme heat, so although they prefer full sun in temperate but windy coastal climates, inland they succeed better in partial shade. Alternatively, grow abutilons as potted plants and move them indoors for the winter.
Propagation In summer take 3-4 in (7.5-10 cm) cuttings of semimature lateral shoots. Root the cuttings in a propagating box at 59-64°F (15-18°C). Pot up the rooted cuttings, and grow on before hardening them off in a cold frame. Plant out in late spring.
Pests/diseases Trouble free.

Abutilon vitifolium, white form

Akebia
akebia

Akebia quinata

- ❏ Height 20-40 ft (6-12 m)
- ❏ Climber
- ❏ Flowers early to late spring
- ❏ Well-drained, moisture-retentive soil
- ❏ Sunny or lightly shaded site
- ❏ Hardy zones 5-8

Hardy, vigorous, and easy to grow, *Akebia quinata* is an attractive climber, valued for its spreading rich tapestry of leaves. The small, round green leaflets that cover its slender, twining stems often persist through winters in the southern part of its range. In early spring the old leaves are joined by purple-flushed new foliage and later by strings of flower buds that open into three-petaled, fragrant reddish-purple blooms.

Cultivation
Plant in fall or spring in any deep, moisture-retentive, well-drained soil in sun or light shade. Train akebias up trees, pergolas, walls, or trellises, using wire or string for the stems. After flowering, prune weak shoots; in tight areas cut other side shoots back hard.
Propagation Layer long shoots in fall, or root cuttings in late summer.
Pests/diseases Trouble free.

Andromeda
bog rosemary

Andromeda polifolia

- ❏ Height 1-2 ft (30-60 cm)
- ❏ Spread 2-3 ft (60-90 cm)
- ❏ Flowers late spring
- ❏ Acid, moisture-retentive soil
- ❏ Sunny or lightly shaded site
- ❏ Hardy zones 2-6

In the wild, as its name suggests, bog rosemary *(Andromeda polifolia)* grows in peaty soil of bogs; in gardens it is an ideal low-growing shrub to pair with rhododendrons or to use in cool, semishady corners in a rock garden.

Throughout the year, its slender, wiry stems are covered in small, leathery gray-green leaves, resembling those of rosemary. Clusters of urn-shaped pink flowers appear at the tips of the stems in late spring. 'Compacta' is a popular cultivar; it is smaller and denser than the species, with bright pink flowers. 'Macrophylla' bears rich pink flowers.

Cultivation
Plant container-grown specimens in spring in moist, acid, humus-rich soil in a lightly shaded or sunny spot. This shrub does not tolerate high heat and humidity.

Pruning is not necessary.
Propagation Increase stock by layering the plants in fall or in spring or by division or hardwood cuttings in fall.
Pests/diseases Trouble free.

ARBORVITAE — see *Thuja*

Arbutus
strawberry tree

Arbutus unedo, fruits

- ❏ Height 8 ft (2.4 m) or more
- ❏ Spread 5 ft (1.5 m) or more
- ❏ Flowers mid- to late summer
- ❏ Any well-drained soil
- ❏ Sunny or partially shaded site sheltered from cold winds
- ❏ Hardy zones 7-9

Among the loveliest of all evergreens is the strawberry tree (*Arbutus unedo*). It flowers in mid- to late summer, bearing pendulous clusters of tiny, creamy white or pale pink blooms. These are followed by red or orange fruits, which resemble strawberries in shape and size. These delightful fruits stand out against the lustrous dark green foliage. The fruits are edible, but they are usually devoured by birds as soon as they ripen in the fall.

In a temperate, moist climate, such as that of the Pacific Northwest, this species reaches treelike proportions (see p.26), but in the East the maximum height is more likely to be 8 ft (2.4 m). When mature, it takes on a splendid gnarled appearance, and as the deep brown bark peels away it exposes older wood beneath. While the plant is usually grown as a multistemmed shrub, you can prune it to a single trunk.

Two popular cultivars are 'Elfin King' (shrubby; fruiting at an early stage) and 'Rubra' (red-tinged flowers).

Cultivation
Plant in fall or spring in full sun or partial shade in a site sheltered from cold winter winds. Although a member of the acid-loving heather family, the strawberry

Arbutus unedo, flowers

tree will tolerate some alkalinity in the soil, provided it is well drained. This species thrives in mild coastal gardens.

Protect young plants in winter with a wrapping of burlap — once established they become hardier. Prune straggly shoots back to the main stems in midspring. To expose the flaking bark on established shrubs, cut out the lower shoots flush with the main stems.

Propagation The best time to take 3-4 in (7.5-10 cm) long heel cuttings is in summer; root them in a propagating unit at a temperature of 64°F (18°C). Cuttings are often difficult to root, but when successful, pot them up singly and grow on in a sheltered nursery bed.

Pests/diseases None serious.

Arctostaphylos
bearberry

Arctostaphylos uva-ursi 'Point Reyes'

- ❏ Height 6 in (15 cm)
- ❏ Spread 4 ft (1.2 m) or more
- ❏ Flowers mid- to late spring
- ❏ Moist, acid soil
- ❏ Sunny or lightly shaded site
- ❏ Hardy zones 2-6

The hardy bearberry (*Arctostaphylos uva-ursi*) is an excellent ground-cover shrub for banks with stony or poor soil. The plant forms a near-prostrate but rapidly spreading mat of oval, dark green, leathery leaves with pointed tips; the wiry stems root where they touch the ground.

In mid- to late spring bearberry produces pendulous sprays of tiny pale pink flowers. It is especially attractive in fall, when the foliage takes on a bronze sheen and the shoots glisten with clusters of bright red berries, which last through the winter. 'Point Reyes' bears blush-pink flowers.

Cultivation
Plant container-grown specimens in early fall or midspring. The bearberry thrives in cool, moist climates and in coastal gardens with sandy or poor acid soil. They prefer full sun, but they also grow, with fewer berries, in light shade. Pruning is unnecessary when the plants are grown for ground cover; wayward shoots can be cut back at any time of year.

Propagation Layer long shoots in spring and separate from the parent plant after 1 or 2 years; or take heel cuttings in late summer and root in a cold frame.

Pests/diseases Trouble free.

Arundinaria

bamboo

Arundinaria japonica

Arundinaria variegata

❏ Height 1-15 ft (30-450 cm)
❏ Spread 3-8 ft (90-240 cm)
❏ Foliage plant
❏ Any moist soil
❏ Sunny or partially shaded site sheltered from cold winds
❏ Hardy zones 5-10, depending on species

These elegant grasses are excellent evergreen screens and windbreaks in gardens with plenty of space, though you can also grow them as specimen plants. They are moisture lovers, and look effective planted by water.

All have long grasslike leaves; some leaves are pale green, others are variegated. The woody stems are gracefully arched and jointed. They rarely flower and when they do, the flowers are inconspicuous.

Popular species

Arundinaria anceps, syn. *Yushania anceps*, forms a dense thicket, growing 10-15 ft (3-4.5 m) high. Bright green stems are topped with narrow, glossy green leaves. A good species for screening, it is highly invasive; set the plants 6-8 ft (1.8-2.4 m) apart. The species is hardy only to zone 9.

Arundinaria humilis, syn. *Pleioblastus humilis*, is a rampant species, forming a low clump 2 ft (60 cm) high and 4 ft (1.2 m) wide. Its slender dark green stems carry light green leaves that are downy underneath. This plant makes an ideal ground cover and is suitable to grow beneath trees. It is hardy to zone 7.

Arundinaria japonica, syn. *Pseudosasa japonica* reaches 7-15 ft (2.1-4.5 m) high, making it ideal for screening. It has olive-green stems and glossy green leaves; it is hardy to zone 7. Set the plants 6-8 ft (1.8-2.4 m) apart.

Arundinaria murielae, syn. *Thamnocalamus spathaceus,* is an ideal specimen plant; it forms clumps and does not spread. Its midgreen leaves are carried on yellow-green arched stems. This species grows to 6-8 ft (1.8-2.4 m) and should be set 3 ft (90 cm) apart. It is hardy to zone 6.

Arundinaria nitida, syn. *Sinarundinaria nitida*, is a noninvasive species with dark purple canes and bright green leaves that are gray-green underneath. It is a good specimen plant and thrives in a tub. It does best in light shade. The plants grow 10 ft (3 m) high; set them 4 ft (1.2 m) apart. It is hardy to zone 5.

Arundinaria vagans, syn. *Sasaella ramosa*, is an invasive carpet-forming species. It reaches 1 ft (30 cm) tall and is an excellent ground cover. The narrow leaves, 4 in (10 cm) long, are midgreen and the thin canes are bright green, becoming darker with age. Set the plants 1½ ft (45 cm) apart. This species is hardy to zone 7.

Arundinaria variegata, syn. *Pleioblastus variegatus*, forms a dense thicket up to 4 ft (1.2 m) high. It has pale green canes and dark green leaves striped with white. Set the plants 6 ft (1.8 m) apart. It is hardy to zone 7.

Arundinaria viridistriata, syn. *A. auricoma*, forms a clump 4 ft (1.2 m) high. It has purple canes and rich yellow-and-green foliage. Set the plants 1½-2 ft (45-60 cm) apart. It is hardy to zone 7.

Cultivation

Plant in early spring to midspring in ordinary moist garden soil in a sunny or lightly shaded spot, sheltered from cold winds.

Pruning is unnecessary, but cut out old dead canes to ground level in early fall.

Propagation In midspring or fall, divide and replant; or remove rooted suckers and replant.

Pests/diseases Trouble free.

Arundinaria viridistriata

Aucuba

Japanese aucuba

Aucuba japonica

- ❏ Height 6-12 ft (1.8-3.7 m)
- ❏ Spread 5-7 ft (1.5-2.1 m)
- ❏ Flowers early spring to midspring
- ❏ Soil rich in organic matter
- ❏ Shaded site
- ❏ Hardy zones 7-10

Its decorative leaves and scarlet berries make this shrub popular with gardeners in the southeastern states.

Japanese aucuba *(Aucuba japonica)* prefers moist but well-drained soil that is rich in organic matter, such as leaf mold or peat. It must be given shade; it is one of the most shade-tolerant shrubs.

Insignificant olive-green star-shaped flowers in spring are followed by scarlet berries on female plants in fall. Expose females to male shrubs for berry production.

Popular cultivars

These common cultivars are listed as male or female:
'Crassifolia' (male) has large glossy deep green leaves.
'Crotonifolia' (male) grows large green leaves speckled gold.
'Longifolia' (female) has narrow, willowlike bright green leaves.
'Nana' (female) bears dark lustrous green foliage.
'Variegata' (or 'Maculata'; female) has green leaves blotched yellow.

Cultivation

Plant in fall or spring in soil rich in organic matter, and in a shady spot. It tolerates air pollution.

Propagation In late summer take 4-6 in (10-15 cm) heel cuttings and root in a cold frame.

Pests/diseases Trouble free.

AZALEA — see *Rhododendron* (azalea)
BAMBOO — see *Arundinaria, Nandia*
BARBERRY — see *Berberis*
BAY LAUREL — see *Laurus*

Aucuba japonica 'Variegata'

Berberis

barberry, berberis

Berberis julianae

- ❏ Height 1½-10 ft (45-300 cm)
- ❏ Spread 1½-12 ft (45-365 cm)
- ❏ Flowers spring or early summer
- ❏ Ordinary soil
- ❏ Sunny or lightly shaded site
- ❏ Hardy zones 6-8

The evergreen barberries are hardy ornamental shrubs that are easy to grow as specimen plants or as barrier hedges. They repay a minimum of care with a year-round display, showing off glossy, green spiny leaves that take on bronze hues in winter, fiercely thorny stems, yellow or orange flower clusters in spring, and long-lasting decorative berries.

Popular species

Berberis buxifolia (Magellan barberry) has dark green, leathery, 1 in (2.5 cm) long, spine-tipped leaves with gray undersides. It grows 6 ft (1.8 m) high and wide. In early spring and midspring it bears yellow flower clusters, followed in fall by blue-black berries with a waxy bloom. This species is hardy to zone 6. The cultivar 'Nana' rarely grows higher than 1½ ft (45 cm) and is suitable for a rock garden or a low hedge; it seldom flowers or fruits.

Berberis darwinii is one of the most popular species. Of bushy habit and with glossy, hollylike dark green leaves, it makes an excellent hedge. It produces an abundance of rich yellow-orange flowers in mid- to late spring, followed by blue berries in fall. This species grows to a height and spread of 8-10 ft (2.4-3 m) and is hardy to zone 7.

Berberis x gladwynensis 'William Penn'

Berberis darwinii

Berberis × gladwynensis 'William Penn' is a dense, mounded shrub that reaches a height and spread of about 4 ft (1.2 m). The foliage is a lustrous dark green and turns a handsome shade of bronze in winter — this plant may have the finest foliage of any evergreen barberry. The bright yellow flowers appear in early spring to midspring. This plant is hardy in the warmer parts of zone 6.

Berberis julianae (wintergreen barberry) is probably the hardiest of the evergreen barberries, overwintering reliably in zones 6-8. It bears leathery, lance-shaped leaves which are tinted copper when young. Reaching 10 ft (3 m) high and 6 ft (1.8 m) wide, with strongly spiny stems, it makes an excellent screening or hedging shrub. Its slightly scented yellow flowers appear in early to late spring and are followed by large clusters of black berries. The cultivar 'Nana' is a compact shrub about half the height and width of the species.

Berberis linearifolia is an erect,

slow-growing species, up to 10 ft (3 m) high and 4 ft (1.2 m) wide. It is one of the best barberries for blossoms, bearing clusters of rich orange flowers in midspring; they are particularly fine in the form 'Orange King.' This species is hardy to zone 6.

Berberis sargentiana (Sargent barberry) is a dense evergreen shrub 6-9 ft (1.8-2.7 m) high and 6 ft (1.8 m) wide. While similar in appearance to *B. julianae*, Sargent barberry has larger leaves, 1½-5 in (3.75-13 cm) long and ½-1¼ in (1.25-3.25 cm) wide. It bears yellow flowers in spring; the fruit is an egg-shaped black berry. The species is hardy to the warmer parts of zone 6.

Berberis × stenophylla grows vigorously, making it an excellent hedging shrub. It reaches up to 8-10 ft (2.4-3 m) high and 10-12 ft (3-3.7 m) wide. The arching stems are clothed with narrow, lance-shaped deep green leaves that are bluish-white on the undersides. Sweetly scented golden yellow flowers are borne from mid- to

late spring and are followed by purple berries. This shrub is hardy to zone 6.

Berberis verruculosa grows slowly to 3-6 ft (1-1.8 m) high and wide. The arching stems are set with tiny warty growths and small, spiny-toothed leaves that are dark green above, white beneath. The golden yellow flowers, borne singly or in pairs, make their appearance in late spring and early summer; they are followed by black berries. A good hedging shrub, this species is hardy to zone 6.

Berberis × wisleyensis (sometimes sold as *B. triacanthophora*) is an open shrub 3-5 ft (1-1.5 m) high and wide, with bright green leaves that turn reddish purple in winter. The flowers are borne in spring and are pale yellow or whitish, tinged red on the outside. The berries are bluish black, ⅓ in (8 mm) in diameter; the thorns are branching with three points. This plant is hardy in zones 6-8.

Cultivation
Plant in fall or in spring in sun or light shade. Ordinary garden soil, including a poor or shallow soil, is suitable. For hedging and screening, space young plants 1½-2 ft (45-60 cm) apart and cut them back by a quarter to encourage bushy growth.

Little pruning is necessary, but you can cut back old, unproductive branches or shoots growing in an undesirable direction to ground level or to healthy young shoots after they flower. Trim hedges to shape when flowering has finished; they will not produce berries.

Berberis x stenophylla

Propagation Take heel cuttings from lateral shoots in late summer and early fall, and root in a cold frame. The following spring pot up the cuttings singly and plunge them in an outdoor nursery bed (with the pot buried but the lip of the pot just above the soil); they will be ready for planting in their permanent positions about 2 years later.

Pests/diseases With the exception of the potential deadly root-rot fungi, these shrubs have few serious problems when grown in a landscape setting.

BOG ROSEMARY — see *Andromeda*
BOWER VINE — see *Pandora*
BOXWOOD — see *Buxus*
BUCKTHORN — see *Rhamnus*

Berberis verruculosa

Buddleia

orange butterfly bush

Buddleia globosa

- ❏ Height 10 ft (3 m)
- ❏ Spread 10 ft (3 m)
- ❏ Flowers late spring to early summer
- ❏ Any fertile, well-drained soil
- ❏ Sunny site
- ❏ Hardy zones 7-9

Unlike the other *Buddleia* species, the deciduous butterfly bush, the orange butterfly bush *(B. globosa)* retains most of its leaves through the winter in the mild-weather regions where it flourishes. Hardy in zones 7-9, this plant grows best in the Southeast and along the Pacific Coast, where it will perform as a semievergreen.

It is of vigorous, upright habit, grows 10 ft (3 m) high and wide, and has lance-shaped, dark green, wrinkled leaves with tawny undersides. In late spring and early summer the shrub is covered with clusters of globular orange-yellow, sweetly scented flower heads. The cultivar 'Lemon Ball' has lemon-yellow flowers.

Cultivation

In fall or spring plant in fertile, well-drained soil in full sun; in exposed gardens, grow them against sheltered west-facing walls.

This buddleia flowers on shoots of the previous season; do any pruning immediately after the flowers fade.

Propagation Take 4 in (10 cm) heel cuttings of semimature side-shoots in late summer, and root in a cold frame. In spring, transfer the rooted cuttings to an outdoor nursery bed and grow them there for a year before transplanting.

Pests/diseases None serious.

BUTCHER'S-BROOM — see *Ruscus*

Buxus

boxwood

Buxus sempervirens, variegated form

- ❏ Height up to 10 ft (3 m)
- ❏ Spread 4-6 ft (1.2-1.8 m)
- ❏ Foliage shrub
- ❏ Ordinary garden soil
- ❏ Sunny or lightly shaded site
- ❏ Hardy zones 5-8, depending on the species

Common boxwood *(Buxus sempervirens)* tolerates shearing well and has a compact growth habit, making it an excellent choice for edge beds or paths; it is also a classic material for topiary. Well adapted to the milder regions of the United States, common box is hardy in zones 6-8. In colder gardens, plant one of the similar-looking varieties of the littleleaf boxwood, such as *Buxus microphylla koreana;* they are winter hardy through zone 5.

Popular cultivars

Buxus microphylla 'Wintergreen' is outstanding for cold climates. *Buxus sempervirens* 'Suffruticosa' is compact and may be kept trimmed to 6 in (15 cm) high. It is ideal for edging.

B. sempervirens also offers a number of variegated cultivars.

Cultivation

In fall or spring plant in ordinary garden soil in sun or light shade. To establish hedges, plant 9-12 in (23-30 cm) high specimens at 12-15 in (30-38 cm) intervals. Clip hedges and topiary specimens in late summer and early fall.

Propagation Take cuttings in late summer and early fall.

Pests/diseases Box psyllids may feed on the leaves; leaf miners and leaf spot can be problems.

Buxus sempervirens

Calluna
heather

Calluna vulgaris 'Silver Queen'

Mixed heather on a bank

- ❏ Height 4-24 in (10-60 cm)
- ❏ Spread 10-30 in (25-75 cm)
- ❏ Flowers late summer and early fall
- ❏ Well-drained, acid to neutral soil
- ❏ Sunny, open site
- ❏ Hardy zones 3-7

Heathers do well in cool, temperate regions of the United States. They cannot tolerate hot, humid summers but they flourish in the coastal Northeast and throughout the Pacific Northwest.

All heathers belong to a single species *(Calluna vulgaris);* from it dozens of cultivars have been developed, offering a wide range of colors in flower and foliage. The spikes of closely set bell-shaped flowers may be purple, mauve, pink, red, or white; the scalelike leaves are green, gold, silver-gray, or bronze and may change color with the seasons.

Heathers are ideal as ground cover for conifers, in a bed of their own, or as individual dwarf shrubs. The flower spikes are excellent for cutting; they keep their colors well and are good dried for winter decoration.

Popular cultivars
'Blazeaway' bears pale lavender flowers; the foliage is golden yellow in summer and red in winter. It grows 12-15 in (30-38 cm) high and spreads to 2 ft (60 cm).
'County Wicklow' bears double shell-pink flowers. It grows 10 in (25 cm) high and spreads widely.
'Foxii Nana' bears mauve flowers.

Only 4 in (10 cm) high and 10 in (25 cm) wide, it is ideal in a pot.
'Gold Haze' grows to 2 ft (60 cm) high. It has white flowers and golden foliage.
'H.E. Beale' has long sprays of double rose-pink flowers and reaches 2 ft (60 cm) high.
'Kinlochruel,' to 10 in (25 cm) high, has bright green foliage and spikes of double white flowers.
'My Dream' has double white flowers tinged pink with age. It is 2 ft (60 cm) high.
'Nana Compacta' grows only to 8 in (20 cm) high, and bears a profusion of purple-pink flowers.

Calluna vulgaris 'My Dream'

Calluna vulgaris 'Kinlochruel'

Calluna vulgaris 'Nana Compacta'   *Calluna vulgaris* 'County Wicklow'   *Calluna vulgaris* 'Blazeaway'

Calluna vulgaris 'Silver Knight'

Calluna vulgaris 'Robert Chapman' and 'Gold Haze'

'Orange Queen' has golden young foliage turning deep orange as it matures, and purple-pink flowers. It grows 1½ ft (45 cm) high.
'Robert Chapman' has purple flowers and gold foliage that deepens to bronze-red in winter. It reaches 1½ ft (45 cm) high.
'Silver Knight' has woolly silver foliage and pink flowers. It grows 1 ft (30 cm) high.
'Silver Queen' has woolly silver foliage and pale mauve flowers. It is 10 in (25 cm) high.
'Spring Torch,' 20 in (50 cm) high and 2½ ft (75 cm) wide, bears mauve flowers. The summer foliage is tipped cream and pink; in winter and spring, pink and red.

Cultivation
Plant in fall or spring in an open, sunny spot. A well-drained, peaty, slightly acid soil provides perfect growing conditions, but heathers thrive in all but alkaline soils as long as the soil is well-drained.

In spring cut off dead flower stems close to the foliage. Prune tall cultivars lightly with shears after flowering or before new growth starts to avoid legginess.
Propagation Take cuttings from young side shoots between midsummer and midfall.

Increase large plants by layering in early spring. The layers should root after a year.
Pests/diseases Root-rot fungi sometimes attack heathers, as do Japanese beetles, two-spotted mites, and oystershell scale.

Calluna vulgaris 'H.E. Beale'

Camellia

camellia

Camellia japonica 'Elegans'

Camellia japonica 'Berenice Boddy'

- ❏ Height 6-15 ft (1.8-4.5 m)
- ❏ Spread 4-10 ft (1.2-3 m)
- ❏ Flowers late fall to midspring, depending on species
- ❏ Fertile, acid to neutral soil
- ❏ Lightly shaded, sheltered site
- ❏ Hardy zones 7-9

Beautiful camellias are prized as much for their rich green, shiny foliage as for their flowers, which range from white to shades of pink and reds of varying intensity. The single, semidouble, or double blooms, shaped like roses, anemones, or peonies, are borne in late winter and early spring.

Camellias are hardy and thrive in dappled shade. They are ideal to grow against west- or north-facing walls and as freestanding tall specimen shrubs. Camellias, especially those that flower in late winter, do well in containers.

Popular species and cultivars

Camellia cultivars have been developed from two species.

Camellia japonica and its cultivars have a height of 10-15 ft (3-4.5 m), and a spread of 6-10 ft (1.8-3 m); they may bloom from November through April, as climate permits. The blossoms are impressive, measuring 3-5 in (7.5-13 cm) in diameter. Popular cultivars — and their flowering season — include:

'Adolphe Audusson': semidouble blood-red flowers with golden stamens; early.

'Berenice Boddy': semidouble light pink flowers; buds resist frost damage; early to midseason.

'Betty Sheffield': semidouble deep pink flowers; midseason.

'C.M. Wilson': pale pink flowers shaped like anemones; early to midseason.

'Debutante': double peonylike flowers in light pink; early.

'Elegans': salmon-rose anemone-shaped flowers, occasionally marbled white; early.

'Flame': semidouble red flowers; cold-hardy buds; late.

'Governor Mouton': red-and-white variegated flowers; cold-hardy buds; midseason.

'Kumasaka': double deep pink flowers; cold hardy; late.

'Lady Clare': semidouble deep peach-pink flowers; early.

'Lady van Sittart': semidouble pinkish-white flowers streaked rose-pink; mid- to late season.

'Magnoliaeflora': compact plant; semidouble light pink flowers; cold hardy; mid- to late season.

'Mathotiana Rubra': crimson double flowers shaped like roses; midseason.

'Rev. John G. Drayton': semidouble carmine-rose flowers; late.

'Tricolor': semidouble white flowers streaked with carmine-pink; midseason.

'White Empress': double white flowers; cold hardy; late.

Camellia sasanqua tends to form a smaller shrub than *C. japonica*, typically reaching a height of 6-10 ft (1.8-3 m), with a correspondingly smaller spread. It is also less cold hardy, but it can survive most winters in zone 7 if trained against a wall or kept in some other protected spot. The flowers of this species also tend to be smaller, measuring only 2-3 in (5-7.5 cm) in diameter; they open earlier, generally from September into December. Popular cultivars include:

'Bonanza': large, peonylike deep red flowers.

'Jean May': large, semidouble to double shell-pink flowers.

'Mine-No-Yuki': large, double white flowers; a heavy-blooming cultivar.

'Pink Snow': large, semidouble, light pink flowers; vigorous.

Camellia japonica 'Magnoliaeflora'

Camellia sasanqua 'Setsugekka'

Camellia japonica 'Mathotiana Rubra'

'Setsugekka': semidouble white flowers with large ruffled petals.
'Sparkling Burgundy': peonylike ruby-red flowers washed with lavender.
'Yuletide': single red flowers with yellow stamens.

Cultivation

Camellias grow in any good acid to neutral soil; enrich sandy soils with organic matter. A site in dappled shade is ideal; they will also thrive against west-facing or north-facing walls. Avoid an east-facing site, as morning sun after night frost damages developing buds; also avoid exposed sites.

Plant in early spring to midspring or in fall. Staking may be necessary until the shrubs are established. In midspring apply a mulch of well-rotted manure or compost.

Deadhead all camellias as the flowers fade.

Propagation Take cuttings of semimature lateral shoots in summer. Alternatively, layer large plants in early fall and separate 18 months later.

Pests/diseases Birds can damage the flowers, and bud drop can occur in dry soil. Canker causes dieback of twigs or whole trunks; tea scale can infest twigs and foliage; and thrips can cause flower buds to brown at the tips, then rot and drop off.

Camellia japonica 'Tricolor'

Camellia japonica 'C.M. Wilson'

Camellia japonica 'Betty Sheffield'

Camellia sasanqua 'Yuletide'

Camellia japonica 'Rev. John G. Drayton'

Carpenteria

carpenteria, tree anemone

Carpenteria californica

Ceanothus

ceanothus, wild lilac

Ceanothus dentatus

- ❏ Height 1-21 ft (30-640 cm)
- ❏ Spread 5-30 ft (1.5-9 m)
- ❏ Flowers spring to early summer
- ❏ Well-drained soil
- ❏ Sunny site
- ❏ Hardy zones 7-9

The blue-flowered evergreen ceanothuses are nearly all native to California. Many are of hybrid origin and generally hardier than the species. The Californian ceanothuses prefer the temperate, dry climate of the southern Pacific Coast and coastal foothills and are rarely grown in the East. They thrive in seaside gardens and do best inland when grown in the shelter of sunny walls.

Ceanothuses range from tall shrubs to prostrate and creeping types. They are prized for their dense clusters or panicles of star-shaped flowers, all in shades of blue, which are borne in great abundance in spring. The evergreen foliage is ovate to lance-shaped and usually glossy green.

Popular species and hybrids
Ceanothus arboreus is a treelike species reaching 10-20 ft (3-6 m) high. 'Owlswood Blue,' a commonly grown form, bears spike-like clusters of dark blue flowers. *Ceanothus* 'Concha' grows to a height of 6-7 ft (1.8-2.1 m) and spreads to 6-8 ft (1.8-2.4 m). It bears dark green, 1 in (2.5 cm) long leaves and dark blue flowers in 1 in (2.5 cm) clusters. *Ceanothus* 'Dark Star,' a shrub 5-6 ft (1.5-1.8 m) tall and 8-10 ft (2.4-3 m) wide, bears tiny, dark

- ❏ Height 10 ft (3 m)
- ❏ Spread 6-8 ft (1.8-2.4 m)
- ❏ Flowers late spring to midsummer
- ❏ Any fertile, well-drained soil
- ❏ Sunny or shaded site
- ❏ Hardy zones 7-10

Sometimes known as the tree anemone, *Carpenteria californica* is a moderately hardy bushy shrub, with rich glossy green, lance-shaped leaves that are gray-green beneath. Its glistening white, anemonelike, sweetly fragrant flowers bloom from late spring to midsummer. Exceptionally drought resistant, the shrub does well in dry western climates.

Cultivation
Plant in mid- to late spring. Carpenterias will thrive in any fertile and well-drained soil, including an alkaline one. Sun or shade is acceptable, though the plant performs best in light shade. Set plants where they will be protected from cold winds.

Shorten straggly shoots after flowering. Otherwise no pruning is required.
Propagation Seed propagation is the most suitable method; it is a slow process.
Pests/diseases Aphids may attack new growth.

Chamaecyparis

false cypress

Ceanothus thyrsiflorus

Chamaecyparis lawsoniana
'Pembury Blue'

❑ Height 1-15 ft (30-450 cm)
❑ Spread 1-6 ft (30-180 cm)
❑ Coniferous shrub
❑ Ordinary well-drained soil
❑ Sunny or lightly shaded site
❑ Hardy zones 5-8

green leaves and dark cobalt blue flowers in 1½ in (3.75 cm) clusters. It is not attractive to deer.
Ceanothus dentatus grows 8 ft (2.4 m) high and wide. Its clusters of dark blue flowers appear in late spring and early summer.
Ceanothus gloriosus (Point Reyes ceanothus) is a prostrate and creeping shrub, forming an evergreen carpet. It reaches a height of only 1-1½ ft (30-45 cm) but a spread up to 12-16 ft (3.7-4.9 m) wide. This species has dark glossy green, toothed leaves. In spring the plant is studded with lovely lavender-blue flower clusters. Hardy to zone 7, it does not flourish in the hot summers of southern California.
Ceanothus griseus horizontalis (Carmel creeper) is another prostrate form. This species reaches a height of 1½-2½ ft (45-75 cm) and a spread of 5-15 ft (1.5-4.5 m). It bears glossy, oval, bright green leaves that reach 2 in (5 cm) long and displays 1 in (2.5 cm) clusters of light blue flowers. A popular cultivar is 'Yankee Point'; it has a more refined appearance than its parent and produces medium blue flowers.

Ceanothus thyrsiflorus, one of the hardiest and largest evergreen ceanothuses, grows to 6-21 ft (1.8-6.4 m) high with a spread of 8-30 ft (2.4-9 m). It bears light to dark blue flowers in 3 in (7.5 cm) spikelike clusters. 'Repens,' a more compact form, grows into a dome 3-4 ft (1-1.2 m) high.

Cultivation

Plant container-grown young shrubs in spring or fall in fertile, well-drained soil in an open, sunny spot. Although new plantings require watering for the first season, irrigation is likely to prove fatal to established ceanothuses; plant them outside the watered part of the garden. In the colder parts of their range, a protected spot or a sunny wall is best.

You can shorten shoots and prune deadwood after flowering.
Propagation Take heel cuttings of firm nonflowering sideshoots in midsummer, and insert in a propagating box. Pot up rooted cuttings in containers of potting soil, and overwinter in a cold frame or other protected spot.
Pests/diseases Chlorosis may occur in strongly alkaline soil.

This genus of hardy evergreen conifers, commonly known as false cypresses, contains several species and cultivars that grow so slowly that they are treated as shrubs. They are ideal in rock gardens and among heathers, and miniatures can provide winter interest in window boxes and other container displays.

Chamaecyparis conifers can be recognized by their leaves, which are formed of small, flat overlapping scales carried in pairs on either side of the shoots. The leaves are arranged in sprays flattened into one plane and come in a huge range of colors — dark, mid-, and light green, and blue and golden

Chamaecyparis lawsoniana
'Pygmaea Argentea'

Chamaecyparis lawsoniana 'Aurea Densa'

Chamaecyparis obtusa 'Crippsii'

Chamaecyparis obtusa 'Nana Aurea'

yellow. After a few years' growth, small round cones appear.

Depending on the species, the shapes of false cypresses vary; they include columnar, conical, prostrate, and round forms.

Popular species and hybrids
Most popular false cypresses come from one of three species. *Chamaecyparis lawsoniana* (Lawson's false cypress), which is hardy in zones 6-7 in the East and through zone 8 on the Pacific Coast, has given rise to numerous cultivars. Their only shared feature is the fanlike arrangement of their scaly leaves.

'Aurea Densa' has bright golden yellow foliage; it grows in a conical form to 4 ft (1.2 m) high.

'Blom' grows slowly, forming a pillar of blue-green foliage 6 ft (1.8 m) tall and 15 in (38 cm) wide after 10 years.

'Ellwoodii' has gray-green foliage and slowly forms a dense pyramidal shape, reaching 6 ft (1.8 m) tall. Also available are a gold-leaved form, 'Ellwood's Gold,' and a variegated form, 'Ellwoodii Variegata' ('Ellwood's White').

'Fletcheri' has a broad columnar shape. It grows extremely slowly but eventually reaches a height of 12 ft (3.7 m). Its gray-green foliage turns bronze in winter.

'Forsteckensis' grows into a small, round dense shrub with light green foliage. After 10 years, it reaches just 1 ft (30 cm) high and 20 in (50 cm) wide.

'Green Globe,' a 1 ft (30 cm) high and wide miniature, has short sprays of bright green foliage.

'Luteocompacta' forms a broad,

dense cone of green foliage tipped with gold, 5 ft (1.5 m) tall and 3 ft (90 cm) wide after 10 years.

'Minima Aurea' has golden soft foliage and forms a rounded pyramid 3 ft (90 cm) high and wide. A blue-green cultivar, 'Minima Glauca,' is also available.

'Pembury Blue' has a conical shape with silver-blue foliage. It reaches 1½-2 ft (45-60 cm) high.

'Pygmaea Argentea' has blue-green foliage tipped white and forms a rounded shrub with a height of 1-1½ ft (30-45 cm).

Chamaecyparis obtusa (Hinoki cypress) has horizontal branches and flattened sprays of foliage. The leaves are arranged in unequal pairs and have blunt tips. This species is hardy in zones 5-8.

'Crippsii,' a bright golden form with an open habit, grows slowly into a loose conical shrub; it eventually reaches 15 ft (4.5 m) high.

'Fernspray Gold' is of open, bushy habit, with golden foliage in fernlike sprays. Pruning can restrain it to 5 ft (1.5 m).

'Nana Aurea' has golden green foliage and forms a flat-topped miniature 2-2½ ft (60-75 cm) high.

'Nana Gracilis,' a conical shrub with shiny dark green foliage, slowly grows to 8 ft (2.4 m) high.

'Spiralis' forms an upright dark green spire with twisted branchlets. It grows 2½ ft (75 cm) high.

Chamaecyparis pisifera 'Filifera Nana'

Chamaecyparis lawsoniana 'Fletcheri'

Chamaecyparis lawsoniana 'Minima Aurea'

Chamaecyparis lawsoniana 'Elwoodii'

Chamaecyparis pisifera 'Boulevard'

Choisya
Mexican orange blossom

Choisya ternata 'Sundance,' foliage

❏ Height 3-6 ft (1-1.8 m)
❏ Spread 3-8 ft (1-2.4 m)
❏ Flowers late spring to early summer, sporadically thereafter
❏ Well-drained, acid to neutral soil
❏ Sheltered site in full sun or partial shade
❏ Hardy zones 7-9

Chamaecyparis pisifera has horizontal spreading branches and sharply pointed leaves. This species is hardy in zones 5-8.
'Boulevard' forms a broad pyramidal shrub with silver-blue foliage. It grows best in light shade; prune it to 4 ft (1.2 m) high.
'Filifera Nana' has midgreen leaves; it grows into a dense, flat-topped dome 2 ft (60 cm) high.
'Nana' forms a flat-topped mound 1 ft (30 cm) high; its foliage is dark green.
'Plumosa Aurea' forms an irregular shape to 5 ft (1.5 m) high. Its young bright yellow growth deepens to yellow-green with age.
'Plumosa Aurea Compacta' forms a dense conical shrub 2 ft (60 cm) high and has bright yellow leaves that fade to green-yellow.
'Squarrosa Intermedia' forms a neat mound of fine blue-gray foliage; after 10 years, it reaches just 20 in (50 cm) high and wide.
'Sungold' has golden yellow foliage on a rounded, flat-topped shrub up to 2 ft (60 cm) high.

Cultivation
False cypresses grow in any well-drained soil in an open spot or in light shade. To preserve their coloring, grow the golden cultivars in full sun. Avoid exposing these shrubs to drying winds.
    Plant in midfall or early spring. An application of fertilizer in mid-

Chamaecyparis lawsoniana
'Green Globe'

spring can improve the leaf color.
    Pruning is not necessary, but if a leading shoot forks, remove the weaker shoot, or if a dwarf cultivar's branch reverts to the parent's vigor, remove the oversized branch at the base. You can prune false cypresses to restrict growth and spread at any time during the growing season.
Pests/diseases Root-rot fungi may kill false cypresses.

CHERRY LAUREL — see *Prunus*
CHILEAN FIRE BUSH or TREE — see *Embothrium*

For a shrub from Mexico, *Choisya ternata* has proven itself to be surprisingly hardy. Indeed, with protection from winter winds it will overwinter successfully in the southern part of zone 7 and will even survive in the colder parts of that zone if espaliered against a sunny wall. It thrives in the mild-winter and cool-summer areas of the Pacific Coast.
    This shrub is particularly suitable for small gardens, being of compact and neat growth and taking many years to reach its ultimate height of 6 ft (1.8 m). The glossy evergreen leaves have three lobes and are highly aromatic when crushed.
    Grow Mexican orange blossom in a mixed border, close to a path or beneath a window — where its sweet scent can be easily savored. It is suitable as an informal hedge and needs only light trimming.
    The blossom resembles orange blossom and the sweet scents of the plants are similar. White flowers blossom in clusters along the branches, even on young plants, and appear in late spring and early summer; often there is a second, smaller display in fall, following warm summers.
    'Sundance,' a relatively new cultivar, is notable for its bright

Cistus

rock rose

Cistus ladanifer

- ❏ Height 1½-8 ft (45-245 cm)
- ❏ Spread 2-9 ft (60-275 cm)
- ❏ Flowers late spring to midsummer
- ❏ Any well-drained soil
- ❏ Open, sunny site
- ❏ Hardy zones 7-9

Choisya ternata

golden yellow foliage, especially on unfolding young leaves. It grows slowly, and rarely exceeds 3 ft (90 cm) in height and spread.

Cultivation

Plant container-grown young specimens in mid- to late spring in well-drained, acid to neutral soil. They do best in sites sheltered from cold winds, and in northern zone 7; preferably, grow them against any south- or west-facing walls. Choisyas revel in full sun, though they will tolerate light shade.

Little pruning is necessary, but cut back frost-damaged shoots to the base in early spring so that new shoots can develop. When the main flowering display has finished, you should cut out any wayward shoots in order to maintain the bushy shape.

Propagation Take 3 in (7.5 cm) long cuttings of semimature side shoots in late summer. Root the cuttings in a propagation unit with a temperature established between 61-64°F (16-18°C). Pot up the rooted cuttings separately in 3 in (7.5 cm) pots using a sterilized potting soil, and overwinter them in a cold frame or other cool but protected spot. In late spring move the specimens to a nursery bed, and grow on for a year before planting them out in their permanent sites.

Pests/diseases Mites or sucking insects, such as aphids or scale insects, may infest choisyas. In poorly drained soils these plants are subject to crown rot and root-rot fungi.

Natives of the Mediterranean shore, the rock roses flourish along the Pacific Coast, in the foothills of the California coastal ranges, and in the warmer parts of southern Arizona. These tough plants tolerate drought, salt spray, and desert heat. However, they do not adapt well to heat combined with humidity, and though the cold-hardier kinds will survive in the coastal areas of the southeastern or mid-Atlantic states, they do not flourish there as they do on the West Coast.

All *Cistus* species and the numerous hybrids have exquisite, usually white, flowers; they resemble single roses, with petals like crumpled silk surrounding a prominent boss of colorful stamens. The individual blooms last only one day, but they are produced in such abundance that the flowering display extends from late spring into midsummer.

Popular species and hybrids

Cistus × corbariensis, syn. *C. hybridus*, is a low, spreading hybrid, reaching 3-4 ft (1-1.2 m) high and 6-9 ft (1.8-2.7 m) wide. Its reddish buds open into white flowers blotched with yellow. The leaves are dull green and oval.
Cistus crispus is low-growing (2 ft/60 cm high and wide), with gray leaves and purple-pink flowers. The cultivar 'Sunset' has

Cistus × cyprius

Cistus crispus 'Sunset'

cerise-pink flowers. This species is exceptionally hardy, overwintering reliably in zone 7.

Cistus × cyprius, one of the taller hybrids, reaches 8 ft (2.4 m) high and wide. It has sticky olive-green leaves and clusters of white flowers blotched crimson-maroon.

Cistus ladanifer (crimson-spot rock rose) grows up to 3-5 ft (1-1.5 m) high with an equal spread. Its erect stems are clothed with narrow, lance-shaped, dull green leathery leaves that exude a fragrant gum. The large white flowers, up to 4 in (10 cm) wide, have bright yellow stamens and crimson blotches at the petal bases. The species is the parent of numerous hybrids. The variety *C.l. latifolius,* often sold as *C. palhinhae,* is a compact shrub that reaches 2 ft (60 cm) tall and wide; it bears large white flowers in late spring.

Cistus laurifolius is 7 ft (2.1 m) high and 6 ft (1.8 m) wide. This species has leathery dark green leaves and white flowers with yellow centers. The hardiest of the rock roses, it can survive in temperatures as low as 0°F (-18°C) and suffer little damage.

Cistus × purpureus (orchid rock rose) grows into a vigorous upright shrub 4-5 ft (1.2-1.5 m) high and wide. It has lance-shaped gray-green leaves and carmine-pink flowers with maroon blotches. It is an excellent choice for seaside gardens.

Cistus salviifolius (sageleaf rock rose) is a spreading shrub that reaches 2 ft (60 cm) high and 6 ft (1.8 m) wide. The leaves are light gray-green and crinkly; they grow up to 1 in (2.5 cm) long. The 1½ in (3.75 cm) wide flowers are white with dashes of yellow near the petal bases. This tough shrub makes an excellent ground cover for a dry, rocky bank.

Cistus × skanbergii is a naturally occurring hybrid. This shrub grows 3-4 ft (1-1.2 m) high and wide, with narrow gray-green leaves. Clear pink flowers are borne in abundant clusters during late spring.

Cultivation

Plant container-grown specimens in mid- or late spring in well-drained soil in an open, sunny site sheltered from cold winter winds. Cut out a few old stems periodically to keep plants compact and neat; a light shearing of new growth has the same effect.

Propagation In mid- to late summer take 3-4 in (7.5-10 cm) long heel cuttings of nonflowering half-hardened shoots. Root them in a propagating unit and overwinter in a cold frame or other protected spot.

Pests/diseases Frost damage may cause dieback.

Cistus × purpureus

Clematis

clematis

Clematis armandii 'Apple Blossom'

Clematis cirrhosa

- ❏ Height 10-25 ft (3-7.5 m) or more
- ❏ Climber
- ❏ Flowers spring to summer, and winter
- ❏ Well-drained, slightly alkaline soil
- ❏ Sunny, sheltered site
- ❏ Hardy zones 7-10

Most of the climbing *Clematis* species and large-flowered hybrids are deciduous. The chief attraction of these species is their display of large and colorful blooms in spring and summer. In winter, though, these deciduous clematises look distinctly unattractive, with their tangles of long, bare stems seemingly lifeless. However, a few species are evergreen, keeping their attractive leaves throughout the year.

Unfortunately, the evergreen clematises are less hardy than the deciduous types, and none flourish north of zone 7. Even there, the evergreen clematises are best planted along a sunny, sheltered wall or fence. Where the climate suits them, however, they make fast-growing vines that quickly cover a fence or arbor with handsome foliage. The flowers, though less spectacular than those of their deciduous relatives, are nevertheless a welcome bonus.

Popular species

Clematis armandii is a vigorous species that clings with extremely strong tendrils; it is capable of climbing up to 25 ft (7.5 m) or more on a sunny wall and spreading as far as 50 ft (15 m). The three-lobed leaves are dark green with prominent veins. The large saucer-shaped flowers, with pointed petals, are creamy white and appear in early spring to midspring; they are followed by silky seed heads. The cultivar 'Apple Blossom' bears white flowers tinged with pink; 'Farquhariana' bears pink flowers; and 'Snowdrift' has pure white blossoms. This species is the hardiest of the evergreen clematises, flourishing in zones 7-10.

Clematis cirrhosa reaches up to 10-15 ft (3-4.5 m) high and bears ovate to heart-shaped or three-lobed leaves. The creamy white bell-shaped flowers grow to 2½ in (6.25 cm) wide; they open in winter and are followed by fluffy seed heads. It is hardy in zones 9-10.

Cultivation

Plant container-grown specimens in spring when all danger of hard frost has passed. The soil should be well drained, ideally with a neutral or slightly alkaline pH (6.0-7.5); but clematises grow satisfactorily on slightly acid soil as well. The best site is a warm, sheltered spot in the sun with some afternoon shade. Clematis roots prefer moist and cool conditions; the soil around the base of the plant should be shaded or covered with an inch or two of shredded bark. Keep the plants well watered during dry spells, and tie the stems to the trellis supports until growth is well developed.

Pruning is generally unnecessary. Frost may damage some stems, but new ones will usually grow again from the base. Cut back frost-damaged shoots in late spring; you can prune back overlong stems that have outgrown their allotted space by up to two-thirds at the same time or after they flower.

Propagation Take stem cuttings of nonflowering young shoots in summer, and root in a propagating unit. Alternatively, layer long young shoots in late spring and sever them after a year, when they should have rooted.

Pests/diseases Clematis borer is a dull white larva that tunnels into the roots and crowns of clematis, stunting its growth. Black blister beetles, mites, and scale insects attack the flowers, stems, and foliage. Leaf spot and stem rot can be troublesome.

Convolvulus

convolvulus, silverbush

Cordyline

cordyline, giant dracaena

Cordyline australis

❑ Height 3-30 ft (1-9 m)
❑ Spread 2-10 ft (60-300 cm)
❑ Foliage shrub
❑ Well-drained soil
❑ Sunny or lightly shaded site
❑ Hardy zones 8-10

Most cordylines are too cold sensitive to be useful as anything but houseplants, but one species, *Cordyline australis* from New Zealand and Australia, succeeds in mild southern gardens where frosts are rare. It is often grown as a container plant that can be moved under cover during winter.

As a container plant, cordyline forms a fountain of gray-green leaves and grows 3 ft (90 cm) tall. But if planted outside in a warm-winter region, it may become a branching tree, 20-30 ft (6-9 m) high and 6-10 ft (1.8-3 m) wide. Sprays of scented creamy white flowers are borne in spring. The cultivar 'Purpurea' bears purple-flushed leaves.

Cultivation
In the open, plant in spring in any good, well-drained soil, in full sun or light shade. Cordylines are tolerant of strong winds and thrive in mild coastal gardens. Elsewhere, grow in 6-8 in (15-20 cm) pots of a peat-enriched potting mix; move them outdoors when all danger of frost has passed and bring them under frost-free cover in fall. Pruning is unnecessary.
Propagation Detach suckers in spring, pot them up, and grow on.
Pests/diseases Leaf spot may disfigure the leaves.

Convolvulus cneorum

❑ Height 2-4 ft (60-120 cm)
❑ Spread 2-4 ft (60-120 cm)
❑ Flowers late spring to early fall
❑ Gritty, well-drained soil
❑ Sunny, sheltered site
❑ Hardy zones 9-10

The large genus *Convolvulus* includes many herbaceous annuals and perennials, some of which are weeds. One species, *Convolvulus cneorum,* is a neat evergreen shrub that, though intolerant of frost, will thrive in warm, dry regions in gritty, well-drained soil. It is ideal in a rock garden or along a dry stone wall.

It grows as a bushy shrub to an equal height and spread of 2-4 ft (60-120 cm). The narrow lance-shaped leaves, which are covered in hairs, give the shrub a silvery appearance. Clusters of pink buds open into funnel-shaped white flowers between late spring and early fall.

Cultivation
Plant in spring or fall in well-drained, sandy or gritty soil in a sunny, sheltered spot. If the plant becomes straggly, prune it back severely in early spring.
Propagation During early summer to midsummer, take 1½-3 in (3.75-7.5 cm) long heel cuttings of basal shoots or lateral growths. Root them in a cool, shaded spot; pot up the rooted cuttings singly and overwinter in a sunny, protected spot. Plant out in spring.
Pests/diseases None serious.

Corokia

corokia

Corokia cotoneaster

❏ Height 2-4 ft (60-120 cm) or more
❏ Spread 2-4 ft (60-120 cm)
❏ Flowers late spring to early summer
❏ Fertile, well-drained soil
❏ Sheltered, sunny site
❏ Hardy zones 8-10

Corokia cotoneaster is a shrub that flourishes in the United States only in the temperate climate of the Pacific Coast. Within this restricted range, it is very hardy, flourishing in the difficult conditions of seaside gardens and in containers.

Corokia can grow into a dense shrub as much as 10 ft (3 m) high but it more commonly reaches only 2-4 ft (60-120 cm) high and wide. The rigid, wiry branches, one of the plant's main attractions, zigzag in a striking pattern.

Small star-shaped yellow flowers appear in spring. The sparse spoon-shaped leaves are dark green, felted white underneath.

Cultivation

Plant in fertile, well-drained soil in a sunny and sheltered site in spring. You can prune the plant to emphasize the zigzag pattern of growth; make cuts immediately after flowering.

Propagation Take 3 in (7.5 cm) long heel cuttings of semimature lateral shoots in late summer. Root them in a cold frame or other protected spot, and grow on in pots for a year or two before planting out.

Pests/diseases None serious.

Correa

Australian fuchsia

Correa pulchella

❏ Height 2-2½ ft (60-75 cm)
❏ Spread 2-8 ft (60-240 cm)
❏ Flowers late fall to early spring
❏ Well-drained, nutrient-poor soil
❏ Sunny or partially shaded site
❏ Hardy zones 9-10

These shrubs flourish only in the warm, dry climates of southern California and Arizona. Their flowers keep blooming throughout the winter. While ideal ground covers for dry, nutrient-poor banks and slopes, correas do not tolerate fertilization or irrigation. They are low, spreading bushes with 1 in (2.5 cm) roundish gray or grayish-green leaves. The small flowers are fuchsialike, hanging down along the stems like bells.

Popular species and cultivars
'Carmine Bells' is a low, spreading shrub (2 ft/60 cm high) with deep red flowers. ('Ivory Bells' is similar but has creamy blossoms.) *Correa pulchella,* which thrives into northern California, grows to 2 ft (60 cm) tall and 8 ft (2.4 m) wide, bearing pink flowers. *C. × Harrisii,* to 2½ ft (75 cm) tall, is compact and bears red flowers.

Cultivation

Plant in spring in sun or partial shade in well-drained soil that is not too rich. Irrigate regularly for the first year after planting, then only during prolonged drought.

Regular pruning is not needed.
Propagation Take semihardwood cuttings in summer or early fall, and root in pots of equal parts sand and sphagnum peat.
Pests/diseases None serious.

Cotoneaster

cotoneaster

Cotoneaster × watereri 'Rothschildianus'

❏ Height 1-20 ft (30-600 cm)
❏ Spread 1-20 ft (30-600 cm)
❏ Flowers midspring to early summer
❏ Well-drained garden soil
❏ Sunny site
❏ Hardy zones 5-8

The hardy evergreen cotoneasters, one of the most accommodating garden shrubs, are easy to grow in almost any type of soil, and require minimal attention. These shrubs are particularly valued in winter, when the glossy-leaved branches are studded with bright berries.

In growth habit, cotoneasters range from creeping species suitable for ground cover to tall dense shrubs ideal for hedging and screening.

Popular species

Cotoneaster congestus is a dwarf species that forms a dense mound of tightly packed branches; it grows to 1½-2½ ft (45-75 cm) high and 1-3 ft (30-90 cm) wide. This species has tiny bright green leaves and small pink flowers which appear in mid- to late spring. The fall berries are red. It is hardy in zones 6-8 and is ideal for rock gardens.
Cotoneaster conspicuus forms a dense mass of arching stems and grows up to 6-7 ft (1.8-2.1 m) high and 5-6 ft (1.5-1.8 m) wide. The white late-spring flowers conceal the small, glossy dark green leaves and are followed in fall by bright red berries. This species is hardy in zones 7-8.

Cotoneaster dammeri

Cotoneaster horizontalis

Cotoneaster dammeri is a ground-hugging shrub, 1-1½ ft (30-45 cm) high and up to 6 ft (1.8 m) wide. It bears small, glossy dark green leaves; white flowers; and red berries. Perfect for carpeting banks and for espaliering on walls, it is hardy in zones 6-8.

Cotoneaster franchetii grows in a graceful arching habit. Reaching 6-10 ft (1.8-3 m) high and 5-8 ft (1.5-2.4 m) wide, it bears oval gray-green leaves, pink and white blooms in late spring or early summer, and orange-red berries. A good hedging shrub, it is hardy to zone 6.

Cotoneaster horizontalis, deciduous or semievergreen, attracts attention with branches arranged in an appealing herringbone fashion. It grows 2-3 ft (60-90 cm) high and 5-8 ft (1.5-2.4 m) wide and is excellent for training up a wall. Pink flowers appear in mid- to late spring and are followed by red berries. 'Variegatus,' a slow-growing form, has small leaves variegated with cream white and tinged pink in fall. This species is hardy in zones 5-7.

Cotoneaster lacteus, an excellent hedging shrub, reaches a height of 6-10 ft (1.8-3 m) and a spread of 5-8 ft (1.5-2.4 m). It has large, leathery, deep green leaves that are gray and hairy below. The cream-white flowers appear in mid- to late spring and are followed by dense clusters of red berries. These ripen late and last well into winter. This species is hardy in zones 6-8.

Cotoneaster microphyllus, a 2-3 ft (60-90 cm) high species, spreads up to 6-8 ft (1.8-2.4 m) wide. It has glossy dark green leaves with gray and hairy undersides. White flowers appear in mid- to late spring, and scarlet berries crowd the branches in fall. Suitable as ground cover and for covering banks and walls, this species is hardy in zones 6-8.

Cotoneaster salicifolius grows to a height and spread of 12-15 ft (3.7-4.5 m). It bears narrow, willowlike, glossy green leaves. In late spring or early summer, white flowers are displayed in downy clusters; red berries appear in fall. Popular cultivars include 'Autumn Fire' (orange-red berries) and 'Repens' (a low, spreading ground-cover type; its foliage turns reddish-purple in winter). This species is hardy in zones 6-8.

Cotoneaster × watereri, which thrives on the Pacific Coast, is evergreen in warmer regions and deciduous in the colder part of its range. Its arching branches can

Cotoneaster lacteus

Cotoneaster salicifolius

form a shrub 15-20 ft (4.5-6 m) high and wide. The cultivar 'Cornubia' bears heavy crops of large red berries. 'John Waterer' is vigorous, with large clusters of red berries; 'Rothschildianus' bears large clusters of cream-yellow fruit. This species is hardy in zones 7-9.

Cultivation
Plant in fall or early spring in well-drained soil, ideally in a sunny spot. For hedging, space the shrubs 2-3 ft (60-90 cm) apart and cut them back by a quarter to encourage bushy growth.

While pruning is not essential, you can prune vigorous forms back hard in spring. Trim hedges to shape after flowering.
Propagation Layer long shoots in fall; they should root within a year. Alternatively, take 3-4 in (7.5-10 cm) long heel cuttings of mature shoots in late summer.
Pests/diseases Aphids may make the plants sticky and foster sooty mold. Root-rot fungi and fire blight may be problems.

Cotoneaster conspicuus

Crinodendron
lily-of-the-valley tree

Crinodendron hookeranum

Cryptomeria
Japanese cedar

Cryptomeria japonica 'Sekkan Sugi'

❏ Height 1½-6 ft (45-180 cm) or more
❏ Spread 1-5 ft (30-150 cm)
❏ Coniferous shrub
❏ Moist well-drained, slightly acid soil
❏ Sunny, sheltered site
❏ Hardy zones 6-9 (northern)

The Japanese cedar (*Cryptomeria japonica*) is a handsome conifer (see p.30). It is too tall and fast-growing for the average garden, but numerous dwarf forms have been developed from it. These are ideally suited for specimen planting in small gardens, rarely exceeding 6 ft (1.8 m) in height; some are compact enough to warrant a place in the rock garden.

These hardy shrubby conifers are easy to grow. Their attractive foliage often takes on rich colors in fall and winter, adding interest in what can be a drab landscape.

Popular cultivars
'Compressa' grows slowly to a height and spread of 3 ft (90 cm). It forms a flat-topped compact globe of dense foliage, which turns reddish-purple in winter. It is suitable for a rock garden.
'Elegans Compacta' has soft, plumelike blue-green foliage. A tall shrub for this species, it reaches 7 ft (2.1 m) high and 5 ft (1.5 m) wide. In winter the leaves are bronze-red.
'Elegans Nana' grows into a compact shrub, reaching 3 ft (90 cm) high and 5 ft (1.5 m) wide. The shrub's blue-green leaves turn bronze in winter.

❏ Height 10-25 ft (3-7.5 m)
❏ Spread 6-10 ft (1.8-3 m)
❏ Flowers late spring and early summer
❏ Rich, moist, acid to neutral soil
❏ Partially shaded, sheltered site
❏ Hardy zones 8-9

In early fall the lily-of-the-valley tree (*Crinodendron hookeranum*, syn. *Tricuspidaria lanceolata*) puts out a mass of small, long-stalked buds. The following year, in late spring and early summer, the buds swell, resembling tiny crimson lanterns. Much like unopened fuchsia buds, these flowers droop from the branches, swinging in a breeze on long slender stalks.

The crinodendron, a sensitive specimen native to Chile, grows in the United States only in a temperate climate found in the Pacific Northwest's coastal area. It cannot tolerate either extreme cold or heat and grows best in areas of humid but cool summers.

Forming a large, dense shrub or small tree up to 25 ft (7.5 m) tall, the crinodendron bears narrow leaves that are dark green and slightly toothed, with a leathery texture.

Cultivation
Plant in spring in rich, moist but well-drained, acid to neutral soil. The site should be partially shaded and, ideally, sheltered from cold winter winds.

Regular pruning is not necessary; remove any dead or frost-damaged stems in late spring.
Propagation Mid- to late summer is the best time to take 3-4 in (7.5-10 cm) long heel cuttings of half-hardened shoots; root them in a propagating unit at a temperature of 61°F (16°C). Pot rooted cuttings in containers of a peat-enriched potting soil, and over-winter in a frost-free frame or other protected spot. Pot on as necessary the following year, and plant the cuttings out in their second spring.
Pests/diseases Root-rot fungi can kill the shrubs.

Cryptomeria 'Globosa Nana'

Cupressus
cypress

Cupressus macrocarpa 'Golden Cone'

❏ Height 2-8 ft (60-240 cm)
❏ Spread 2-10 ft (60-300 cm)
❏ Coniferous shrub
❏ Ordinary well-drained soil
❏ Sunny site
❏ Hardy zones 7-9

'Globosa Nana' is a compact domed shrub; it grows to a height of 3 ft (90 cm) and a spread of 5 ft (1.5 m). A good specimen cultivar, its rich green leaves, borne on arching branchlets, are blue-green in winter.
'Sekkan Sugi' grows with an upright treelike habit and reaches a height of 5-6 ft (1.5-1.8 m). In winter the foliage is a cream color or tinged with bronze.
'Spiralis' has bright green foliage, which spirals around the branches. This plant has a dense and spreading habit and grows slowly to a height of about 3 ft (90 cm).
'Vilmoriniana' forms a compact globular shrub just 1½ ft (45 cm) high and 2 ft (60 cm) wide. In winter the foliage turns a dull bronze color. It is a popular dwarf conifer for a rock garden.

Cultivation
Plant in fall or spring in a moist but well-drained, slightly acid soil in a sunny, sheltered site.
Do not allow young plants to dry out, and keep them free of weeds. In late spring apply a general fertilizer on the soil surface over the root run. Pruning is rarely necessary, but in midspring cut out any new shoots forking off the main stem.

Propagation In early fall, take 2-4 in (5-10 cm) long cuttings and root in a cold frame. Pot up the cuttings when roots are established. In spring plunge the pots into a protected, well-drained bed outdoors; the lip of the pot should be above the soil. The following fall, plant the cuttings out in a nursery bed, and let them increase in size for a couple of years before moving to permanent planting sites.
Pests/diseases Leaf spot and leaf blight may attack the foliage; branch dieback may be a problem in the Southeast.

This group of conifers includes the picturesque trees Monterey and Italian cypresses (see p.31) and several dwarf cultivars.

Popular cultivars
Cupressus arizonica glabra 'Compacta,' a rounded conical dwarf shrub, is 2 ft (60 cm) high and wide with gray-green foliage.
Cupressus macrocarpa 'Golden Cone' and 'Golden Pillar' make compact cones of golden foliage that can be clipped to 8 ft (2.4 m).
Cupressus sempervirens 'Swane's Golden' grows into a narrow golden column 6 ft (1.8 m) high.

Cultivation
Plant in any well-drained soil in fall or early spring in a sunny spot. Pruning is not needed, but keep leading shoots down to one.
Propagation Take heel cuttings in early fall; root in a cold frame.
Pests/diseases Root-rot fungi can kill the shrubs.

CYPRESS, FALSE — see *Chamaecyparis*

Daboecia

Irish heath

Daboecia cantabrica 'Cinderella'

❏ Height 1½ ft (45 cm)
❏ Spread 1½ ft (45 cm)
❏ Flowers early summer to midfall
❏ Rich, acid, moisture-retentive soil
❏ Sunny or lightly shaded site
❏ Hardy zones 6-8

This small evergreen shrub resembles its better-known relative, the heather *(Calluna vulgaris)*. Irish heath *(Daboecia cantabrica)* grows up to 1½ ft (45 cm) high. It carries long, one-sided spikes of bright rose-purple urn-shaped flowers from June into October in the northern part of its range; in warmer areas, they start to flower in April.

Irish heath is ideal for rock gardens and for ground cover; it makes suitable underplanting for rhododendrons, as long as the shade from these is not too dense.

Popular cultivars

'Alba' bears lovely white flowers.
'Atropurpurea' produces deep purple flowers.
'Cinderella' has a mixture of pink, white, and bicolored flowers.
'Praegerae' displays deep cerise flowers.

Cultivation

In spring or fall, plant in full sun or partial shade in rich, acid, and moisture-retentive soil. Set the plants 1½ ft (45 cm) apart.

Deadhead in spring; to prevent legginess, lightly shear in late fall.
Propagation Layer large plants in early spring. Allow a year for the layers to root.
Pests/diseases Trouble free.

DAISYBUSH — see *Olearia*

Daphne

daphne

Daphne laureola

❏ Height 6-72 in (15-180 cm)
❏ Spread 2-6 ft (60-180 cm)
❏ Flowers any time of year
❏ Good, well-drained soil
❏ Sunny or partially shaded site
❏ Hardy zones 5-9

The evergreen daphnes, like their deciduous relatives, are mainly grown for their richly scented flowers, which appear in winter, spring, summer, or fall, depending on the species. They are generally hardy and easy to grow.

Daphnes grow into small or medium-sized shrubs, making them suitable for rock gardens or the front of mixed flower and shrub plantings.

Popular species

Daphne bholua displays its flowers in winter, bearing a profusion of white or purplish-pink blooms with white interiors. Though the species is evergreen, some of the cultivars are deciduous; check with your nursery before buying. This species is an upright, open

Daphne × burkwoodii 'Somerset'

shrub with a height of 6 ft (1.8 m) and a spread of 5 ft (1.5 m). It is hardy only in zones 8-9.

Daphne blagayana, with a height of just 6 in (15 cm), forms a mat with its spread of 6 ft (1.8 m). It has midgreen leaves and cream-white flowers, which appear in early spring to midspring. It grows best in light shade and is hardy to zone 6.

Daphne cneorum

Daphne × burkwoodii grows into a neat, well-branched, bushy shrub, about 3-4 ft (1-1.2 m) high and wide. A semievergreen, it bears clusters of soft pink flowers in late spring and again in late summer. It is hardy in zones 5-8. 'Somerset,' a popular cultivar, has pale mauve-pink flowers.

Daphne cneorum (garland flower) is a popular species but can be difficult to establish. It grows 6 in (15 cm) high and 2-3 ft (60-90 cm) wide. It has deep green leaves and highly scented rose-pink flowers, which are borne in dense clusters in late spring and early summer. This species is hardy in zones 5-7. Cultivars include 'Alba' (white flowers), 'Eximia' (crimson buds opening to rose-pink flowers), and 'Ruby Glow' (deep pink).

Daphne collina, syn. *D. sericea,* reaches 2½-3 ft (75-90 cm) high and wide. It is of compact habit. The shoots are clothed with ovate, glossy dark green leaves and bear clusters of scented rose-purple flowers in late spring. Ideal for a rock garden, this species is hardy to zone 7.

Daphne laureola (spurge laurel) is a useful ground-cover plant. It reaches 2-4 ft (60-120 cm) high and 3-5 ft (1-1.5 m) wide. It bears tiny green-yellow flowers between late winter and early spring, and is hardy to zone 7.

Daphne × mantensiana slowly forms a dense shrub 1½ ft (45 cm) high and 3 ft (90 cm) wide. The narrow leaves are 1½ in (3.75 cm) long. The perfumed pink or purple flowers are borne at the branch tips intermittently from late spring through the summer. This daphne is hardy to zone 6.

Daphne odora grows into a bushy shrub 5-6 ft (1.5-1.8 m) high and wide. It has lance-shaped, glossy green leaves and pale purple flowers between late winter and midspring. This species is hardy in zones 7-9; at the northern edge of its range it benefits from being grown under the protection of a wall. 'Alba' produces white flowers; 'Aureo-marginata' bears leaves with yellow edging and is slightly hardier.

Daphne tangutica, from China, grows to 3 ft (90 cm) high and 2 ft (60 cm) wide. The foliage is glossy green. The plant bears sweetly scented flowers in late spring and early summer; the blooms are white, tinged rose-purple on the outside. The species is hardy to zone 6.

Cultivation
Plant in early fall or midspring in good, well-drained garden soil. The site can be in sun or partial shade. Select container-grown plants, as daphnes dislike root disturbance.

Regular pruning is not necessary, but remove straggly growth in early spring.

Propagation From midsummer to early fall, take 2-4 in (5-10 cm) long heel cuttings of lateral non-flowering shoots. Root them in a cold frame or other protected spot. The following spring pot up the rooted cuttings singly; plunge them in an outdoor nursery bed with the lip of the pot above the soil. Transplant to their permanent positions 1 or 2 years later.

Pests/diseases Aphids may infest young growth; leaf spot may attack foliage, causing disfigurement and premature drop. Twig canker fungi may cause dieback.

Dodonaea

hop bush

Dodonaea viscosa 'Purpurea'

- ❏ Height 6-15 ft (1.8-4.5 m)
- ❏ Spread nearly equal to height
- ❏ Foliage shrub; attractive fruit in late summer
- ❏ Any, even poor, soil
- ❏ Full sunny site
- ❏ Hardy zones 8-10

The hop bush *(Dodonaea viscosa)* is an Arizona native that forms a dense evergreen shrub 6-8 ft (1.8-2.4 m) tall and wide on dry sites, though if irrigated it will shoot up as high as 15 ft (4.5 m). Because it is sensitive to cold, it will not survive extreme winters; otherwise, it is remarkably tough. This species tolerates extreme drought and heat, as well as poor and alkaline soil, polluted air, and the salt sprays of coastal gardens. Unlike most desert plants, it also thrives in irrigated environments and performs quite well as an accent plant in a mixed border.

Its fast growth and its dense green willowlike foliage make the hop bush an ideal shrub for use as a screen or hedge — and it withstands shearing well. By cutting away all but one stem, you can train this plant as a small tree; it also lends itself to espaliering.

The cultivar 'Purpurea' offers bronze-colored foliage that deepens to purple in winter. While the clusters of greenish flowers are insignificant, the pinkish winged fruit that follows in late summer is decorative.

Cultivation
Plant in fall or early spring in a site with full sun. For the first year of growth, water the shrubs regularly during dry weather; once established, these shrubs flourish even in arid regions with only occasional irrigation.
Propagation In summer, take 4-6 in (10-15 cm) long semihard shoot cuttings; in late summer take firm shoot cuttings. Or grow plants from seeds.

Prune only to maintain specimens as trees or hedges.
Pests/diseases Trouble free.

DRACAENA — see *Cordyline*

Drimys

pepper tree, winter's-bark

Drimys winteri

- ❏ Height 6-25 ft (1.8-7.5 m)
- ❏ Spread 6-15 ft (1.8-4.5 m)
- ❏ Flowers winter and spring
- ❏ Fertile, moist soil
- ❏ Sheltered site with dappled sun or shade
- ❏ Hardy zones 9-10

In mild climates drimyses grow into handsome specimen shrubs or small trees. These natives of South America and Australia cannot tolerate more than an occasional light frost. However, the clean foliage borne on reddish-brown or purplish twigs and the early season of bloom make these a welcome addition to southern and southwestern gardens.

Popular species
Drimys lanceolata, syn. *D. aromatica,* is a slow-growing shrub, 6-8 ft (1.8-2.4 m) high and wide. It is of upright, slender habit and highly aromatic, with purple-red shoots. The leathery leaves are oval to lance-shaped, glossy dark green above, pale green on the undersides; they have copper tints when young. Numerous clusters of small white flowers are produced in mid- and late spring; they are followed by small fruit on female plants.

Drimys winteri grows much taller, to 25 ft (7.5 m) high and 15 ft (4.5 m) wide, into a conical shrub or small tree. It has aromatic bark and large, leathery oval leaves, soft green above and bluish-gray beneath. It flowers when young, bearing loose clusters of attractive, fragrant creamy white flowers in winter and spring.

Elaeagnus
elaeagnus

Drimys lanceolata

Elaeagnus pungens 'Maculata'

Cultivation

Plant in good loamy, well-drained, moisture-retentive soil in midfall or early spring. These shrubs require a warm and sheltered site to protect them from cold winds. In temperate coastal gardens they flourish in dappled sun; in hotter inland gardens they do better in shade. The shrubs thrive in woodland conditions.

Pruning is occasionally necessary to remove straggly growth and maintain a compact form.

Propagation In fall take 6-8 in (15-20 cm) hardwood cuttings, and root in a cold frame or other protected spot. In spring transfer the rooted cuttings to a sheltered nursery bed, and grow them on for a couple of years before moving them to their permanent sites. Long shoots can also be layered in spring; they should root by the following year.

Pests/diseases Trouble free.

❑ Height 8-15 ft (2.4-4.5 m)
❑ Spread 6-15 ft (1.8-4.5 m)
❑ Foliage shrub; flowers fall
❑ Ordinary, even poor, well-drained soil
❑ Sunny or partially shaded site
❑ Hardy zones 6-9

The evergreen *Elaeagnus* species produces tough, adaptable shrubs that are grown mainly for their handsome foliage and their ability to flourish even in adverse conditions. These plants will grow in a wide range of soils, both alkaline and acid. They tolerate both drought and air pollution, flourish in coastal gardens despite salt sprays, and succeed in either full sun or shade. When considering all these strengths and their attractive evergreen foliage, these shrubs are invaluable as hedges and screens on difficult sites.

Evergreen elaeagnus shrubs bloom in fall. Though the flowers are small, they are sweetly scented and freely produced when little else is in bloom.

Popular species

Elaeagnus × ebbingei is a fast-growing hybrid that bears leathery silver-gray leaves. Its foliage may thin with the onset of winter at the northern edge of its range (zone 6), but it never drops all its leaves; towards the South it performs as a true evergreen. Silvery flowers appear in mid- to late fall, followed by small red or orange fruit. It grows 10-15 ft (3-4.5 m) high and wide. 'Gilt Edge' has gold-margined leaves, and 'Limelight' has green leaves with broad deep yellow markings.

Elaeagnus pungens, one of the parents of *Elaeagnus × ebbingei*, is a vigorous, spreading shrub that will grow out of control unless kept in check by regular pruning. It bears leathery leaves that are glossy green above and dull white underneath. The silver flowers, which are borne in mid- to late fall, are sometimes followed by small red or orange fruit. With a height of 8-10 ft (2.4-3 m) and an equal spread, this species is excellent for hedging. Popular cultivars include 'Dicksonii' (slow-growing and erect; gold-edged leaves), 'Fruitlandii' (more symmetrical in outline than the species; narrow creamy yellow leaves edged with bright green), 'Maculata' (leaves splashed with gold in the center), 'Marginata' (leaves edged with silvery-white), and 'Variegata' (vigorous; cream-edged leaves).

Embothrium

Chilean fire tree or fire bush

Erica

heath

Elaeagnus × ebbingei 'Gilt Edge'

Embothrium coccineum

Erica vagans 'Lyonesse,' flowers

Cultivation

Plant in spring or fall in virtually any soil, even nutrient-poor, shallow, sandy soil. Evergreen elaeagnus does equally well in sun and partial shade.

For hedges, space young plants 1½ ft (45 cm) apart; for screens, 2-3 ft (60-90 cm) apart. After planting, cut all shoots back by at least one-third to promote bushy growth from below.

Regular pruning is necessary to contain the long straggling shoots that spring up from *Elaeagnus pungens*; these can be shortened in mid- to late spring. Branches of variegated cultivars of *E. pungens* can revert to green-leaved shoots; it's best to remove these branches immediately by cutting them off at the base.

Propagation Take 4 in (10 cm) long heel cuttings in late summer or early fall; root in a cold frame or other protected spot. Pot up the rooted cuttings singly in spring; plunge them in an outdoor nursery bed until fall, when the young plants can be moved to their permanent positions.

Pests/diseases Leaf spot can cause brown blotches on the leaves, and spider mites may attack foliage in hot, dry weather.

- ❏ Height 15-20 ft (4.5-6 m)
- ❏ Spread 7-10 ft (2.1-3 m)
- ❏ Flowers late spring
- ❏ Lime-free, moisture-retentive soil
- ❏ Sunny, sheltered site
- ❏ Hardy zones 8-9

The fire tree *(Embothrium coccineum)* from Chile and Argentina can be grown outdoors only in the milder regions of the United States, such as southern California. Under favorable conditions, however, this species grows into a magnificent shrub, with stiff upright stems reaching 15-20 ft (4.5-6 m) high and 10 ft (3 m) wide from numerous suckers. The shiny, oval midgreen leaves provide year-round interest, and in late spring the shrub bears numerous clusters of scarlet flowers. These blooms are tubular, approximately 2 in (5 cm) long, and brilliantly colored.

Cultivation

Plant in spring in good, acid to neutral, moist soil in a sunny site. In the northern part of their range, the shrubs must be protected from cold winds and frost until they are well established; set them on the south side of a sunny wall or wrap them with burlap before a cold spell sets in.

Pruning is not required, though straggly growth can be shortened after flowering.

Propagation Increase by detaching suckers from the base and growing in pots.

Pests/diseases None serious.

- ❏ Height ¾-20 ft (23-600 cm)
- ❏ Spread ¾-8 ft (23-240 cm)
- ❏ Flowers throughout the year
- ❏ Moist, but well-drained, acid soil
- ❏ Sunny, open site
- ❏ Hardy zones 4-8, depending on species

Ericas are grown mainly for their flowers. At almost any time of the year at least one species or cultivar is producing spikes of white, pink, purple, or bicolored bell-shaped blooms at the end of their stems. The flowers are excellent for cutting and drying for winter decoration.

The neat needlelike foliage is composed of dense green whorls, though some cultivars have handsome leaves in shades of orange, red, or yellow.

The hardy ericas, which are closely related to true heathers *(Calluna),* range in height from ¾-20 ft (23-600 cm). Low-growing types are ideal as ground cover, and the taller ones can be treated as specimen plants or grown as hedges. All ericas will blend easily with conifers.

Popular species and hybrids

Erica arborea (tree heath) reaches 12 ft (3.7 m) high and 6-8 ft (1.8-2.4 m) wide, though in mild climates it may grow to a height of 20 ft (6 m). It has midgreen leaves and slightly fragrant ash-white flowers, which appear in early spring to midspring. The species is hardy only to zone 6; but 'Alpina,' with bright green foliage, is somewhat hardier.

Erica australis, a tree heath from southern Europe, is hardy in

Erica carnea 'Aurea' in winter

Erica arborea 'Alpina'

zones 7-9, and even in zone 10, in dry climates. It grows up to 4 ft (1.2 m) wide and 6 ft (1.8 m) high, and flowers from early to late spring, bearing dense spikes of rich rose-pink flowers. The cultivar 'Mr. Robert' is pure white; 'Riverslea' is pink.

Erica carnea, syn. *E. herbacea*, a dwarf compact species, flowers from early winter to late spring. It is parent of a large number of garden cultivars. With a height of 1 ft (30 cm) and a spread of 2 ft (60 cm), it is ideal as a ground cover. The species and its cultivars tolerate alkaline soils and are hardy to zone 4 with winter protection of a blanket of evergreen boughs. The following popular cultivars all have midgreen leaves unless otherwise stated: 'Aurea' (deep pink flowers fading to white; golden foliage in spring and early summer), 'December Red' (purple-red flowers), 'Foxhollow' (pale pink flowers; golden foliage in summer), 'Heathwood' (rose-purple flowers; dark green or bronze leaves), 'King George' (carmine-pink flowers), 'Myretoun Ruby' (ruby-red flowers; dark green leaves), 'Pink Spangles' (abundant pink flowers), 'Ruby Glow' (ruby-red flowers in spring; bronze foliage), 'Springwood Pink' (rose-pink flowers), 'Springwood White' (dense pure white flowers; dark green leaves), and 'Vivellii' (red flowers and bronze leaves in winter; dark green leaves in summer).

Erica ciliaris (fringed heath) is hardy to zone 7. It forms a low, pale green shrub that grows to 12-15 in (30-38 cm) high and 2 ft (60 cm) wide. The flower spikes, in shades of pink, rose, and purple as well as white, appear in early summer and continue until winter. Popular cultivars include 'Corfe Castle' (salmon-pink flowers; bronze winter foliage), 'David McClintock' (pink, white-tipped flowers; gray-green leaves), 'Mrs. C.H. Gill' (clear red flowers; dark green foliage), and 'Stoborough' (pure white).

Erica cinerea (twisted heath or bell heather), an ideal ground-cover plant, grows to a height and spread of 9-12 in (23-30 cm). It is hardy to zone 6 or to zone 5 with winter protection. The flowers, which appear in late spring and summer, are white or striking shades of deep pink, red, maroon, or mahogany. When they fade in fall they resemble russet-brown bells. The following popular cultivars all have midgreen foliage unless otherwise stated: 'Alba Minor' (white flowers; light green leaves), 'Atrorubens' (ruby-red flowers), 'Atrosanguinea' (magenta flowers; dark green leaves), 'C.D. Eason' (rose-red flowers), 'Cindy' (bright pink flowers; bronze-green foliage), 'Eden Valley' (bicolored lavender-and-white flowers), 'Golden Drop' (pale purple flowers; its coppery yellow leaves turn bronze-red in winter), 'Pink Ice' (pink flowers; bright dark green foliage), and 'Velvet Night' (dark purple flowers; dark green leaves).

Erica × darleyensis is a hybrid between *E. carnea* and *E. erigena*. Up to 2 ft (60 cm) high, with a spread of 3 ft (90 cm) or more, it grows well in acid or alkaline soils and is hardy to zone 5. The leaves are usually midgreen; the white, pink, or purple flowers appear between fall and late spring, though they are at their finest in early

Erica carnea 'Aurea' in spring

Erica vagans

spring and midspring. Popular cultivars include 'Arthur Johnson' (rose-colored flowers), 'Darley Dale' (pale pink flowers), 'Jack H. Brummage' (deep pink flowers; greenish-yellow leaves tinged red in winter), and 'White Perfection' (pure white flowers; bright green foliage).

Erica erigena, syn. *E. mediterranea*, is a tall species capable of reaching 10 ft (3 m) or more high and 4 ft (1.2 m) wide. Hardy only as far north as zone 7, it thrives in a wide range of soils, both acid and alkaline — and unlike other heaths, it tolerates damp ones. Popular cultivars include 'Brightness' (low-growing; rose-purple flowers; bronze-green leaves), 'Irish Dusk' (clear pink flowers; dark green foliage), and 'W.T. Rackliff' (cream-white flowers; dark green leaves).

Erica terminalis, syn. *E. stricta*, is the hardiest of the tree heaths, overwintering successfully in zone 5 if given winter protection. Reaching 8 ft (2.4 m) high and 4 ft (1.2 m) wide, it makes a good hedging shrub. This heath grows in alkaline soil. The pink or purple flowers appear in abundance in early summer and continue until fall. The leaves mature from bright to dark green.

Erica tetralix (cross-leaved heath) thrives in gardens in any acid to neutral soil, growing to a height and spread of 9-12 in (23-30 cm). It bears gray, often hairy, leaves. Soft pink flowers are produced in summer and early fall. It is hardy

Erica cinerea 'Atrorubens'

Erica vagans 'Lyonesse'

Erica × darleyensis 'Darley Dale'

in zones 4-8. Popular cultivars include 'Alba Mollis' (white flowers; silver-gray foliage), 'Con Underwood' (crimson flowers; gray-green foliage), and 'Hookstone Pink' (clear rose-pink flowers; light silver-gray foliage).

Erica vagans (Cornish heath) is a vigorous species that is hardy in zones 5-8. It grows to a height of 4 ft (1.2 m) and a spread of 8 ft (2.4 m). Its pale pink or purple flowers, borne between midsummer and midfall, are set off by midgreen leaves. Cultivars include 'Lyonesse' (white flowers), 'Mrs. D.F. Maxwell' (cerise-pink flowers), and 'St. Keverne' (clear salmon-pink flowers).

Cultivation

Plant in an open, sunny spot in mid- to late spring or mid- to late fall. Most of these species and cultivars will grow best in acid soil; however, *E. carnea*, *E. × darleyensis*, *E. erigena*, *E. terminalis*, and *E. tetralix* tolerate alkalinity. All except *E. erigena* require well-drained soil.

Winter- and spring-flowering ericas rarely need pruning, but trim off any faded flower spikes with scissors. The spikes of summer- and fall-flowering types remain ornamental as they fade, and deadheading can be delayed until spring.

With age, it is not unusual for ericas that flower in the summer

and fall to become straggly, producing inferior flowers; cut old woody stems back hard in spring. If you wish to prevent legginess in tree heaths, lightly prune them in late fall or before new growth starts in spring.

Propagation All ericas are easily increased. Layer low-growing types in spring or fall. They usually root within a year; at this point sever them from the parent plants and transplant. Or take

1-2 in (2.5-5 cm) cuttings of non-flowering side shoots in late summer or early fall, and root in a cold frame.

Pests/diseases Stem rots, rust, and powdery mildew (a gray discoloration of the foliage caused by a fungus) may affect the plants. Chlorosis may occur on strongly alkaline soil.

Erica erigena 'W.T. Rackliff'

Eriobotrya
loquat

Eriobotrya japonica, foliage

plants, with winter protection, until they are both large enough and strong enough to be planted in the ground.

Pests/diseases Fire blight may cause browning and wilting of leaves and shoots.

Eriobotrya japonica

- ❏ Height 15-25 ft (4.5-7.5 m)
- ❏ Spread similar to height
- ❏ Flowers fall or early winter
- ❏ Any moisture-retentive soil
- ❏ Sunny or lightly shaded, sheltered site
- ❏ Hardy zones 8-10

The fragrant loquat tree *(Eriobotrya japonica)* thrives in our southern states. It commonly grows as a multistemmed shrub and can be kept compact through shearing, but it may also be trained as a single-trunked tree. Loquats have been used for street and specimen plantings.

The white flowers, which resemble hawthorn clusters, appear from early fall onward; the plant rarely bears fruit in the mid-South, but it produces a heavy crop of edible globular yellow fruit in spring in the Deep South.

Most loquats are grown for the architectural beauty of their foliage. The firm, leathery leaves are 1 ft (30 cm) or more long and have corrugated surfaces and sawtooth edges. They are oblong, glossy dark green above and coated with a fuzzy brown wool on the undersides.

Cultivation
Plant in fall or spring in ordinary moisture-retentive, well-drained soil. The site can be in full sun or light shade and should be sheltered from cold winds; mild maritime locations are ideal. Loquats make excellent espaliers and are notably drought tolerant. This species tolerates pruning quite well but should not be overfertilized; this promotes susceptibility to fire blight.

Propagation In late summer take 4-6 in (10-15 cm) long heel cuttings of semimature young shoots, and root them in a propagating unit. When the roots are established, pot up the cuttings singly and overwinter in a frost-free greenhouse. In late spring plunge the pots outdoors in a sheltered, lightly shaded spot; the lips of the pots should protrude above the soil. Grow the young

Eriobotrya japonica, fruits

Escallonia

escallonia

Escallonia 'C.F. Ball'

❏ Height 4-8 ft (1.2-2.4 m) or less
❏ Spread 4-6 ft (1.2-1.8 m)
❏ Flowers late spring to midfall
❏ Any well-drained soil
❏ Sunny site
❏ Hardy zones 7-10

Escallonias are South American natives that are sensitive to cold but tolerant of wind. They thrive on exposed coastal headlands and can tolerate moderate drought once well rooted into the soil. Fast-growing, they make an excellent informal screen and may be cultivated as a formal hedge, though shearing reduces the numbers of flowers they bear. The clusters of small tubular blossoms appear between late spring and midfall, set among small, lance-shaped, glossy midgreen to deep green leaves.

Popular species and cultivars

Escallonia rubra, hardy to zone 8, is an upright shrub that grows to 6-15 ft (1.8-4.5 m) high. It bears smooth, very glossy dark green leaves; in the winter months it produces red to crimson flowers in 1-3 in (2.5-7.5 cm) clusters. *Escallonia virgata* is the most cold-tolerant species, surviving into zone 7.

Escallonia 'Apple Blossom'

Eucryphia
eucryphia

Escallonia rubra

The following garden cultivars, although hardy only into zone 8, offer superior performance when grown in suitable conditions.
'Apple Blossom' is a slow-growing compact shrub 5 ft (1.5 m) high and wide, with cup-shaped pink-and-white flowers.
'C.F. Ball' has large tubular crimson flowers. Its dark green leaves are aromatic when crushed. You can maintain this compact cultivar at 3 ft (90 cm) high by pinching back the shoots.
'Frades' grows into a dense shrub 5-6 ft (1.5-1.8 m) high; but you can maintain it at a lower height by pinching back the new growth. It bears a fine show of clear pink to rose-colored flowers almost throughout the year.
'William Watson' is a compact shrub that reaches a height of just 4 ft (1.2 m); it bears 3 in (7.5 cm) clusters of deep rose flowers from spring through summer.

Cultivation
Plant in midfall or in early spring in any ordinary well-drained soil. In mild coastal gardens, the site should be sunny and open; in hot interior regions, grow in partial shade. Trim flowering shoots after the blooms fade. With mature, taller specimens, remove one third of the old shoots each year; cut them back to the shoot bases.
Propagation You can take 3-4 in (7.5-10 cm) long heel cuttings of semimature nonflowering shoots in late summer and early fall; root them in a cold frame or other protected spot.
Pests/diseases Trouble-free.

Eucryphia × nymansensis

- Height 15 ft (4.5 m)
- Spread 7 ft (2.1 m)
- Flowers late summer to early fall
- Well-drained, neutral or acid soil
- Sheltered, sunny or lightly shaded site
- Hardy zones 8-9

There comes a time in late summer when a fresh effect is needed to cheer up the garden — *Eucryphia × nymansensis* fills the bill perfectly, with glossy dark foliage that sets off cream-colored blooms. In August and September it bears delicately fragrant cup-shaped flowers with a satiny sheen. Two cultivars are usually available: 'Mount Usher,' which forms a small column of toothed evergreen leaves, and the faster-growing 'Nymansay.'

Cultivation
Plant in fall or spring in well-drained, neutral to acid soil with a cool root run (this can be provided by a thick blanket of mulch or by shading the roots with a low-growing shrub). Eucryphias need a sunny or partially shaded site, ideally in the shelter of light woodland or a west-facing wall. They prefer the combination of mild summers and winters offered by the Pacific Northwest

Eucryphia × nymansensis, flowers

coast. Even there, however, they need protection from the wind on exposed sites.

Propagation In late summer to early fall take 3-4 in (7.5-10 cm) long heel cuttings of lateral nonflowering shoots. Root in a propagating unit at a temperature of 61°-64°F (16°-18°C). Pot the rooted cuttings singly in containers of sterilized potting mix; overwinter in a frost-free greenhouse, cold frame, or other protected spot. In late spring, pot on and plunge them outdoors, with the lips of the pots protruding above the soil; overwinter in a cold frame, then plant out in permanent positions the following spring.
Pests/diseases Trouble free.

Euonymus

euonymus

Euonymus fortunei 'Emerald 'n' Gold'

Euonymus fortunei 'Silver Queen'

❑ Height ½-15 ft (15-450 cm) or more
❑ Spread 1-8 ft (30-240 cm)
❑ Climber
❑ Foliage shrub
❑ Any kind of soil
❑ Sunny or partially shaded site
❑ Hardy zones 5-9

The evergreen euonymuses supply valuable year-round interest in the garden. They are moderately to very cold hardy and flourish in many conditions. Leaves are generally in shades of glossy green, but may have gold or silver variegations. Some species are excellent for close ground cover; other, upright and climbing types are suitable for hedging and as wall coverings.

Evergreen euonymuses are grown mainly for their handsome foliage of small oval and leathery leaves. Although they do bloom in late spring or summer, the clusters of small pale green to white flowers are less conspicuous than the pink or orange fruit in fall.

Popular species and cultivars

Euonymus fortunei is a variable species, creeping and prostrate in the young stages and shrubby or climbing in the adult form, rather like ivy *(Hedera)*. At ground level the long stems sprawl to 6 ft (1.8 m), rooting where they touch the soil; as a self-clinging climber on a wall, the species easily reaches a height of 10 ft (3 m). Only adult forms produce flowers, in early summer, followed by orange seeds enclosed in pink capsules. This species is hardy in zones 5-8.

Numerous cultivars have been bred from *E. fortunei;* they include 'Carrierei' (large-leaved glossy shrub; to 9 ft/2.7 m against a wall; bears flowers and fruit), 'Coloratus' (glossy green leaves tinged red-purple in winter; trails or climbs to 26 ft/8 m against a wall), 'Emerald Cushion' (prostrate, mound-forming shrub; rich green leaves), 'Emerald Gaiety' (bushy shrub; 2 ft/60 cm high and 3 ft/90 cm wide; deep green leaves edged in white which turns pinkish in winter), 'Emerald 'n' Gold' (dense dwarf shrub; 1½ ft/45 cm high and 2 ft/60 cm wide; glossy

Euonymus fortunei 'Emerald 'n' Gold'

green leaves with broad margins of yellow, turning pink in winter; climber if supported), 'Gold Tip' (upright shrub; 1½ ft/45 cm high; dark green leaves tipped golden yellow), 'Kewensis' (prostrate shrub; 6 in/15 cm high; miniature green leaves), 'Sarcoxie' (upright shrub; 6 ft/1.8 m high; glossy dark green leaves; large white fruit tinted pink), and 'Silver Queen' (small compact shrub; adult reaches 10 ft/3 m against a wall; creamy yellow young leaves become green with broad creamy white margins).

Euonymus japonica is a densely branched shrub reaching 10-15 ft (3-4.5 m) in height, with a spread of 5 ft (1.5 m). It bears narrow, ovate, shallow-toothed leaves that are leathery and glossy dark green. Small clusters of green-white flowers are borne in late spring and may be followed by pink and orange fruit. Although the species is not reliably hardy north of zone 7, it will grow as far south as zone 9 and thrives in coastal gardens where it is extremely tolerant of salt sprays.

The numerous forms raised from *E. japonica* include 'Albomarginata' (pale green young leaves aging to blue-green with narrow white edges), 'Aurea' (syn. 'Aureopicta'; green leaves with broad yellow centers), 'Latifolius Albomarginata' (syn. 'Macrophylla Alba'; variegated form with broad white edges to the leaves), 'Microphylla Variegata' (small and slow-growing;

Fabiana
fabiana

Euonymus japonica 'Aurea'

Fabiana imbricata

❏ Height 7 ft (2.1 m)
❏ Spread 7 ft (2.1 m)
❏ Flowers early summer
❏ Neutral or acid soil
❏ Sunny, sheltered site
❏ Hardy to zone 9

dense habit; small narrow leaves margined with white; similar to boxwood in appearance), and 'Ovata Aurea' (syn. 'Aureovariegata'; slow-growing; compact habit; leaves edged and suffused with creamy yellow; requires a site in full sun to retain its bright leaf colors).

Euonymus kiautschovica, syn. *E. patens*, is a wide-spreading shrub, 8 ft (2.4 m) high and wide. This species bears bright green pointed leaves. In early fall it produces comparatively large yellow-green flower clusters; they are followed by pink seeds hidden in orange capsules in early winter. It is hardy in zones 6-8.

Cultivation
Plant euonymuses in early fall to midfall or in early spring. They thrive in almost any kind of soil, moist or dry, acid or alkaline; the site can be in full sun or partial shade. The variegated cultivars tend to be less cold hardy than the green-leaved ones and should be protected by sheltered sites in the North.

For hedging, use young plants about 1 ft (30 cm) high and space them 15-18 in (38-45 cm) apart.

After planting and during the first year of growth, pinch the tips of leading shoots to encourage branching.

Specimen shrubs need little regular pruning, though you can trim them to shape with shears at any time of the year. Prune established hedges in midspring and, if necessary, again in late summer.

Propagation In late summer or early fall take 3-4 in (7.5-10 cm) heel cuttings; root them in a cold frame or other protected spot. Late next spring, transplant the cuttings to an outdoor bed, and grow on for a couple of years before planting out.

Pests/diseases Scale insects can infest stems and leaves. Powdery mildew is common on *E. japonica* and shows as a white coating. Crown gall, anthracnose, and various fungal leaf spots are also common problems.

Fabiana imbricata is an oddity and a rarity: it resembles the tree heaths (see *Erica arborea*) but is not related to them. It is actually a member of the potato family.

The shrub is not frost tolerant and requires a warm, sheltered spot; but it does not thrive in hot, humid summers. It is best suited to temperate seaside gardens, especially those along the Pacific Coast. It is well worth growing for the dense plumes of white flowers it produces in early summer. This shrub bears green leaves that are small and needlelike.

Cultivation
Plant in good, moist but well-drained soil in a sheltered, sunny site. The shrub thrives in acid to neutral soil, although it is tolerant of an alkaline pH.

Pruning is not necessary, but you can keep its shape by trimming the shrub in midsummer.

Propagation Take semimature cuttings in summer and root in a propagating unit.

Pests/diseases Trouble free.

EVERLASTINGS — see
Helichrysum

FALSE CYPRESS — see
Chamaecyparis

×*Fatshedera*

fatshedera

× Fatshedera lizei

❑ Height 4-8 ft (1.2-2.4 m)
❑ Spread 3-4 ft (1-1.2 m)
❑ Foliage shrub
❑ Any well-drained soil
❑ Sunny or partially shaded site
❑ Hardy zones 8-10

× *Fatshedera lizei* is a hybrid between *Fatsia* and *Hedera helix* (English ivy). A hardy sprawling shrub, you can use it for ground cover, allow it to trail over low walls, or train it up vertical surfaces as a climber (but tie it up; it cannot cling to the support itself).

Fatshedera is grown for its handsome foliage; it has shiny, leathery deep green leaves that are palmate with five deep lobes. Pale green flowers are borne in terminal bunches that are 8-10 in (20-25 cm) long and 4 in (10 cm) wide. The cultivar 'Variegata' has leaves edged with white.

Cultivation
Plant in early fall to midfall or early spring to midspring in ordinary well-drained soil in a sunny or partially shaded site.

Though regular pruning is not necessary, lateral growths can be shortened in early spring to midspring. If growing fatshedera as ground cover, stake the upright shoots down into the soil when they are 1½ ft (45 cm) high.

Propagation In mid- to late summer take 4-5 in (10-13 cm) long cuttings of tip or side shoots. Root the cuttings in a cold frame.

Pests/diseases Trouble free.

Fatsia

Japanese fatsia

Fatsia japonica

❑ Height 8-15 ft (2.4-4.5 m)
❑ Spread 8-15 ft (2.4-4.5 m)
❑ Foliage shrub
❑ Any moist but well-drained soil
❑ Sheltered, shaded site
❑ Hardy zones 8-10

Despite its exotic appearance, this Japanese relation of the common ivy *(Hedera)* is at home in southern gardens and is often grown as a houseplant. *Fatsia japonica* is an erect shrub, with strong stems that rarely branch, supporting glossy hand-shaped leaves that are often more than 1 ft (30 cm) across. The leaves are midgreen above and paler green on the undersides. In fall each stem bears a multiple head of creamy white ivylike flower clusters, sometimes followed by black berries.

To show fatsia at its best, set it against a wall, where it will provide a comforting backdrop of greenery throughout the year. It thrives in city gardens, as it tolerates pollution and shade.

Cultivation
Plant in early fall to midfall or spring in any kind of moist but well-drained soil. Choose a sheltered spot in full or partial shade. In areas where occasional frosts may be expected, plant it against a south- or west-facing wall.

Pruning is not essential, but hard cutting back of straggly shoots in midspring will lead to lush new growth.

Fatsia japonica, flowers

Propagation Detach suckering shoots in early spring to midspring. Pot singly in potting compost; root in a cold frame. Pot on as necessary, then plant out in the permanent spot in midspring the following year.

Pests/diseases Frost damage and mites may distort the leaves.

FIRE BUSH, CHILEAN — see *Embothrium*
FIRETHORN — see *Pyracantha*
FLANNEL BUSH — see *Fremontodendron*

Fremontodendron

flannel bush

Fremontodendron californicum

Fremontodendron californicum
'California Glory'

- ❏ Height 10-25 ft (3-7.5 m)
- ❏ Spread 6-15 ft (1.8-4.5 m)
- ❏ Flowers late spring and summer
- ❏ Good, well-drained soil
- ❏ Sunny, sheltered site
- ❏ Hardy zones 8-10

Native to California and the Southwest, fremontodendrons are magnificent tall shrubs that are suitable for dry and sunny mild-winter climates. They require a very well-drained soil and are notably drought tolerant once established. Because their roots are shallow, these tall shrubs (or small trees) require staking while they are young. This characteristic also makes them the perfect partners for such deeper-rooted drought survivors as *Ceanothus* species; the two types of shrubs can grow in close proximity without competing.

Fremontodendrons are relatively short-lived — but they do grow fast, soon reaching a height of 10-25 ft (3-7.5 m) and a spread of 15 ft (4.5 m) on favorable sites. The yolk-yellow flowers measure 2¹/₂-3 in (6.25-7.5 cm) wide, and mount a brilliant display when the shrubs are in peak bloom in late spring.

Popular species

Fremontodendron californicum is the hardier species, overwintering through zone 8. Its slender stems are set with dark green three-lobed leaves that are covered with a pale brown felt on the undersides. In May and June the shrub's branches are practically hidden in yellow blossoms. 'California Glory' is hardier than the species and flowers even more profusely, over a longer season. *Fremontodendron mexicanum* resembles *F. californicum* but has five-lobed glossy foliage; its narrower flowers open out to stars of lemon-yellow flushed with red on the outside. This species blooms over a longer season; however, because the flowers are borne in among the leaves, the show is not as dramatic. It is hardy to zone 9.

Cultivation

Plant in fall or spring in any fertile, well-drained soil; fremontodendrons are drought resistant and thrive on alkaline soil. They require full sun and shelter from cold winds; because they have shallow roots, the shrubs appreciate the support of a trellis or a sunny wall.

Pruning is rarely required, but cut back straggly shoots and frost-damaged stems to healthy buds in early spring.

Propagation Take heel cuttings, 3-4 in (7.5-10 cm) long, in late summer, and root in a propagating unit at a temperature of 61°F (16°C). Pot up the rooted cuttings singly, and overwinter in a frost-free, sunny spot. Plunge the pots in a sunny bed through the next summer, moving them back into shelter in fall if frost threatens. Plant out in the permanent sites the following spring.

Pests/diseases Trouble free.

FUCHSIA, AUSTRALIAN — see *Correa*

Garrya

silk-tassel bush

Garrya elliptica

× *Gaulnettya*

gaulnettya

× *Gaulnettya wisleyensis*

❏ Height 3 ft (90 cm)
❏ Spread 3 ft (90 cm)
❏ Flowers late spring to early summer
❏ Well-drained, acid soil
❏ Sunny or partially shaded site
❏ Hardy zones 6-9

By crossing two species, breeders have added another shrub to the small collection of acid-loving plants: × *gaulnettya wisleyensis* (syn. × *gaulthettya wisleyensis*).

Reaching just 3 ft (90 cm) high and wide, this hardy bushy shrub spreads by means of suckers. As well as being evergreen, the shrub is laden with clusters of dark wine-red fruit through the coldest months of the year.

Gaulnettyas have ovate, leathery dark green leaves and sprays of small white or pink flowers appearing between late spring and early summer.

'Wisley Pearl,' a widely available gaulnettya, bears dark green leaves on branches that are tipped with pearly white flower clusters in spring; oxblood-red fruit is produced in fall and winter. Other cultivars of merit, which may be difficult to obtain, are 'Pink Pixie' (dwarf; pink-tinged white flowers; purple-red berries) and 'Ruby' (vigorous; profuse bloom of white flowers; ruby-red fruit).

Cultivation

Plant in early fall to midfall or early spring to midspring in well-drained, acid soil in sun or partial shade. Thin out any old wood in early spring.

Propagation Detach and replant rooted suckers in early fall.

Pests/diseases Trouble free.

❏ Height 8-30 ft (2.4-9 m)
❏ Spread 6-12 ft (1.8-3.7 m)
❏ Flowers midwinter to early spring
❏ Well-drained garden soil
❏ Sunny or partially shaded site
❏ Hardy zones 8-10

Few plants bear as lovely catkins as the male specimens of *Garrya elliptica*. Their festoons of silvery lime-green catkins, which grow to 9 in (23 cm) long, sway in the breeze from midwinter to early spring. The smaller, less attractive silver-gray catkins on female shrubs are followed by round clusters of silky purple-green berries. To produce fruit, grow male and female shrubs together to allow cross-pollination. The leaves are thick, oval, and leathery with a gray-green appearance.

Garryas can grow 30 ft (9 m) high and half as wide; however, with thinning and cutting back, you can maintain them at 4-8 ft (1.2-2.4 m). On the Pacific Coast plant them as screens or hedges.

Cultivation

Plant container-grown garryas in spring in any well-drained soil. A sunny or lightly shaded site is suitable, but the catkins do better in the sun. On exposed sites in zone 8, plant the shrubs against a west- or south-facing wall.

Pruning is not necessary, but you can thin out straggly and crowded shoots after they flower. Garryas dislike root disturbance, and established shrubs should not be moved.

Propagation You can take 3-4 in (7.5-10 cm) long heel cuttings of semimature side shoots in late summer to early fall. Root in a cold frame or other protected spot; pot up the cuttings singly the following spring. Plunge the pots in a sunny bed (with the lips of the pots above the soil); grow on for a year before transplanting to their permanent sites. Or layer long shoots in early fall.

Pests/diseases Trouble free.

Gaultheria
gaultheria

Gaultheria procumbens

- ❏ Height 3-72 in (7.5-180 cm)
- ❏ Spread 3-6 ft (1-1.8 m)
- ❏ Flowers late spring to early summer
- ❏ Moist, acid soil
- ❏ Partially shaded site
- ❏ Hardy zones 3-9

Gaultherias are hardy shrubs characterized by their habit of spreading through underground stems. Suitable for large-scale ground cover on acid soil, they are particularly handsome in spring and early summer with their sprays of small urn-shaped flowers; they are followed by large clusters of fleshy berries.

Popular species
Gaultheria procumbens (wintergreen, checkerberry, or teaberry), a Northeastern native, is hardy in zones 3-8. This prostrate shrub grows only 3-6 in (7.5-15 cm) high but spreads to 3 ft (90 cm) or more. It has tufts of shiny dark green leaves that are oval and toothed. The small white or pink flowers appear in late spring; bright red round berries follow.
Gaultheria shallon, a native of the Pacific Coast, is hardy in zones 6-9 and grows to a height and width of 4-6 ft (1.2-1.8 m). It spreads using suckers and forms a dense thicket of upright stems bearing midgreen to dark green, oval, leathery leaves. Sprays of pale pink or white flowers appear in late spring to early summer; purple-black round berries follow.

Cultivation
Plant in early fall or early spring to midspring in a moist, acid, and organic-enriched soil. Gaultherias grow best in partial shade.

Cut *G. shallon* back hard in mid- to late spring to keep shape.
Propagation Take heel cuttings of lateral shoots in mid- to late summer. Alternatively, increase *G. shallon* by detaching and replanting rooted suckers in fall.
Pests/diseases Trouble free.

GAULTHETTYA — see *Gaulnettya*

Gaultheria shallon

Griselinia
griselinia

Griselinia littoralis 'Variegata'

- ❏ Height 10-25 ft (3-7.5 m)
- ❏ Spread 6-15 ft (1.8-4.5 m)
- ❏ Foliage shrub
- ❏ Any ordinary soil
- ❏ Sunny or shaded site
- ❏ Hardy zones 9-10

A tall native New Zealand tree, this plant does well in the warmer regions of the Pacific Coast where it often forms a shrub 10 ft (3 m) high and wide. Oval, leathery, shiny yellow-green leaves are the griselinia's main attraction; its greenish flowers (borne in mid- to late spring) are insignificant.

Griselinia littoralis makes an excellent screening or hedging shrub for seaside gardens; it tolerates both salt spray and strong winds. The cultivar 'Variegata' has white-variegated leaves.

Cultivation
Plant in fall or midspring in any soil in a sunny or shaded site. For hedging, set plants 1½ ft (45 cm) apart; to encourage bushy growth from the base, remove the shoots' growing tips after planting.

Regular pruning is not necessary, but you can shorten loose, straggly growth in midspring or late summer. Trim hedges annually in summer.
Propagation In late summer to early fall take 3-4 in (7.5-10 cm) heel cuttings of side shoots; root them in a cold frame.
Pests/diseases Trouble free.

GERMANDER — see *Teucrium*
GORSE — see *Ulex*

Halimium

halimium

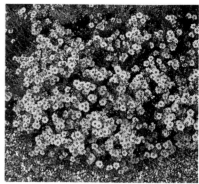

Halimium ocymoides

Halimium lasianthum

- ❏ Height 1½-3 ft (45-90 cm)
- ❏ Spread 2-4 ft (60-120 cm)
- ❏ Flowers spring
- ❏ Any well-drained soil
- ❏ Full sun
- ❏ Hardy zones 8-10

Halimiums resemble their relatives, Mediterranean sun roses (*Helianthemum*), and are sometimes sold under that name. Like sun roses, frost-sensitive halimiums perform particularly well in mild seaside gardens. These compact shrubs are valuable for their profusion of yellow flowers, which resemble single roses and have prominent blotches at the base of each of the five petals.

Popular species

Halimium lasianthum, syn. *Cistus formosus* and *Helianthemum lasianthum,* is hardy in coastal regions and inland valleys, and thrives along the temperate seaside strip into southern Oregon. It grows 1½-3 ft (45-90 cm) high and 4 ft (1.2 m) wide with thick, oblong gray-green leaves. In mid- to late spring the foliage is almost hidden by loose clusters of lovely golden yellow flowers marked with purple-brown blotches. *Halimium ocymoides,* syn. *Helianthemum ocymoides,* is the

hardiest species. It grows 2-3 ft (60-90 cm) high, with a spread of 4 ft (1.2 m). This species is of branching habit and has narrow, oblong gray-green leaves. In mid- to late spring it bears clusters of bright yellow flowers with blotches of chocolate-brown.

Halimium umbellatum grows about 2 ft (60 cm) high and wide. Its narrow leaves are similar in appearance to those of rosemary, and it bears white flowers in mid- to late spring.

Cultivation

Plant in early fall or early spring in any kind of soil, including a poor one, as long as the drainage is excellent. A rocky slope or a niche in a south- or west-facing stone wall is ideal. It is essential that the shrubs are sited in full sun. At the northern edge of their range, halimiums should be set where they will be protected from cold winter winds.

Pruning is rarely necessary, but cut back frost-damaged tips to healthy wood in spring. Take care that you avoid overwatering these drought-tolerant shrubs.

Propagation In mid- or late summer take 2-3 in (5-7.5 cm) long heel cuttings of lateral non-flowering shoots. Root the cuttings in a propagating unit at a

temperature of 61° F (16° C), and pot the rooted cuttings up singly in a sterilized potting mix. Overwinter in a frost-free, sunny spot. Pot them on the following spring; plunge outdoors until transplanting the young shrubs to their permanent sites in early fall.

Pests/diseases Trouble free.

Halimium umbellatum

HEATH — see *Erica*
HEATHER — see *Calluna*
HEAVENLY BAMBOO — see *Nandina*

Hebe

hebe

Hebe pinguifolia 'Pagei'

❏ Height ½-6 ft (15-180 cm)
❏ Spread 1½-6 ft (45-180 cm)
❏ Flowers late spring to early fall
❏ Ordinary well-drained soil
❏ Sunny site
❏ Hardy zones 8-9; a few to zone 7

Hebe 'Autumn Glory'

The shrubs in this large New Zealand genus are grown mainly for their attractive evergreen foliage and neat, compact form. A number of species also provide an appealing floral display, which sometimes continues from late spring until early fall. Hebes are fast growers but they dislike both extreme heat and extreme cold. They flourish in the temperate climates found along the California coast; on inland sites they should be given partial shade to protect them from the sun. Being resistant to salt spray and air pollution, hebes are excellent shrubs for both seaside and city gardens, and they may fare well in protected sites in the Pacific Northwest.

Popular species and cultivars
Hebe albicans forms a dense, round shrub reaching 2 ft (60 cm) high and wide. The lance-shaped leaves are gray-green, and dense spikes of white flowers appear in early summer to midsummer. This species is hardy to zone 8.
Hebe 'Amy' reaches 1½ ft (45 cm), producing deep purple new leaves that gradually age to green. Its flowers are a rich violet. This cultivar is hardy to zone 8.
Hebe armstrongii grows in a round habit to 3 ft (90 cm) high and 2-3 ft (60-90 cm) wide. Its golden green foliage has scalelike overlapping leaves. The sparse

clusters of white flowers appear between early and late summer. The species is hardy to zone 8. *Hebe ochracea* is similar to this species (and often confused with it), although it has coppery leaves and flowers more freely.
Hebe 'Autumn Glory,' also hardy to zone 8, is a compact shrub with a height and spread of 2-3 ft (60-90 cm). It bears conical spikes of violet-blue flowers in late summer; they continue into fall. The dark green oval leaves are carried on purple stems.
Hebe brachysiphon, syn. *H. traversii* is a hardy shrub of bushy habit, 6 ft (1.8 m) high and 4-6 ft (1.2-1.8 m) wide. Its 2 in (5 cm) long sprays of white flowers are produced in early summer and midsummer.
Hebe buxifolia (boxleaf hebe) is the hardiest species, overwintering successfully in zone 7. A shrub with a rounded, symmetrical profile, it reaches a height of 5 ft (1.5 m) but may be trimmed into a 3 ft (90 cm) tall hedge. Clusters of small white flowers ornament the deep green foliage in summertime. This species is outstandingly heat and drought tolerant. One cultivar is 'Patty's

Hebe armstrongii

Purple,' which produces wine-red stems and slender spikes of purple flowers in summer.
Hebe 'Carl Teschner' grows in a dense, spreading habit, reaching 1 ft (30 cm) high and 2-2½ ft (60-75 cm) wide. It is a moderately hardy shrub and is suitable for ground cover. In early summer and midsummer small spikes of violet-blue flowers appear among gray-green leaves.
Hebe cupressoides grows slowly, eventually reaching a height of 4-5 ft (1.2-1.5 m). The scalelike

Hebe x franciscana 'Blue Gem'

Hedera

ivy

Hebe cupressoides

Hedera colchica 'Dentata Variegata'

foliage resembles that of the cypress, as the botanical name suggests. 'Nana,' a dwarf cultivar, grows to only 2 ft (60 cm) tall and is commonly cultivated in containers or as a bonsai.

Hebe × franciscana 'Blue Gem' is a compact hybrid with a height and spread of 4 ft (1.2 m). The bright blue flowers appear intermittently throughout the summer. The plant has rich green rounded leaves. The smaller 'Variegata' has cream-edged leaves and mauve-blue flowers.

Hebe pinguifolia is a spreading or upright shrub that reaches a height of 1-3 ft (30-90 cm). 'Pagei' is a hardy cultivar; while it grows only 6-9 in (15-23 cm) high, it spreads up to 5 ft (1.5 m). It has gray-green foliage and white flower spikes, which appear in late spring and early summer. This is a good ground cover or specimen plant for rock gardens.

Cultivation

Plant in early fall to midfall or early spring to midspring in any well-drained soil and in a warm sunny site.

Deadhead as soon as flowering is over. In midspring prune back hard any leggy shrubs.

Propagation Take tip cuttings of nonflowering shoots in summer, and root in a cold frame or other protected spot.

Pests/diseases Downy mildew, leaf spot, and fusarium wilt can be problems.

- ❏ Height 2-100 ft (60-3,000 cm)
- ❏ Climber or ground cover
- ❏ Foliage plant
- ❏ Any soil
- ❏ Sunny or shaded site
- ❏ Hardy zones 4-10

Hedera are among the easiest and hardiest climbers to grow, tolerating almost any soil or situation, including extreme heat, severe winters, heavy shade, and city or industrial pollution. Though they produce both flowers and fruit, it is their evergreen foliage that makes ivies popular. The leaves comes in a range of shapes and in different shades of green, often with cream, gold, or silver variegations and frequently with pink tints in winter.

Ivies have two distinct stages of growth. In the juvenile stage the stems climb, clinging by means of aerial roots to any available support; they bear deeply lobed leaves. Adult growth is triggered when the climbing stems reach the top of their supports. Then the plant ceases to climb and becomes bushy. It begins to produce greenish flowers; they are followed by black fruit. Ivies propagated from the adult form retain the bushy characteristics and will grow into shrubs, often known as tree ivies.

In addition to climbing, ivies may trail, forming dense ground cover beneath trees and seeding themselves in cracks between paving and in walls. They survive neglect and submit to hard pruning. Tree ivies are favorite subjects for topiary designs.

Popular species

Hedera canariensis (Algerian ivy) is hardy only from zone 10 north into the warmer parts of zone 8. It overwinters reliably where temperatures remain above 20°F (-7°C). It grows rapidly to 15-20 ft (4.5-6 m) tall and is a good species for training up a trellis — it has a more upright habit than *H. helix*. The leathery lobed leaves are bright green in summer and turn bronze-green in winter. 'Gloire de Marengo,' syn. 'Variegata,' is less hardy than the species but is a vigorous climber or trailer. It has large lobed leaves with dark green centers that merge through silver-gray to white margins, which are most pronounced on young foliage. 'Margine Maculata' resembles 'Gloire de Marengo,' but the red-stalked leaves are mottled with creamy white. 'Striata' bears unlobed dark green leaves with centers that are lightly splashed with yellow.

Hedera colchica (Persian ivy) is recognized by its large leathery leaves, which are heart-shaped or oval. A rapid climber, it can reach a height of 20-30 ft (6-9 m), and is hardy in zones 6-9. The young growth is covered with yellow down. In this species the leaves are dark green, but several cultivars have been developed offering more interesting foliage: 'Arborescens' (shrubby adult form; large ovate leaves), 'Dentata' (the largest-leaved ivy, also called elephant's ears; extremely vigorous; rich green foliage drooping from purplish stalks), 'Dentata Variegata' (bright green shading to

Hedera helix 'Buttercup,' foliage

Hedera helix 'Goldheart'

gray leaves with conspicuous and irregular creamy yellow margins) and 'Sulphur Heart' (leaves boldly splashed with yellow merging into shades of green; occasionally leaves are wholly yellow).

Hedera helix (English ivy) is the hardiest ivy, overwintering reliably in zone 5 (some cultivars are hardy in zone 4). It is also one of the most useful of all climbing plants, good for covering ground where little else will grow, as well as walls. Its three- to five-lobed leaves are glossy dark green, often marked with silver veins.

The species is capable of reaching 50-100 ft (15-30 m) high, but cultivars developed from it are less vigorous. Popular choices include 'Arborescens' (a bushy form), 'Baltica' (small leaves with whitish veins; hardy to zone 4), 'Bulgaria' (similar to 'Baltica,' but more reliably cold hardy), 'Buttercup' (outstanding golden form; five-lobed rich yellow leaves that turn lime-green in shade and with age), 'Cavendishii' (triangular gray-mottled green leaves with broad creamy white margins), 'Chicago' (small leaves blotched bronze-purple), 'Congesta' (upright, nonclimbing form; arrow-shaped dark green leaves with pale veins; a good choice for rock gardens), 'Glacier' (silver-gray leaves edged white),

'Goldheart' (green leaves that have yellow centers), 'Green Ripple' (green leaves with frilled edges), 'Hibernica' (syn. *H. helix hibernica*; large, five-lobed dark green leaves; good for ground cover), 'Ivalace' (large, crimped dark green leaves, turning coppery-green in winter), 'Little Diamond' (dwarf shrubby form; excellent as ground cover in rock gardens; gray-green, white-edged leaves), 'Parsley Crested' (strong grower; cascading stems with glossy pale green leaves twisted and crimped at edges, turning pinkish-red and crimson in winter), 'Pedata' (slow grower; narrowly lobed dark

gray-green leaves conspicuously veined with white), 'Sagittifolia' (dark purple-green arrowhead-shaped leaves), 'Thorndale' (large leaves for the species; more cold hardy), and 'Tricolor' (small leaves, which are grayish-green edged white and usually flushed pink in winter).

Hedera nepalensis is a Southeast Asian species that is moderately cold hardy (to zone 7). It bears narrow triangular leaves that are green marked with gray along the stems; these hang from wine-red stems. The cultivar 'Suzanne' offers slender, elongated leaves of darker green.

Cultivation

Plant in early fall to midfall or early spring to midspring. Almost any soil and any site is suitable, from full sun to deep shade, although ivies grow more slowly in a sunny site. Full sun often burns variegated forms, but these types

Hedera helix 'Ivalace'

Hedera helix 'Buttercup'

Hedera helix 'Hibernica'

Hedera canariensis 'Gloire de Marengo'

still need good light to retain their leaf colors; preferably, they should be grown in light shade or on a west-facing wall. Ivies are highly tolerant of air pollution.

Ivy grown on walls or fences can be cut back close to its support during late winter to early spring. In the summer prune again to remove any unwanted growth. Prevent growth from becoming too matted and heavy by thinning out occasionally. Cut back hard before climbing stems reach gutters or roofs.

Propagation In mid- to late summer take 3-4 in (7.5-10 cm) cuttings from the tips of shoots. For shrubby tree ivies, take cuttings from mature growth; for climbing, trailing, and ground-cover ivies, take cuttings from juvenile growth. Root the cuttings in a cold frame or other protected spot; pot them up and grow on outdoors until they are large enough to be planted in permanent sites.

Pests/diseases Scale insects can infest the leaves; leaf spot or stem canker may be a problem. Sooty mold may flourish on ivy leaves covered with the secretions from aphids in overhanging trees.

Hedera colchica 'Sulphur Heart'

Helianthemum

rock rose, sun rose

Helianthemum nummularium 'Wisley Pink'

- ❏ Height 2-6 in (5-15 cm)
- ❏ Spread 1-2 ft (30-60 cm)
- ❏ Flowers late spring to midsummer
- ❏ Any well-drained soil
- ❏ Sunny site
- ❏ Hardy zones 5-10

Few plants can equal rock roses when it comes to fast-spreading ground cover in dry, sunny areas; in one year a single specimen can spread up to 2 ft (60 cm). These hardy, low-growing shrubs provide 2-6 in (5-15 cm) high carpets of glossy deep green to soft silver-gray evergreen foliage. In summer the plants are covered with brightly colored flowers in white, cream, yellow, scarlet, orange, bronze, crimson, and pink.

Rock roses are suitable for banks, terrace walls, raised beds, and rock gardens, but they should be sited carefully so they don't overrun less vigorous plants.

Popular species

Helianthemum apenninum grows to a height of 1½ ft (45 cm) and a spread of 2 ft (60 cm). It has long gray leaves; in late spring and

Helianthemum nummularium 'Amy Baring'

Helianthemum nummularium 'Raspberry Ripple'

Helianthemum nummularium
'Fire Dragon'

early summer it bears white flowers. It is hardy in zones 5-10.
Helianthemum nummularium (common rock rose or sun rose), hardy in zones 5-10, is the parent of many cultivars. These cultivars are 4-6 in (10-15 cm) high and 2 ft (60 cm) wide; they display flowers in late spring and early summer. Popular choices include 'Afflick' (orange flowers with buff centers; green leaves), 'Amy Baring' (yellow flowers; green foliage), 'Ben Nevis' (deep yellow flowers with bronze-red centers; green leaves), 'Buttercup' (golden yellow flowers; gray-green foliage), 'Fire Dragon' (orange-scarlet flowers; gray-green leaves), 'Jubilee' (double primrose-yellow flowers), 'Raspberry Ripple' (red-and-white flowers; green leaves), 'St. Mary's' (white flowers; dark green leaves), 'Wisley Pink' (soft pink flowers; gray leaves), 'Wisley Primrose' (yellow flowers; gray leaves), and 'Wisley White' (pure white flowers; gray leaves).

Helianthemum oelandicum alpestre, syn. *H. alpestre,* grows 3-4 in (7.5-10 cm) high and 1 ft (30 cm) wide; it is hardy to zone 6. Bright yellow saucer-shaped flowers appear in early and midsummer. *H. alpestre roseum,* a more prostrate species, is 2-3 in (5-7.5 cm) high and 2 ft (60 cm) wide; it has smaller, hairy gray-green leaves and silver-pink flowers.

Cultivation
Plant in early fall or early to mid-spring in any type of well-drained soil in a sunny spot.

To keep *H. nummularium* cultivars under control and maintain a neat shape, cut them back hard with shears after flowering.

Propagation In summer take heel cuttings, 2-3 in (5-7.5 cm) long, of nonflowering lateral shoots. Root them in a cold frame or other protected spot. Pot up the cuttings singly; overwinter them in a frost-free but cool area. Plant them out in midspring.

Pests and diseases Powdery mildew and leaf spot may occur.

Helianthemum nummularium 'Wisley White'

Helichrysum

everlastings

Helichrysum rosmarinifolium

❏ Height ⅔-9 ft (20-270 cm)
❏ Spread 1-5 ft (30-150 cm)
❏ Primarily foliage shrub
❏ Ordinary well-drained soil
❏ Sunny site
❏ Hardy zones 8-10

Shrubby everlastings have attractive gray-green or white woolly foliage, which stays evergreen in areas with mild winters.

Popular species

Helichrysum angustifolium (curry plant), hardy in zones 8-10, reaches 8-15 in (20-38 cm) high and 1-2 ft (30-60 cm) wide. It has narrow, needlelike silver-gray leaves and bears small mustard-yellow flower clusters in late spring or summer.

Helichrysum petiolatum is less hardy, overwintering successfully

Helichrysum angustifolium

only in zones 9-10. This species' great attraction is its superb foliage. It has semitrailing stems that bear round, felted gray leaves and cream-colored flowers. Reaching 2 ft (60 cm) high and wide, it is sometimes grown as an annual and used for bedding displays; it may be grown in hanging baskets in regions where it is not winter hardy. Two of the preferred cultivars are 'Limelight' (pale chartreuse-yellow leaves) and 'Variegatum' (leaves variegated with cream).

Helichrysum rosmarinifolium, syn. *Ozothamnus rosmarinifolius*, is an upright shrub, reaching 6-9 ft (1.8-2.7 m) high and 2-5 ft (60-150 cm) wide. It is hardy to zone 8. The young woolly white stems bear narrow leaves that are dark green above and white beneath. White flowers appear in early summer to midsummer.

Cultivation

In late summer and early fall or in spring, plant in any well-drained soil and in a sunny and sheltered site. Trim the shrubs to shape in spring.

Propagation Take 3 in (7.5 cm) long heel cuttings of lateral shoots in mid- to late summer.

Pests/diseases Downy mildew can affect the foliage.

HEMLOCK — see *Tsuga*
HOLLY — see *Ilex*
HONEYSUCKLE — see *Lonicera*
HONEY FLOWER — see *Melianthus*

Helichrysum petiolatum

Hypericum

St.-John's-wort

Hypericum calycinum

- ❏ Height 6-48 in (15-120 cm)
- ❏ Spread 1-4 ft (30-120 cm)
- ❏ Flowers midspring to early fall
- ❏ Any well-drained soil
- ❏ Sunny site
- ❏ Hardy zones 6-9

The true evergreen species of St.-John's-wort are dwarf or prostrate shrubs. They are usually classified as semievergreen because they behave like deciduous plants in the northern parts of their ranges; however, in milder climates they retain their leaves through the winter. The species included here are winter hardy in most of the United States.

Valued for their year-round carpet of foliage, hypericums are suitable for ground cover on sunny banks and for growing in rock gardens. The shrubs are prized for their golden or yellow flowers borne for many weeks, mostly in summer and early fall. Each cup-shaped flower displays a prominent center of golden stamens.

Popular species and cultivars

Hypericum balearicum is hardy in southern and southwestern areas; it can overwinter in most of zone 7. It is an erect shrub, reaching 2 ft (60 cm) high and wide. It bears tiny leaves and small, heavily fragrant yellow flowers from early summer to early fall.

Hypericum calycinum (Aaron's-beard) is a vigorous shrub. While it grows to a height of only 1-1½ ft (30-45 cm), underground runners allow it to spread far, forming a lovely carpet of foliage. The ovate leaves are bright green above and bluish-green beneath. Large golden yellow flowers are borne singly or in pairs in great profusion from early summer onward. The species is excellent for large-scale ground cover and flourishes in shade. It is hardy in zones 6-8.

Hypericum coris is suitable for a rock garden. It grows 6 in (15 cm) high and 1 ft (30 cm) wide, with tufts of gray-green heatherlike leaves along wiry stems. The golden yellow flower clusters are borne from mid- to late spring at the tips of the stems. This species thrives on poor and alkaline soil.

Hypericum patulum 'Hidcote' is a spreading shrub that reaches 4 ft (1.2 m) high and wide. Its ovate leaves grow 2½ in (6.25 cm) long. This species bears bright golden, 3 in (7.5 cm) wide flowers in the summer. It is hardy to zone 7.

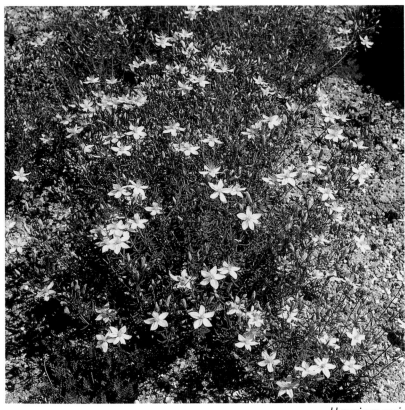

Hypericum coris

Cultivation

Evergreen hypericums do best on well-drained, warm, and sunny sites. These plants, particularly *H. calycinum,* tolerate light shade but flower most profusely in full sun. In cold winters they may lose not only their leaves but also the tips of their stems; however, fresh growth usually sprouts from the base in spring.

Hypericums thrive in any fast-draining soil, and many prefer poor soil. Plant them in early spring to midspring; set out small container-grown specimens.

Pruning is unnecessary, though cut back frost-damaged shoots to healthy wood in midspring. Keep the invasive *H. calycinum* within bounds by cutting it back almost to ground level in spring every few years.

Propagation In late spring or early summer take 2 in (5 cm) long softwood cuttings. Ideally, root them in a moist propagation unit; otherwise in a closed cold frame or other protected, humid spot. When rooted, pot the cuttings up singly in sterilized potting mix; overwinter them in a frost-free location. Set the young plants in their permanent sites in spring of the following year.

H. calycinum can also be increased by division of the roots between midfall and midspring; replant the divisions at once.

Pests/diseases Powdery mildew, rust, and leaf spot may attack the foliage, and root-rot fungi may attack the roots.

Hypericum patulum 'Hidcote'

Ilex

holly

Ilex crenata 'Golden Gem'

- ❏ Height 2-15 ft (60-450 cm)
- ❏ Spread 2-15 ft (60-450 cm)
- ❏ Foliage shrub with berries
- ❏ Ordinary garden soil
- ❏ Sunny or shaded site
- ❏ Hardy zones 5-10, depending on species

Holly is one of the most adaptable of our broad-leaved evergreens, with species that thrive from the chilly North to the Deep South. The glossy dark green or variegated leaves supply interest all year; the colorful berries of the female hollies serve as a welcome source of winter color.

Some of the evergreen hollies attain tree proportions (see p.35), but many others naturally form compact shrubs. These shrubby forms make admirable specimen plants and are often excellent for hedging. They are adaptable to most soils and sites, withstanding pollution and exposure to wind.

Popular species and hybrids

Ilex × altaclarensis incorporates a group of large-leaved hybrids that grow 10-15 ft (3-4.5 m) tall. The hardiness varies with the hybrid, but in general they overwinter well through zone 7. They make good windbreaks and hedges and thrive in urban and seaside gardens. Popular cultivars include 'Camelliifolia' (pyramid- shaped female clone; spineless leaves; large red berries) and 'Wilsonii' (vigorous; glossy and spiny green leaves, up to 5 in/13 cm long and 3 in/7.5 cm wide; red berries).

Ilex aquifolium (English holly) naturally reaches the proportions

117

Ilex aquifolium

Ilex cornuta, flowers

of a small to medium-size tree, but with regular pruning you can maintain many of the cultivars as large shrubs. These are hardy to zone 7 and usually bear red berries. Popular shrublike cultivars include 'Ferox Argentea' (male; leaves spined on upper surfaces and on the cream-white margins), 'Golden Queen' (male; spiny dark green leaves shaded gray and light green, with broad yellow edges), and 'Teufel's Zero' (female; thin, gracefully drooping branches; hardy in lower zone 6). *Ilex cornuta* (Chinese holly) can grow 8-10 ft (2.4-3 m) high with an equal or greater spread; it is hardy in zones 7-9. This species has oblong-rectangular, spiny dark green leaves and bright red berries (yellow in some cultivars) that persist through winter.
Ilex crenata (Japanese holly) is a hardy shrub (zones 6-8), reaching 5-10 ft (1.5-3 m) high and wide. It bears small (½ in/1.25 cm long), elliptical glossy green leaves and inconspicuous black berries. This species withstands shearing well, making it ideal for hedging or topiary. The cultivar 'Convexa' is

1-2 ft (30-60 cm) tall; it has shiny leaves and a profusion of berries. The flat-topped 'Golden Gem,' to 1-2 ft (30-60 cm) high, has golden yellow foliage. The female 'Helleri,' with tiny glossy leaves, forms a mound 2 ft (60 cm) high. *Ilex latifolia,* hardy in zones 7-9, can reach 20-25 ft (6-7.5 m) high, but is commonly maintained as a

10-15 ft (3-4.5 m) tall shrub. It bears large glossy dark green leaves with toothed edges and clusters of dull deep red berries. *Ilex × meserveae,* a hybrid of English holly, forms a shrub 8-12 ft (2.4-3.7 m) high; it is hardy to zone 5. The species offers a number of fine cultivars with deep purple twigs and bluish-green leaves. These include 'Blue Girl' (female clone with red berries; broad pyramid shape), 'Blue Princess' (more abundant dark red fruit; darker bluish foliage), and 'Blue Stallion' (relatively fast-growing male form; effective pollinator for female forms). *Ilex vomitoria* is one of the best hedging shrubs for the Southeast;

Ilex aquifolium 'Ferox Argentea'

Ilex vomitoria

it is hardy in zones 7-10. 'Nana' is an excellent compact cultivar that grows to a dense mound approximately 3-5 ft (1-1.5 m) tall.

Cultivation
In spring or early fall to midfall, set out container-grown young plants in either sun or shade; however, set out the variegated forms only in a sunny position. Hollies will grow in any soil but thrive in moist loam. With the exception of the self-fertile *I. cornuta*, plant the female and male hollies together if you want the females to bear fruit. Water them during dry weather until the plants are established. Set hedging plants 2 ft (60 cm) apart.

Trim hedges and specimens in midspring or late summer. On variegated hollies remove any green-leaved shoots that appear.
Propagation Layer long shoots in midfall, and separate from the parent plant 2 years later. Alternatively, take 2-3 in (5-7.5 cm) long heel cuttings in late summer and root in a cold frame or other protected spot. Cuttings are often slow to root.
Pests/diseases Holly leaf miners cause blotches on the foliage. Leaf spot may attack foliage, and fungal cankers may cause dieback.

IVY — see *Hedera*
JAPANESE CEDAR — see *Cryptomeria*
JASMINE NIGHTSHADE — see *Solanum*

Ilex cornuta

119

Jasminum polyanthum

Jasminum

jasmine

Juniperus

juniper

Juniperus communis 'Compressa'

- ❏ Height 2-72 in (5-180 cm)
- ❏ Spread 6-72 in (15-180 cm)
- ❏ Coniferous shrub
- ❏ Ordinary well-drained soil
- ❏ Sunny site
- ❏ Hardy zones 2-9, depending on species

Many junipers grow to treelike proportions (see pp.37-38), but a large number of slow-growing dwarf cultivars have been developed. They rarely grow more than 4-5 ft (1.2-1.5 m) tall, making them ideal for smaller gardens.

These shrubs vary in growth habits, including columnar, prostrate, semiprostrate, and rounded. They are suitable for rock gardens or as specimen shrubs, and also blend well with heathers.

Junipers have two types of foliage: juvenile leaves on young growth are small, pointed, and awl-shaped; the leaves on older growth are scalelike and densely packed. Some dwarf cultivars never produce adult foliage. The small black or blue cones on the shrubs resemble berries.

Popular species and cultivars
Juniperus chinensis, hardy in zones 3-9, has given rise to numerous cultivars, which generally have a columnar habit. 'Kaizuka Variegata' grows to 6 ft (1.8 m) tall. Its mainly adult foliage is green marked with cream. 'Pyramidalis,' a pyramid-shaped, slow-growing conifer, grows to 5 ft (1.5 m) high and 2 ft (60 cm) wide. It has blue-gray juvenile foliage.

Jasminum humile 'Revolutum'

- ❏ Height 5-25 ft (1.5-7.5 m)
- ❏ Climber
- ❏ Flowers year-round
- ❏ Any well-drained soil
- ❏ Warm, sheltered site
- ❏ Hardy zones 7-10

Evergreen jasmines, grown for the scent of their flowers, are only moderately hardy. In the upper South many grow best if trained against a sunny wall. But in the Deep South or Southwest, they are ideal as shrubs and climbers.

Popular species and cultivars
Jasminum humile 'Revolutum,' a semievergreen shrub, is hardy in zones 8-10. It grows 6 ft (1.8 m) high and wide; in summer it bears leathery dark green leaves and clusters of yellow flowers. *Jasminum mesnyi,* syn. *J. primulinum,* is hardy in zones 8-9. It bears semidouble yellow flowers from fall through early spring in warmer regions, in early spring elsewhere. This climbing species reaches a height of 15 ft (4.5 m).

Jasminum polyanthum is hardy in zone 10, into zone 7 in a protected spot. A vigorous vine, it can reach a height of 25 ft (7.5 m). The white flowers are borne from late winter to early summer, depending on the local climate. *Jasminum* × *stephanense* is also hardy into zone 7. This 10-15 ft (3-4.5 m) high climber is ideal for covering archways and pergolas. Clusters of fragrant pale pink flowers appear in summer.

Cultivation
Plant in early to late spring (depending on the climate) in any well-drained but moist soil. Full sun and a sheltered spot are essential in northerly regions; partial shade is fine in warmer areas. Prune after flowering; cut out old weak shoots and straggly stems.
Propagation In fall layer long shoots. Alternatively, take heel cuttings in late summer and root in a propagation unit.
Pests/diseases Frost damage may encourage botrytis.

Juniperus x media 'Pfitzerana Aurea'

Juniperus chinensis 'Pyramidalis'

Juniperus communis (common juniper) is hardy in zones 2-7 and is the parent of numerous dwarf cultivars.

'Compressa,' a neat conical shrub only 1½ ft (45 cm) high and 6 in (15 cm) wide, is ideal for a rock garden. The foliage is dark green.

'Depressa Aurea' is a prostrate juniper, growing 1 ft (30 cm) high and 4-5 ft (1.2-1.5 m) wide. The summer foliage is golden yellow, and the winter foliage is bronze.

'Hornibrookii,' a mat-forming cultivar, grows only 6 in (15 cm) high but spreads to 3 ft (90 cm); it is excellent for ground cover. It has silvery-green leaves.

'Repanda' is a low carpet-forming conifer 10 in (25 cm) high and 6 ft (1.8 m) wide. Its dark green foliage may turn bronze in winter.

'Sentinel' has a very narrow and columnar habit and dense erect branches. It grows 6 ft (1.8 m) high and 1 ft (30 cm) wide. This cultivar bears deep blue-green foliage on purple shoots.

Juniperus horizontalis (creeping juniper), hardy in zones 3-9, is a useful ground cover in full sun. The main stems root where they touch the soil; the wholly adult foliage is blue-green. The species includes several fine cultivars.

'Blue Chip' reaches 1 ft (30 cm) high and 4-5 ft (1.2-1.5 m) wide. It has feathery silver-blue foliage.

'Emerald Spreader' is a prostrate ground-hugging cultivar that reaches 2-4 in (5-10 cm) high but spreads to 5 ft (1.5 m) wide. The foliage is bright green.

'Glauca' is a carpeting juniper that forms low mounds of blue-green foliage. It is 4 in (10 cm) high and 4 ft (1.2 m) wide.

'Hughes,' a prostrate but vigorous cultivar, reaches 1 ft (30 cm) high and 5-6 ft (1.5-1.8 m) wide. It has gray-green foliage.

'Wiltonii,' syn. 'Blue Rug,' is 4 in (10 cm) high. Its long branches spread to form a silver-blue mat.

Juniperus × media is hardy to zone 3. This hybrid group of junipers is sometimes listed under *J. chinensis;* it includes cultivars of conical or spreading habit.

'Gold Coast,' a dense, flat-topped, semiprostrate juniper, can reach 2-3 ft (60-90 cm) high and 3-4 ft (90-120 cm) wide. The green foliage is tipped with golden yellow.

'Mint Julep' is a semiprostrate conifer 2½ ft (75 cm) high and 4 ft (1.2 m) wide; rich green foliage covers its arching branches.

'Old Gold,' a compact and semiprostrate form, can reach 3-4 ft (90-120 cm) high with a spread of 4-5 ft (1.2-1.5 m). It has bronze-gold leaves throughout the year.

'Pfitzerana' grows to a height of

Juniperus communis 'Depressa Aurea'

Juniperus squamata 'Meyeri'

3 ft (90 cm) and a spread of 6 ft (1.8 m). The branches curve at the tips, bearing gray-green juvenile foliage. A flat-topped cultivar with gold-tipped foliage, 'Pfitzerana Aurea,' is also available.

'Plumosa Aurea' is a semiprostrate shrub, with branches that droop at the tips. It grows 2½ ft (75 cm) high and 3 ft (90 cm) wide; the foliage is feathery and yellow-bronze.

'Sulfur Spray' gradually grows to 6 ft (1.8 m) high with a spread of 4-5 ft (1.2-1.5 m). The foliage is a pale sulfur-yellow.

Juniperus sabina (savin juniper) is hardy in zones 3-9. 'Tamariscifolia,' the most common cultivar, is a dense, spreading shrub with feathery blue-green foliage. It grows 1½ft (45 cm) high, spreading up to 10 ft (3 m) or more, and is an excellent ground cover.

Juniperus squamata, hardy in zones 5-7, is the parent of several outstanding cultivars with blue-gray foliage.

'Blue Carpet' is prostrate and grows 1 ft (30 cm) high and 5 ft (1.5 m) wide.

'Blue Star,' a dense, mounded form, reaches 12-15 in (30-38 cm) high and 1½ft (45 cm) wide.

'Meyeri' has ascending branches with the deepest blue foliage of all junipers. This irregularly shaped shrub is 4-5 ft (1.2-1.5 m) high and 5 ft (1.5 m) wide.

Juniperus virginiana is hardy in zones 2-9. This species has two excellent dwarf cultivars.

'Globosa' is 3 ft (90 cm) high and wide; it has a dense rounded form and bright green adult foliage.

'Grey Owl,' a vigorous cultivar, eventually grows 5 ft (1.5 m) high and wide, with silver-gray leaves.

Cultivation

Plant in early spring to midspring in ordinary well-drained garden soil in full sun. In summer keep young plants well watered in dry periods; once established, they are drought tolerant. No pruning is required.

Propagation Take heel cuttings in early fall. Because they are difficult to root, it is usually more prudent to buy new stock.

Pests/diseases Juniper scale and spider mites may attack the foliage; juniper blight (phomopsis) may cause the dieback of twigs or whole plants.

Juniperus virginiana 'Globosa'

123

Kalmia

kalmia

Kalmia latifolia

- ❑ Height 3-10 ft (1-3 m)
- ❑ Spread 3-8 ft (1-2.4 m)
- ❑ Flowers late spring to early summer
- ❑ Moist, acid soil
- ❑ Partially shaded site
- ❑ Hardy zones 2-9, depending on species

Kalmias grow best in open woodland conditions where the soil is moist and acidic and there is light shade. They are often planted with azaleas and rhododendrons.

Clusters of cup-shaped flowers appear in late spring or early summer at the tips of the previous season's growth. In foliage the shrubs resemble rhododendrons, though the glossy leaves are slightly narrower.

Popular species

Kalmia angustifolia (sheep laurel), hardy in zones 2-6, reaches 3-4 ft (1-2.4 m) high and wide. It has lance-shaped, glossy green leaves; in early summer clusters of rose-red flowers appear. The cultivar 'Rubra' has deep red flowers and deep green foliage.
Kalmia latifolia (mountain laurel) is hardy in zones 5-9. It bears bright pink flowers with conspicuous stamens in late spring. Reaching 6-10 ft (1.8-3 m) high and 8 ft (2.4 m) wide, it has lance-shaped, leathery midgreen leaves.

Cultivation

In early to midfall or in spring, plant in moist but well-drained, acid soil in a partially shaded site.

No pruning is required, but remove faded flower clusters. After flowering, cut back overlong and crowded shoots hard.

Propagation Layer shoots of the new season's growth in late summer to early fall. By the next fall the layers will root and be ready to sever from the parent plant.

Pests/diseases Leaf spot may afflict the foliage. Whiteflies, scale insects, and lace bugs may also be troublesome, and borers may tunnel into twigs or main stems.

Kalmia angustifolia 'Rubra'

Laurus

bay laurel, sweet bay

Laurus nobilis

- ❑ Height 10-15 ft (3-4.5 m)
- ❑ Spread 10-15 ft (3-4.5 m)
- ❑ Foliage shrub
- ❑ Ordinary garden soil
- ❑ Sheltered, sunny site
- ❑ Hardy zones 8-10

This aromatic shrub provided the laurels with which the ancient Romans and Greeks crowned victors at games and festivals; today it is used in ornamental wreaths.

Bay laurel *(Laurus nobilis)* is grown for its lance-shaped, glossy dark green leaves, which have culinary as well as decorative uses. Insignificant yellow-green flower clusters in midspring are followed by purple-black berries on female plants.

Although bay laurel can attain tree size, it usually grows no more than 10-15 ft (3-4.5 m) high. It is frequently grown in tubs and pruned to a neat pyramid or lollipop (standard) shape.

Cultivation

In early spring to midspring, plant in any soil in a sunny, sheltered spot. Laurus is tolerant of salty coastal winds and air pollution. In the North grow in containers; move indoors in winter.

In summer trim trained bay laurel to shape. Remove any sucker shoots that appear from stems of trained standards.

Propagation In late summer to early fall, take 4 in (10 cm) heel cuttings of semimature lateral shoots, and root in a cold frame or other protected spot.

Pests/diseases Scale insects may infest the stems and undersides of the leaves, secreting a sticky juice that encourages sooty mold.

Lavandula
lavender

Lavandula angustifolia 'Munstead'

Lavandula stoechas

❏ Height 1-4 ft (30-120 cm)
❏ Spread 1-4 ft (30-120 cm)
❏ Flowers late spring to early fall
❏ Any well-drained soil
❏ Sunny site
❏ Hardy zones 5-9, depending on species

Lavender has been grown and loved for so long that most gardeners are familiar with this hardy little shrub. Both the flowers and the leaves are aromatic, and the unique lavender scent is exuded as much in winter by the silver-gray foliage as in summer by the dense flower spikes. The flowers range in color from deepest purple to white.

Lavenders make excellent low-growing informal hedges and are also useful as edging plants. They tend to grow leggy with age unless regularly pruned.

You can dry the flowers for use in potpourris. Pick the blooms when they are showing color but before they open fully. Hang them in bunches and let dry in a cool, airy place.

Popular species
Lavandula angustifolia (English lavender), syn. L. spica, is hardy in zones 5-8. It grows to 1-2 ft (30-60 cm) high and has narrow silver-gray leaves. Between early summer and midsummer pale gray-blue flowers appear in 2½ in (6.25 cm) spikes. The species is responsible for many cultivars. Popular cultivars include 'Alba' (pinkish-white flowers), 'Hidcote' (compact; 2-2¾ ft/60-80 cm high; dense violet flowers), 'Loddon Pink' (compact; 2½ ft/75 cm high; pale pink flowers), 'Munstead' (compact; 1-2 ft/30-60 cm high; clear blue flowers; green leaves), 'Nana Alba' (just 1 ft/30 cm high; white flowers), and 'Twickel Purple' (2-3 ft/60-90 cm high; long purple-blue flower spikes).

Dutch lavender is sometimes listed as *L. vera,* but is correctly known as *L. angustifolia angustifolia.* This robust shrub, up to 4 ft (1.2 m) high and wide, has gray foliage and blue-purple flowers. *Lavandula stoechas* (Spanish lavender), hardy to zone 8, grows up to 3 ft (90 cm) high and wide. It has gray-green leaves and displays spikes of dark purple tubular flowers from late spring to early summer. The flower spikes are shorter than those of *L. angustifolia,* and each is topped by a tuft of purple bracts.

Cultivation
Plant in fall or early spring in any well-drained soil in a sunny spot. Lavenders dislike humid heat. In the Southeast cultivate them in an open, airy spot with perfect drainage; a rock garden or raised bed is ideal. For hedges, set young plants 9-12 in (23-30 cm) apart.

Remove dead flower stems and lightly trim the plants in late summer. You can encourage new growth from the base by cutting back hard any straggly plants in early spring to midspring. Clip hedges to maintain shape in early spring to midspring.

Propagation In late summer take 3-4 in (7.5-10 cm) cuttings of nonflowering shoots, and root in a cold frame or other protected spot. Transplant to the flowering position in spring.

Pests/diseases Shoots injured by frost may die back. Leaf spot may attack foliage, and root-rot fungi may kill whole plants.

LAVENDER — see *Lavandula*

Lavandula angustifolia 'Hidcote'

Leptospermum

tea tree

Leptospermum scoparium

Leptospermum scoparium 'Ruby Glow'

Leucothoe

leucothoe

Leucothoe fontanesiana

- ❏ Height 4 ft (1.2 m)
- ❏ Spread 8 ft (2.4 m)
- ❏ Flowers late spring
- ❏ Moist, acid soil
- ❏ Lightly shaded site
- ❏ Hardy zones 5-9

- ❏ Height ½-15 ft (15-450 cm)
- ❏ Spread 3-15 ft (1-4.5 m)
- ❏ Flowers late winter to early summer
- ❏ Well-drained, acid to neutral soil
- ❏ Sunny, sheltered site
- ❏ Hardy zones 8-10

Leptospermums are hardy only in mild-winter areas. They thrive in coastal areas and in arid climates.

In late winter they begin to bear a profusion of small, saucer-shaped white or pink flowers. Some plants are prostrate; others have an upright growth habit and branch freely. All bear narrow, oblong, pointed dark green leaves.

Tea trees are unrelated to the tea plant. The common name derives from a beverage brewed from its leaves to prevent scurvy.

Popular species

Leptospermum laevigatum grows to 15 ft (4.5 m) high and wide. It has twisting trunks with shaggy bark. Showy white flowers open from mid- to late spring. This species is tolerant of heat, salt, and aridity, and will grow in almost pure sand; it is an ideal shrub for southern California and the warmer parts of the Southwest. 'Reevesii' is a compact cultivar that forms a dense mound 3-5 ft (1-1.5 m) high.

Leptospermum rupestre, a prostrate mat-forming species, grows 6 in (15 cm) high and 3 ft (90 cm) wide. In early summer the white flowers almost hide the foliage.

Leptospermum scoparium grows up to 6-8 ft (1.8-2.4 m) high and 10-12 ft (3-3.7 m) wide. In late winter or early spring it starts to bear star-shaped white flowers; this display may continue into early summer. Popular cultivars from the species include 'Chapmanii' (rose-red flowers; bronze leaves), 'Kiwi' (dwarf; 1 ft/30 cm high; crimson flowers), 'Pink Cascade' (weeping dwarf; 1 ft/30 cm; single pink flowers), 'Pink Pearl' (6-10 ft/1.8-3 m; double blush-pink flowers), and 'Ruby Glow' (6-8 ft/1.8-2.4 m; profuse crop of oxblood-red double flowers).

Cultivation

In spring plant container-grown shrubs in good, well-drained, acid to neutral soil in a sunny, sheltered spot. You can grow plants without protection in mild coastal areas; inland they need shelter from cold winter winds.

No pruning is required other than removing straggly branches in midspring.

Propagation In early summer to midsummer take 2 in (5 cm) cuttings of semimature nonflowering shoots, and root in a propagating unit at a temperature of 61°F (16°C). Set rooted cuttings in pots of sterilized potting soil; overwinter in a protected spot. Grow on for a year before planting out in spring.

Pests/diseases Expect root troubles in sites with poor drainage.

Thriving on acid soil, the hardy but elegant leucothoe is valuable for the contrasting shapes and textures it can bring to gardens dominated by rhododendrons and heathers. From fall onward its thick and leathery lance-shaped leaves develop bronze and purple tints. In late spring the shrub is equally spectacular, with drooping spikes of small, urn-shaped white flowers.

Leucothoe fontanesiana is useful for ground cover, developing a wide-spreading thicket of gracefully arching stems. A mature specimen can grow 4 ft (1.2 m) high and spread up to 8 ft (2.4 m).

Popular cultivars

Three outstanding cultivars have been bred from *L. fontanesiana:* 'Nana' is a compact, low-growing version of the species. 'Rainbow' has leaves variegated with cream, yellow, and pink. The young shoots are pink. 'Rollisoni' resembles the species but has narrow green leaves.

Cultivation

In fall or spring plant in moist, acid soil in a lightly shaded site; a cool, shady site is essential in the South. In early spring prune old and overgrown shoots back to ground level.

Propagation Increase by removing and replanting rooted suckers in fall or spring.

Pests/diseases Leaf spot can be troublesome.

Ligustrum

privet

Ligustrum lucidum 'Variegata'

Ligustrum ovalifolium (right) and 'Aureum' (left)

- ❑ Height 6-18 ft (1.8-5.4 m)
- ❑ Spread 4-10 ft (1.2-3 m)
- ❑ Flowers late spring to midsummer
- ❑ Ordinary garden soil
- ❑ Sunny or shaded site
- ❑ Hardy zones 5-10, depending on species

The evergreen privets are excellent for hedging and screening. They are tough, fast-growing shrubs that tolerate shade and air pollution and are amenable to severe pruning and topiary work.

Privets also make fine specimen shrubs. If allowed to grow naturally, they produce clusters of pungent cream-white flowers in summer, followed by long-lasting small blue-black berries.

Popular species

Ligustrum japonicum (Japanese privet), hardy in zones 7-9, grows 6-8 ft (1.8-2.4 m) high and 4-6 ft (1.2-1.8 m) wide. It has a dense, compact habit and camellialike glossy dark green leaves. Panicles of white flowers appear in late spring or early summer.
Ligustrum lucidum is an elegant symmetrical shrub, growing to 10-18 ft (3-5.4 m) high and 10 ft (3 m) wide. It is hardy only in zones 8-10. The large ovate leaves are glossy dark green; it produces handsome white flower panicles in early summer. The cultivar 'Variegata,' syn. 'Tricolor,' has narrower leaves that are marked with gray-green and have white or cream-yellow margins; they are tinged pink when young.
Ligustrum ovalifolium (oval-leaved privet), hardy in zones 6-9, is evergreen only in the southern part of that range; in the North it sheds its foliage in winter. It has oval, glossy midgreen leaves and, if left unclipped, bears panicles of pungent cream-white flowers in early summer or midsummer. One cultivar is 'Aureum,' whose leaves have broad yellow edges.
Ligustrum × vicaryi is hardy to zone 5. A densely branched species, it grows 10 ft (3 m) high and wide. The broad oval leaves are golden yellow, turning bronze-purple in winter. Unpruned, this shrub bears dense white flower clusters in midsummer.

Cultivation

In fall or spring plant privets in any kind of soil in sun or shade. They tolerate poor soil, drought, and neglect; but for a long-lived hedge, prepare the soil thoroughly, improving drainage if necessary and digging in plenty of organic matter.

For hedging, place plants that are 1-3 ft (30-90 cm) high about 1-1½ ft (30-45 cm) apart; to encourage bushy growth from the base, cut them back by at least half in midspring. The following spring prune all new shoots by half again, and repeat in early fall. Continue this hard pruning annually, in late summer to early fall, until the hedge has reached the desired height.

Trim established hedges and topiary at least twice a year, in late spring and in early fall. Free-growing shrubs need little pruning, except for cutting long shoots back to side shoots in spring.
Propagation Take 1 ft (30 cm) hardwood cuttings of *L. ovalifolium* in midfall, and insert them in a sheltered outdoor nursery bed. A year later plant out the rooted cuttings in their permanent sites.

For *L. japonicum* and *L. lucidum*, take 4-6 in (10-15 cm) hardwood cuttings in early fall to midfall; root in a cold frame or other protected spot. The following spring transfer to a sheltered nursery bed. Plant out in fall.
Pests/diseases While serious problems are rare, twig blight can cause dieback; galls, powdery mildew, and scale insects can also infest privets.

LILY-OF-THE-VALLEY TREE —
see *Crinodendron*

Ligustrum japonicum

Ligustrum x vicaryi

Ligustrum x vicaryi, hedge

Lonicera

honeysuckle

Lonicera hildebrandiana

Lonicera japonica

- ❏ Height 5-80 ft (1.5-24 m)
- ❏ Spread 5-6 ft (1.5-1.8 m)
- ❏ Climber
- ❏ Flowers spring to fall
- ❏ Ordinary well-drained soil enriched with humus
- ❏ Sunny or partially shaded site
- ❏ Hardy zones 4-10, depending on species

The large *Lonicera* genus contains both shrubby and climbing plants, which may be evergreen or deciduous, cold hardy or frost sensitive. They display great diversity in their growth habits; however, some can become weeds if not controlled.

The typical honeysuckle flowers are tubular, borne in pairs, clusters, or whorls. They are often, but not always, sweetly fragrant and are usually followed by clusters of berries.

The honeysuckles described here are, with one exception, all climbers. Climbing honeysuckles have woody twining stems, which

need sturdy supports, such as strong trellises fixed to walls and fences. These climbers are excellent for tumbling over arbors and pergolas and for hiding sheds and other eyesores. Without support,

Lonicera japonica 'Aureo-reticulata'

vining honeysuckles will sprawl over the ground; some types, notably *Lonicera japonica* and the less vigorous *L. henryi,* can successfully be grown as ground covers to prevent soil erosion on large sunny banks.

Most of the following species will perform as semievergreen or deciduous plants in the northern parts of their ranges, dropping some or all of their leaves where winters are severe.

Popular species

Lonicera henryi, hardy in zones 5-9, is a vigorous but noninvasive species growing to 30 ft (9 m) tall. The slender, downy stems are set with dark green heart-shaped leaves. Yellow and purple-red flowers are borne in pairs during summer; the berries are black.

Lonicera hildebrandiana (giant honeysuckle) is hardy only in zones 9-10. In a favorable climate it can grow to 80 ft (24 m) high. The glossy dark green leaves are up to 6 in (15 cm) long; they provide a handsome foil for the richly fragrant flowers borne in clusters throughout summer. The flowers are creamy white on opening, maturing to deep yellow flushed with orange. The large berries are nearly black.

Lonicera japonica (Japanese honeysuckle) is hardy in zones 4-9. This vigorous climber grows into a tangled mass of slender stems 25-30 ft (7.5-9 m) high and soon becomes a weed if not kept in check. Its fragrant white to pale yellow flowers are borne from late spring to midfall. The pale green ovate leaves are downy on both sides. 'Aureo-reticulata,' which has bright green leaves veined with yellow, is a common garden

Lonicera sempervirens

cultivar. 'Halliana' bears outstandingly fragrant flowers that change from white to yellow with age; however, it is also one of the weediest Japanese honeysuckles. Although it is a highly successful ground cover for banks and useful for erosion control, consider how much trimming and weeding you are willing to do before planting this cultivar.

Lonicera nitida is a dense shrub that reaches a height and spread of 5-6 ft (1.5-1.8 m); it is hardy in zones 6-9. Its oval, glossy dark green leaves are tiny and respond well to clipping, making it ideal for hedging. Insignificant yellow-green flowers open in mid- to late spring; if the shrub is left unpruned, globular, semitranslucent violet berries will follow. 'Baggesen's Gold' is a popular cultivar, with round golden yellow leaves that turn yellow-green in fall.

Lonicera sempervirens (trumpet honeysuckle), a semievergreen climber, is hardy in zones 4-9. It grows 10-20 ft (3-6 m) high and has ovate midgreen leaves. Its bright orange-scarlet blooms are borne in whorls during summer. They are followed by dark red berries. This species is deciduous in the North but performs as an evergreen in zones 8-9.

Cultivation

Plant evergreen honeysuckles in spring in any ordinary well-drained soil enriched with organic matter. Most species grow well in sun or partial shade; *Lonicera japonica* flourishes even in fairly dense shade, though it bears few flowers there. Mulch around the roots with well-rotted manure or leaf mold annually in spring.

For hedging with *L. nitida*, place the young plants 9-12 in (23-30 cm) apart; at the time of planting cut the plants back by half. To encourage bushy growth, cut off the tips of young shoots two or three times in the summer.

Lupinus

tree lupine

Lupinus arboreus

Lonicera nitida 'Baggesen's Gold'

Each year cut all new growth back by half until the hedge grows to the desired height. Thereafter, maintain its shape by shearing the hedge twice annually in late spring and early fall.

Prune climbing honeysuckles after flowering, thinning out older shoots and removing entirely a proportion from the base of the plants to encourage new shoots.

Propagation For climbing species and cultivars, in mid- to late summer take 4 in (10 cm) long stem sections; root them in a cold frame. The following spring pot the rooted cuttings individually and plunge them outdoors; the lips of the pots should be above the soil. Move them to a frost-free spot for the winter; plant out in the permanent flowering sites in midspring.

For *L. nitida* and its cultivars, take 9-12 in (23-30 cm) hardwood cuttings in fall and root in a sheltered outdoor spot. They will be ready for transplanting in a year.

Pest/diseases Leaf spot shows as small green or large round brown spots; powdery mildew appears as a white powdery deposit on the leaves. Leaf blight may attack foliage in rainy seasons. Aphids, leaf rollers, sawflies, plant hoppers, and whiteflies can also be troublesome. In general, though, honeysuckles are vigorous plants that easily hold their own.

❏ Height 5-8 ft (1.5-2.4 m)
❏ Spread similar to height
❏ Flowers early spring to early summer
❏ Well-drained, acid to neutral soil
❏ Sunny site
❏ Hardy zones 8-10

Despite its common name, the tree lupine (*Lupinus arboreus*) is only a shrub, rarely exceeding a height of 8 ft (2.4 m). Nonetheless, it is an extremely attractive and useful plant, for it tolerates drought, poor soil, and seaside conditions. It grows rapidly and flowers in the second year, even from seed, making it an excellent shrub for creating an almost instant effect in new gardens. By the end of its third year, it reaches full size. Though comparatively short-lived, tree lupines will seed themselves freely on sunny sites with sandy soil, providing constant replacements. They are good for preventing soil erosion on dry banks and make excellent beachside plantings.

Like its more familiar annual and perennial relatives, *Lupinus arboreus* bears large, deeply divided leaves and 6 in (15 cm) long spikes of pealike flowers from early spring to early summer. The flowers are mainly yellow, though occasionally individual plants will bear lilac, bluish, or white blossoms. Whatever the color of the flowers, they will provide a delicate fragrance.

Being more or less evergreen, the fingerlike pale green foliage provides year-round interest.

Cultivation

In fall or early spring, plant in any well-drained, acid to neutral soil. Though they will grow on heavy soil, tree lupines live longer on sandy soil; on fertile soil they produce excessive foliage rather than flowers. This species is particularly suitable for growing in seaside gardens.

Deadhead unless you require seeds for propagation. After flowering, prune any wayward shoots back to shape.

Propagation Increase by seed sown in fall or spring.

Pests/diseases Powdery mildew sometimes shows as a white powdery coating on the leaves. Root-rot fungi can kill the plants.

LOQUAT — see *Eriobotrya*

Mahonia

mahonia

Mahonia aquifolium

Mahonia aquifolium, fruit

- ❏ Height 2½-10 ft (75-300 cm)
- ❏ Spread 5-12 ft (1.5-3.7 m)
- ❏ Flowers early winter to midspring
- ❏ Any well-drained soil
- ❏ Lightly shaded site
- ❏ Hardy zones 5-9, depending on species

The hardy mahonias have sweetly scented winter flowers, attractive foliage, grapelike berries, and an architectural habit suitable for specimen plants.

The bell-shaped or globular yellow flowers appear between early winter and late spring, held in upright or pendent clusters. The spiny foliage is glossy green.

Popular species and cultivars

Mahonia aquifolium (Oregon grape) is hardy in zones 5-9. This suckering shrub grows to 3-5 ft (1-1.5 m) high and spreads up to 5-6 ft (1.5-1.8 m). In spring it bears rich yellow flowers in dense clusters; berries follow. Cultivars include 'Atropurpureum' (purplered leaves in winter) and 'Moseri' (pink-tinted young leaves).
Mahonia japonica grows 8-10 ft (2.4-3 m) high and up to 8-12 ft

(2.4-3.7 m) wide; it is hardy in zones 6-8. Its glossy green hollylike leaflets may become flushed with red as they age. This species bears lemon-yellow flowers with a lily-of-the-valley scent in drooping spikes as early as late winter in mild climates and in early spring to midspring elsewhere.
Mahonia × media 'Charity,' hardy only in zones 8-9, grows 8-10 ft (2.4-3 m) high and spreads 6-8 ft (1.8-2.4 m). It has leathery dark green leaves; in late winter or early spring it bears deep yellow flowers in upright spikes. 'Winter Sun' displays upright, densely packed flower spikes.
Mahonia repens, a suckering species to 2½ ft (75 cm) high, spreads to form ground-covering colonies; it is hardy in zones 5-9. It has spineless matte green leaves and rounded yellow flower clusters in mid- to late spring; black berries follow. 'Rotundifolia' has rounded leaves and rich yellow flowers.

Cultivation

Plant in spring or fall in any well-drained soil. A partially shaded site is best. Pruning is unnecessary, but in spring cut back hard mahonias grown as ground cover.
Propagation In fall take tip or leaf cuttings and root in a propagation unit.
Pests/diseases Leaf spot and rust can affect shrub, as can leaf scorch from winter wind and sun.

Mahonia x media 'Charity'

Mahonia x media 'Winter Sun'

Mahonia japonica, winter   *Mahonia japonica,* mature foliage   *Mahonia repens* 'Rotundifolia'

Mahonia repens

Melianthus

honey flower

Melianthus major

- ❏ Height 12-14 ft (3.7-4.3 m)
- ❏ Spread 10 ft (3 m)
- ❏ Primarily foliage shrub
- ❏ Any well-drained soil
- ❏ Sunny or partially shaded site
- ❏ Hardy zones 8-10

The honey flower *(Melianthus major)* is grown for its striking foliage. The large gray-green leaves are deeply divided, serrated along the edges, and have a pungent aroma. In spring the young leaves are pale green and give the impression of being luminous. Footlong (30 cm) deep maroon flower spikes are produced in late winter or early spring.

The honey flower is not cold hardy but will tolerate the heat and arid atmosphere of desert conditions. It can reach 12-14 ft (3.7-4.3 m) tall but is easily kept shorter through pruning.

Cultivation

Plant in spring in well-drained soil. Choose a sunny spot for temperate coastal gardens and semi-shade for hot inland sites.

Prune by shortening any taller stems in early spring before new growth begins.

Propagation Buy new stock, or in summer take tip cuttings and root in a propagation unit.

Pests/diseases Whiteflies may be a problem.

MEXICAN ORANGE BLOSSOM — see *Choisya*

Myrtus

myrtle

Myrtus communis

- ❏ Height 2-20 ft (60-600 cm)
- ❏ Spread 2-15 ft (60-450 cm)
- ❏ Flowers summer
- ❏ Ordinary well-drained soil
- ❏ Sunny or partially shaded site
- ❏ Hardy zones 8-10

Myrtle *(Myrtus communis)* is an easily grown shrub that thrives in mild seaside gardens and in much of the Southwest. Because it does not tolerate summer heat combined with humidity, plant it in an airy, well-drained spot.

The lance-shaped, oval leaves are dark green and lustrous; they give off an aromatic scent when bruised. In summer rounded buds open into fragrant white flowers with prominent stamens; they are followed by purple-black berries.

Common myrtle grows into a rounded shrub 5-6 ft (1.5-1.8 m) high and 4-5 ft (1.2-1.5 m) wide, though older specimens can reach 20 ft (6 m) high. 'Compacta' is a dwarf form, 2-3 ft (60-90 cm) high and wide, with dense foliage finer than that of the species.

Cultivation

Plant shrubs in spring in any well-drained soil in a site with sun or partial shade.

In spring remove straggly and damaged shoots from the base.

Propagation In summer take heel cuttings of nonflowering side shoots, 2-3 in (5-7.5 cm) long, and root in a propagation unit.

Pests/diseases Branch tips yellow in poorly drained soil.

Nandina

heavenly bamboo

Nandina domestica

- ❏ Height 4-6 ft (1.2-1.8 m)
- ❏ Spread 2-3 ft (60-90 cm)
- ❏ Flowers late spring
- ❏ Rich, moist but well-drained soil
- ❏ Sunny or shaded site
- ❏ Hardy zones 7-9

This shrub is a traditional favorite in the Southeast, where it has adapted to a wide range of soils, although it does best in moist, rich soil. It grows well in direct sun or in shade.

With its erect stems, heavenly bamboo *(Nandina domestica)* resembles bamboo in habit, but the leaves, which are pale green to midgreen, are tinted red and purple in spring and fall. Clusters of white flowers appear in late spring; they are followed by scarlet fruits, which ripen in early fall and persist throughout winter.

A dwarf cultivar with purplish leaves, 'Nana Purpurea,' is also available.

Cultivation

In spring plant in rich, moist but well-drained soil in sun or partial to moderate shade. Thin out deadwood and weak shoots after flowering.

Propagation In early fall take 3-4 in (7.5-10 cm) heel cuttings of side shoots, and root in a cold frame or other protected spot. Transfer to a nursery bed the following late spring, and grow on for 2 or 3 years before planting out in midspring.

Pests/diseases Trouble free.

Olearia

daisybush

Olearia x haastii

Olearia macrodonta

❏ Height 4-15 ft (1.2-4.5 m)
❏ Spread 4-15 ft (1.2-4.5 m)
❏ Flowers late spring to late summer
❏ Any well-drained soil
❏ Sunny, sheltered spot
❏ Hardy zones 8-10

Daisybushes, native to Australasia, are excellent hedging shrubs for mild seaside gardens. Their sensitivity to cold and their intolerance for humid heat limit their use to southern California, to the temperate regions of the Southwest, and to some sections of the Southeast. Within these confines daisybushes have proven remarkably hardy and easy to grow. They require a well-drained soil and flourish in arid, sunny spots, where the choice of flowering shrubs is otherwise severely limited. In addition, daisybushes flourish in the full sun, salt spray, and strong winds of coastal settings. The lower humidity found along the coast makes this the most favorable spot for olearias in the Southeast.

Most olearias display large clusters of daisylike white flowers at any time from late spring to late summer. The foliage, which in some species may resemble spineless holly leaves, has white-felted undersides.

Popular species

Olearia × haastii is a good choice for urban settings because of its tolerance for air pollution. Ultimately reaching 6-8 ft (1.8-2.4 m) high and 8-10 ft (2.4-3 m) wide, it is more often seen as a medium-size shrub with a height and spread of 4 ft (1.2 m). It produces a mass of fragrant flowers from mid- to late summer. The leaves are broad ovals, glossy midgreen on the upper surfaces. This shrub is exceptionally drought tolerant.

Olearia macrodonta is another medium-size shrub; it can reach a height of 6-8 ft (1.8-2.4 m), but is more commonly 4 ft (1.2 m) tall and wide. This species has sage-green hollylike leaves and bears large clusters of tiny, scented, daisylike flowers in late spring or early summer.

Olearia × scilloniensis is a smaller species that doesn't grow beyond 4-5 ft (1.2-1.5 m) tall and wide. It flowers between late spring and early summer and is usually covered with a profusion of brilliant white blooms. The narrow leaves are silvery-green, making this an exceptional choice for foliage interest.

Olearia stellulata is an erect shrub that reaches a height of 5 ft (1.5 m). Its broad oval leaves measure 3 in (7.5 cm) long and are covered with a rust-colored nap underneath. It bears small daisylike flowers in branch-tip clusters in midsummer

Cultivation

Plant in fall or early spring to midspring. These shrubs do well on any well-drained soil and thrive in alkaline conditions. The site should be sunny and sheltered from cold winter winds; while olearias thrive in mild seaside areas, they also withstand exposure to the hot western sun. In midspring cut any dead shoots back to healthy wood.

Propagation Take 4 in (10 cm) semimature cuttings of lateral shoots in late summer, and root in a propagation unit. Pot the rooted cuttings up singly, and overwinter in a frost-free, protected spot. Pot on and plant out a year later in midspring.

Pests/diseases Trouble free.

ORANGE BALL TREE — see *Buddleia*
OREGON GRAPE — see *Mahonia*

Osmanthus

osmanthus

Osmanthus delavayi, flowers

Osmanthus delavayi

❏ Height 6-20 ft (1.8-6 m)
❏ Spread 6-15 ft (1.8-4.5 m)
❏ Flowers spring, fall, and winter
❏ Well-drained soil
❏ Sunny or partially shaded site
❏ Hardy zones 6-10, depending on species

Osmanthus combines both attributes of a fine ornamental shrub — handsome foliage and attractive fragrant flowers. The shrubs, which often resemble hollies *(Ilex),* do well in almost any kind of soil. Although osmanthus is too sensitive to cold to thrive in the northern states, it flourishes across the South, in the heat and humidity of the Southeast, and the dry heat of the Southwest.

These slow-growing graceful shrubs have a neat habit. They can be used as specimen shrubs or included in shrub and mixed borders. Some are also good for hedging and screening.

Popular species

Osmanthus × burkwoodii, syn. × *Osmarea burkwoodii,* is hardy to zone 6. It has a height and spread of 6-10 ft (1.8-3 m) and oval, glossy dark green leaves. The fragrant white flower clusters appear during mid- and late spring. *Osmanthus decorus* is hardy to zone 7. It grows in a robust dome shape to a height and spread of 6-10 ft (1.8-3 m). Its leathery, lance-shaped, glossy rich green leaves can grow as much as 5 in (13 cm) long on young plants.

Clusters of scented white flowers are freely displayed in spring; they are sometimes followed by purple-black berries.
Osmanthus delavayi, hardy only in zones 8 or 9-10, reaches 6-8 ft (1.8-2.4 m) and has glossy dark green oval and toothed leaves. In early spring to midspring it bears

in profusion sweetly scented white flowers.
Osmanthus × fortunei is a vigorous shrub that is hardy to zone 7. It naturally grows to a height of 15-20 ft (4.5-6 m) but can easily be contained through pruning. Its large, spiny-toothed hollylike leaves are shiny dark green with prominent veins. It produces fragrant white flower clusters in fall.
Osmanthus heterophyllus, syn. *O. aquifolium,* is hardy to zone 7. This slow-growing species will

Osmanthus heterophyllus 'Variegatus'

Pachysandra

Alleghany or Japanese spurge

Pachysandra terminalis 'Variegata'

- ❏ Height 10-12 in (25-30 cm)
- ❏ Spread 2-3 ft (60-90 cm)
- ❏ Primarily foliage shrub
- ❏ Fertile, moist soil
- ❏ Shaded site
- ❏ Hardy zones 5-9, depending on species

Pachysandras are excellent hardy ground covers for shady or partially shaded sites; they have a low, spreading habit and evergreen foliage. Flowers appear in midspring, but these blossoms are tiny and have no petals — only white, purple-tinted stamens.

Popular species

Pachysandra procumbens (Alleghany spurge), hardy to zone 5, grows to 1 ft (30 cm) high and 3 ft (90 cm) wide. It has glossy semievergreen leaves; dense flower spikes are borne in spring.

Pachysandra terminalis (Japanese spurge), hardy only to zone 8, reaches 10 in (25 cm) high but spreads to 2 ft (60 cm). This species has smaller, narrower leaves than *P. procumbens*. 'Variegata' has white-variegated leaves.

Cultivation

Plant in fall or spring in any moist, fertile soil. These plants thrive in a shady site, even deep shade. The Japanese spurge will also tolerate considerable sun in the North if the soil is moist. Pruning is not necessary.

Propagation Lift, divide, and replant in spring.

Pests/diseases Trouble free.

Osmanthus x burkwoodii

eventually reach a height and spread of 6-10 ft (1.8-3 m). With its dark, glossy green leaves, it is often mistaken for a holly. The leaves vary considerably on the same plant, some being prickly, others only spine tipped. Dense clusters of scented white flowers are borne in early fall and midfall. The species and its cultivars are good for dense hedging. Several cultivars include 'Aureomarginatus' (deep yellow leaf margins), 'Gulftide' (lobed or twisted, very spiny foliage), 'Myrtifolius' (compact habit; small spineless foliage), and 'Variegatus' (leaves edged cream-white).

Cultivation

Plant in fall or early spring in sun to medium shade. Osmanthus prefers moist, well-drained acid soil but will tolerate an alkaline pH. At the northern edge of its range, osmanthus needs a site sheltered from cold winter winds.

Pruning is rarely necessary with specimen plantings, but trim established hedges to shape in mid- to late spring.

Propagation Take 4 in (10 cm) heel cuttings of semimature shoots in summer. Root in a propagation unit at a temperature of 64°F (18°C).

Pests/diseases Trouble free.

Pandorea

bower vine, wonga-wonga vine

Pandorea jasminoides

- ❏ Height 20-30 ft (6-9 m)
- ❏ Climber
- ❏ Moist, well-drained soil
- ❏ Sunny or partially shaded site
- ❏ Hardy zones 9-10

These fast-growing exotic vines need plenty of space. Pandorea climb by twining; because they quickly overrun the average trellis, the vines are better suited to a large arbor. Do not allow them to grow unchecked; if the shoots are not cut back regularly, the vine develops a sparse appearance.

Trumpet-shaped flowers are borne from early summer to early fall. The handsome leaves are divided into glossy oval leaflets.

Popular species

Pandorea jasminoides (bower vine), an Australian native, is well adapted to the warmer, moister regions of the Southeast. However, it has also proven very drought tolerant in the garden and grows well in the coastal region of southern California. The cultivar 'Alba' has 2 in (5 cm) long white flowers; 'Rosea' bears pink flowers with rose-colored throats.

Pandorea pandorana (wonga-wonga vine) displays small, ³⁄₄ in (19 mm) long yellow or pinkish-white blossoms that have throats spotted with purplish-brown.

Cultivation

Plant in fall or spring in a moist but well-drained soil. Choose a sunny site near the coast but partial shade in hot inland regions. To give these vines a full appearance, cut back regularly.

Propagation Sow seeds in fall or spring. Or, take 4 in (10 cm) long softwood cuttings in late spring; root in a shaded, protected spot.

Pests/diseases Trouble free.

Passiflora

passionflower

Passiflora caerulea 'Constance Elliott,' flowers

- ❏ Height 20-30 ft (6-9 m)
- ❏ Climber
- ❏ Flowers summer to early fall
- ❏ Moist but well-drained soil
- ❏ Sheltered, sunny or lightly shaded site
- ❏ Hardy zones 8-10

The evergreen passionflowers come from South America, where they are grown commercially for their edible fruits. The maypop (*Passiflora incarnata*), native to eastern North America, is a deciduous species that flourishes as far north as zone 7. None of the evergreen species will withstand a severe frost.

The passionflower takes its name, according to legend, from the shape of its dramatic blooms, usually borne singly on long stalks. Each bloom consists of a long tube that opens out into five petals and five sepals surrounding a center, or corona, of thread-like filaments, above which rise five prominent anthers and three stigmas. The corona is said to represent the crown of thorns and the five petals and sepals the Apostles, with Peter and Judas absent; the flower structure is likened to the passion of Christ.

Climbing shrubs, the evergreen and semievergreen passionflowers put on a magnificent display throughout summer and early fall when fully established. If raised in favorable conditions, they may produce edible fruits.

Popular species

Passiflora caerulea is one of the hardier species, overwintering successfully in zone 8. Given full sun and a moist soil, it is a vigorous, even rampant climber up to 30 ft (9 m) high. It bears light green to midgreen, five- or seven-lobed leaves and slightly fragrant flowers, up to 4 in (10 cm) wide, colored white with blue-purple coronas. At the end of the summer orange-red ovoid fruits are sometimes produced. The cultivar

Passiflora caerulea 'Constance Elliott'

Pernettya

pernettya

Pernettya mucronata 'Rubra'

Passiflora caerulea

'Constance Elliott' is outstanding, with ivory-white flowers; it is hardier than the species.
Passiflora mollissima is another vigorous species that is hardy to zone 8. It bears soft green, three-lobed leaves and tubular pink flowers up to 3 in (7.5 cm) wide. The fruits are yellow and 4-6 in (10-15 cm) long. Rampant growth makes this a good vine for covering a bank, but keep it away from nearby trees and shrubs.

Cultivation

Plant in midspring in a loose, evenly moist, but well-drained soil. Choose a sheltered site in full sun or light shade. Train the climbers up a trellis or wire mesh attached to a wall; although they cling by tendrils, tie them in until they become self-supporting. After the second year of growth, prune annually in early spring, thinning the vine by removing overgrown shoots at ground level or by cutting them back to the main stems.
Propagation In summer you can take 3-4 in (7.5-10 cm) long stem sections, and root in a propagation unit.
Pests/diseases Trouble free.

PEPPER TREE — see *Drimys*
PERIWINKLE — see *Vinca*

❏ Height 2-3 ft (60-90 cm)
❏ Spread 2-3 ft (60-90 cm)
❏ Flowers late spring to early summer
❏ Moist, acid soil
❏ Sunny or shaded site
❏ Hardy zones 6-9

This Chilean shrub displays its beauty at two different times of year. First, in late spring and early summer, the wiry stems are whitened with tiny heatherlike flowers. Then, through the fall and winter, the shrubs are laden with bright, marble-sized berries.
    As a hardy low-growing shrub, *Pernettya mucronata* and its cultivars make ideal ground-cover plants in gardens with acid soil.

Popular cultivars

For a female cultivar to produce colorful fruits, you must grow a male plant in close proximity. The species has several cultivars.
'Alba' has white fruits lightly tinged with pink.
'Lilacina' is laden with reddish-lilac berries.
'Rosea' bears rose-pink fruits.
'Rubra,' a self-pollinating cultivar, bears pink flowers and dark carmine-red berries.

Cultivation

Plant pernettyas in fall or early spring in moist, acid soil. They

Pernettya mucronata 'Rosea'

flower and fruit best if you position them for full sun in cold winter regions; however, in areas where summers are long and hot, they benefit from partial shade.
    Old plants tend to become leggy; to encourage new growth, cut back hard into the old wood in late winter or early spring.
Propagation Take 2 in (5 cm) long cuttings in early fall to mid-fall, and root in a cold frame or other protected spot.
Pests/diseases Trouble free.

Phlomis

Jerusalem sage

Phlomis fruticosa

- ❑ Height 3-4 ft (1-1.2 m)
- ❑ Spread 2 ft (60 cm)
- ❑ Flowers late spring or summer
- ❑ Any well-drained soil
- ❑ Sunny site
- ❑ Hardy zones 7-10

Jerusalem sage *(Phlomis fruticosa)* is a low-growing Mediterranean shrub valued for its textured foliage — wedge-shaped, woolly gray-green leaves — and for its whorls of hooded bright golden flowers appearing in late spring or summer.

Reaching 3-4 ft (1-1.2 m) high, it is ideal grown with other sun-loving shrubs and perennials and as ground cover for large sunny banks. Its tolerance for drought makes it a good choice for arid southwestern gardens.

At the northern edge of its range, the above-ground growth may suffer winterkill, but new growth usually appears in spring.

Cultivation
Plant in fall or spring in any well-drained fertile soil in a sunny, sheltered site.

To maintain a compact form, cut back at the end of the season's growth.

Propagation Take heel cuttings in late summer to early fall, and root in a cold frame or other protected spot. Plant out in a nursery bed the following spring, and grow on for a year before transplanting to the permanent site.

Pests/diseases Trouble free.

Photinia

photinia

Photinia x fraseri 'Red Robin'

- ❑ Height 6-10 ft (1.8-3 m)
- ❑ Spread 5-8 ft (1.5-2.4 m)
- ❑ Foliage shrub
- ❑ Any well-drained soil
- ❑ Sunny or partially shaded site
- ❑ Hardy zones 8-9

If you do not have the acid conditions needed for growing *Pieris, Photinia × fraseri* is an excellent substitute. In spring this near-hardy shrub becomes a mass of rich coppery-red as the young leaves unfurl. As summer arrives, the leathery leaves mature to dark green.

Popular cultivars
Two cultivars of *Photinia × fraseri* are commonly grown.
'Red Robin' is the smaller cultivar, reaching 6 ft (1.8 m) high and 5 ft (1.5 m) wide; it bears sharply toothed leaves and brilliant red young foliage.
'Robusta,' a vigorous shrub 10 ft (3 m) high, is the hardiest type.

Cultivation
In fall or early spring, plant in any well-drained but moist soil in a sunny or partially shaded site.

Prune in early summer to keep the shrubs tidy.

Propagation Take semimature cuttings in summer, and root in a propagation unit. Alternatively, layer in spring and sever from the parent plant a year later.

Pests/diseases Fungal leaf spot may cause defoliation in humid weather.

Phyllodoce

phyllodoce

Phyllodoce empetriformis

- ❑ Height 6-15 in (15-38 cm)
- ❑ Spread 6-15 in (15-38 cm)
- ❑ Flowers midspring to early summer
- ❑ Moist, acid soil
- ❑ Cool, shaded site
- ❑ Hardy zones 4-7

The species in this genus of hardy, heatherlike shrubs thrive in cool, moist, acid soil. Plants of the Far North, they are useful as ground cover for chilly, shady sites. They will not, however, tolerate hot summers elsewhere.

The narrow heathlike foliage is pale to dark green and arranged in whorls along the stems. Flowers appear between mid- and late spring, though some blooms may arrive in fall.

Popular species
Phyllodoce aleutica bears green-yellow pitcher-shaped flowers. This species reaches only 6-12 in (15-30 cm) high but spreads 1 ft (30 cm) or more.
Phyllodoce empetriformis grows 9-15 in (23-38 cm) high and up to 15 in (38 cm) wide; it bears rosy-purple flowers.

Cultivation
Plant in spring or fall in moist, nutrient-poor, acid soil in a cool, shaded site. Regular pruning is not necessary.

Propagation Take heel cuttings from young lateral growth between midsummer and fall; root in a cold frame or protected spot.

Pests/diseases Trouble free.

Pieris

Japanese pieris

Pieris formosa

Pieris formosa 'Forest Flame'

Pieris japonica 'Blush'

❏ Height 4-12 ft (1.2-3.7 m)
❏ Spread 4-15 ft (1.2-4.5 m)
❏ Flowers mid- to late spring
❏ Moist, acid soil
❏ Sheltered, partially shaded site
❏ Hardy zones 5-8, depending
  on species

These hardy shrubs are favorites in gardens with acid soil. They are grown for their attractive foliage and beautiful flowers. As soon as the spring flowers fade, new, brightly colored leaves unfurl and put on yet another eye-catching display. In winter the narrow, oval leaves provide a handsome mass of glossy dark green foliage.

Popular species

Pieris floribunda, syn. *Andromeda floribunda,* grows only 4-6 ft (1.2-1.8 m) high and wide; hardy in zones 5-7, it's useful for small gardens. It has narrow, leathery dark green foliage year round and dense, erect spikes of white flowers in mid- to late spring.

Pieris formosa grows best in the cool, moist climate of the Pacific Northwest. Hardy in zones 7-8, it grows 6-12 ft (1.8-3.7 m) high and has a spread of 10-15 ft (3-4.5 m). This species has brilliant red young foliage and sprays of white flowers. 'Forest Flame' has red young leaves that fade to pink, then cream, and finally green.

Pieris japonica, syn. *Andromeda japonica* is hardy in zones 6-8. They grow 6-10 ft (1.8-3 m) high and wide. These shrubs have attractive young leaves, which are copper-red at first and then turn light green; they bear an abundance of drooping, waxy white flowers in spring. Popular cultivars include 'Blush' (rose-colored buds opening to pale pink flowers), 'Christmas Cheer' (early, deep pink buds opening to rose-colored flowers), 'Purity' (compact; pure white flowers), and 'Variegata' (white flowers; cream-edged leaves tinted pink).

Cultivation

Plant in fall or spring in moist but well-drained, acid loam in a sheltered, partially shaded site.

In midspring top-dress the shrubs with leaf mold or compost; do not allow the soil to dry out during the summer months.

After flowering, remove faded flower heads and lightly cut back any straggly shoots.

Propagation In late summer take 3-4 in (7.5-10 cm) cuttings of semimature shoots, and root in a cold frame or other protected spot. In spring transfer to pots of peat-enriched potting mix, and grow on for 2 or 3 years before planting out.

Pests/diseases Dieback, lace bugs, and leaf spot all attack these shrubs.

PINE — see *Pinus*

Pieris japonica 'Purity'

Pinus

pine

Pinus pumila 'Glauca'

Pinus heldreichii 'Compact Gem'

- ❑ Height ⅔-7 ft (20-210 cm)
- ❑ Spread ⅔-5 ft (20-150 cm)
- ❑ Coniferous shrubs
- ❑ Well-drained soil
- ❑ Open, sunny site
- ❑ Hardy zones 3-9, depending on species

Pinus is a large genus of coniferous trees and shrubs, native to most forested areas in the Northern Hemisphere. Tall-growing forest trees, ornamental garden trees (see pp.43-45), and compact, shrubby conifers suitable for rock gardens and specimen planting can all be found in this genus.

Pines are distinguished by their needlelike leaves ranging in color from blue to green to golden yellow, depending on the cultivar. The woody cones are broad and squat or long and tapering.

The shrubby, compact pines described here thrive in full sun; they do not tolerate air pollution.

Popular species and cultivars
Pinus densiflora 'Umbraculifera' is hardy in zones 5-7. It grows slowly into a domed shrub that is typically 3 ft (90 cm) high and wide with an umbrella-like head of branches. It bears a profusion of tiny cones.

Pinus heldreichii is tolerant of both alkaline soil and drought; it is hardy to zone 5. Shrubby cultivars include 'Compact Gem' (rounded form; dark green foliage; slowly grows 7 ft/2.1 m high and 5 ft/1.5 m wide) and 'Pygmy,' (dwarf pine; dense globular or pyramid form; 10 in/25 cm high and wide; bright green leaves).

Pinus mugo (mountain pine) is parent to a number of dense and shrubby cultivars, all of which are hardy in zones 3-7 and tolerant of alkaline soil. 'Gnome' grows into a dense, globular dark green mound up to 20 in (50 cm) high and 2½ ft (75 cm) wide. 'Mops' is a dense, globular cultivar that reaches only 15 in (38 cm) high and 20 in (50 cm) wide. The variety *pumilio* is a compact cushion-like form; it reaches a height of just 15 in (38 cm) in 4 to 5 years of growth.

Pinus nigra 'Hornibrookiana,' growing to 1½ ft (45 cm) high and 3 ft (90 cm) wide, has a broad, spreading habit. The needles are rich dark green. Hardy in zones 4-8, it grows extremely slowly and thrives on alkaline soil.

Pinus parviflora and its cultivars are distinguished by their conical habit and light blue-green needles. In general, they are hardy in zones 5-9. A popular shrubby type is 'Adcock's Dwarf,' a compact pine with a height of 5 ft (1.5 m) and a spread of 2½ ft (75 cm); its gray-green foliage is borne in bunches at the tips of the shoots.

Pinus pumila (dwarf stone pine) is hardy in zones 4-7. It's the parent of two cultivars often found in heather and large rock gardens. 'Dwarf Blue' bears bluish needles banded with white. It reaches 2 ft (60 cm) high and 4 ft (1.2 m)

Pinus mugo 'Mops'

Pinus sylvestris 'Aurea'

Pittosporum
pittosporum

Pittosporum tenuifolium

wide. 'Glauca' is rounded and grows up to 2½ ft (75 cm) high and wide with blue-gray foliage.

Pinus strobus 'Nana' (hardy in zones 3-9), a bushy pine, is 2½ ft (75 cm) high and 3 ft (90 cm) wide with dense blue-green leaves.

Pinus sylvestris (Scots pine) is hardy in zones 3-8. This species has given rise to several dwarf cultivars, including 'Argentea Compacta' (slow-growing cushionlike form; silver-blue needles), 'Aurea' (slow-growing, 6 ft/1.8 m high and 3 ft/90 cm wide, eventually developing into a small tree; striking golden winter foliage), 'Beuvronensis' (broad domed or flat-topped shrub; 2½ ft/75 cm high and 3 ft/90 cm wide; gray-green foliage), and 'Watererei' (slow-growing to 10 ft/3 m; dense growth; pyramidal or flat-topped).

Cultivation
Plant in fall or early spring in well-drained soil of an acid or neutral pH (unless otherwise noted above). While some species succeed on poor soil, few dwarf pines can tolerate shallow soil. The site should be open and in full light.

Pruning is not recommended.

Propagation These cultivars should only be increased by grafting techniques that are best left to professionals.

Pests/diseases Canker and dieback may affect injured or weak trees. Root-rot fungi can kill these plants; sawflies and webworms may also prove troublesome.

❏ Height 1-15 ft (30-450 cm)
❏ Spread 1-7 ft (30-210 cm)
❏ Primarily foliage shrub
❏ Well-drained fertile soil
❏ Sunny, sheltered site
❏ Hardy zones 8-10

These shrubs from Australia and eastern Asia are hardy only in the southernmost regions of North America. Where winters are mild, though, they are popular landscape shrubs as hedges, specimens, and in tubs. Because they tolerate salt spray, these shrubs are useful in seaside gardens.

Pittosporums are grown for their attractive foliage, which comes in a range of variegations and colors. With the exception of *Pittosporum tobira*, they respond well to clipping and are suitable as hedges. Bell-shaped flowers appear in spring; they are small but wonderfully fragrant.

Popular species
Pittosporum crassifolium has oval, leathery gray-green leaves and bears maroon flowers in late spring. Hardy only to zone 9, it reaches 10-15 ft (3-4.5 m) high and 6 ft (1.8 m) wide. Notably wind-resistant, this species is a good seaside plant.

Pittosporum tenuifolium, hardy to zone 9, reaches 15 ft (4.5 m) high and 5-7 ft (1.5-2.1 m) wide. Almost-black stems carry pale green oval leaves with waved edges; cultivars may have bronzy-purple foliage. Chocolate-purple flowers with a strong vanillalike fragrance appear in late spring. Popular cultivars include 'Irene Paterson' (creamy young leaves

Pittosporum tobira, flowers

Prunus
cherry or Portugal laurel

Pittosporum tobira, foliage

Prunus laurocerasus 'Otto Luyken'

that become green mottled with white — in winter, with pink).

Pittosporum tobira is the hardiest species, overwintering successfully in the warmer parts of zone 8. It has dark green 2-5 in (5-13 cm) long leaves, and bears creamy white flowers with a fragrance of orange blossoms in early spring. 'Wheeler's Dwarf' is a compact form that reaches a height and spread of only 1-2 ft (30-60 cm); it is ideal for growing in containers.

Cultivation
In spring place container-grown plants in well-drained, fertile soil in a spot sheltered from cold winter winds. For hedging, set plants 1½ ft (45 cm) apart. Cut off the tips of the leading shoots twice in the first growing season. When a hedge reaches the desired size, clip to shape yearly in midspring and midsummer. Trim specimen pittosporums in spring.

Propagation In midsummer take 3-4 in (7.5-10 cm) heel cuttings of semimature lateral shoots; root in a propagation unit. Overwinter rooted cuttings in a frost-free spot; plant out the following spring.

Pests/diseases Aphids and scale insects may be troublesome.

PORTUGAL LAUREL — see *Prunus*
POTATO VINE — see *Solanum*
PRIVET — see *Ligustrum*

❑ Height 4-20 ft (1.2-6 m)
❑ Spread 6-30 ft (1.8-9 m)
❑ Primarily foliage shrub; flowers spring
❑ Deep, well-drained soil
❑ Sunny or shaded site
❑ Hardy zones 6-9, depending on species

The evergreen laurels are easily grown shrubs, tolerant of shade and invaluable for screening and tall hedging. Although grown mainly for their attractive glossy foliage, laurels also make fine specimen shrubs bearing clusters of cream-white flowers in spring.

Popular species
Prunus laurocerasus (cherry laurel), hardy in southern zone 6 to zone 8, is 15-20 ft (4.5-6 m) high and 20-30 ft (6-9 m) wide. The leathery leaves are shiny midgreen above, pale green beneath. Spikes of white flowers appear in midspring followed by small black fruits. Cultivars include 'Marbled White' (syn. 'Variegata'; slow-growing; gray-green leaves marbled with white), 'Otto Luyken' (narrow leaves, 4 ft/1.2 m high and 6 ft/1.8 m wide), and 'Schipkaensis' (very cold hardy; narrow leaves; 4-5 ft/1.2-1.5 m high).

Prunus lusitanica (Portugal laurel) is hardy in zones 7-9. It grows 15-20 ft (4.5-6 m) high and wide and bears dark green foliage. Sprays of cream-white scented flowers are borne in late spring or early summer, followed by small red fruits. 'Variegata' is slow-growing with white-edged leaves.

Cultivation
Plant in fall or spring in well-drained soil in a shady or sunny spot. *P. lusitanica* thrives on shallow alkaline soil. For hedging, set young plants 2-3 ft (60-90 cm) apart; after planting, cut them back by one-third to promote bushy growth.

Prune large, unsightly laurels back hard into old wood in spring. Trim hedges in spring or summer.

Propagation In late summer or early fall take 3-4 in (7.5-10 cm) long heel cuttings; root in a cold frame or other protected spot.

Pests/diseases Leaf spot and scale insects may be troublesome.

Prunus lusitanica 'Variegata'

Prunus laurocerasus, fruit

Prunus laurocerasus 'Marbled White'

Prunus lusitanica, flowers

Pyracantha

firethorn

Pyracantha 'Orange Glow'

- ❏ Height 5-16 ft (1.5-4.9 m)
- ❏ Spread 6-15 ft (1.8-4.5 m)
- ❏ Flowers midspring to early summer
- ❏ Any fertile, well-drained soil
- ❏ Sunny or partially shaded site
- ❏ Hardy zones 6-9

Pyracantha (firethorns) are particularly valued for their clusters of berries — unlike those on some other evergreen shrubs, these fruits are persistent from fall through winter. The decorative masses of orange, red, or yellow berries hang from the thorny branches in heavy swags.

The leaves are attractive too, being glossy and a particularly fresh bright green on the young shoots. In spring to early summer, small creamy white flowers cluster thickly on the stems.

Firethorns are usually trained up a wall or grown as hedging plants; but this requires pruning to shape, and the shrubs will not bear many berries when pruned. Alternatively, if you prefer the spectacular masses of berries, you can treat them as specimen shrubs and leave them unpruned to grow into large, broad shrubs. Firethorns will thrive on exposed sites and despite air pollution.

Popular species and cultivars

Pyracantha angustifolia is hardy only to zone 7. It bears rounded clusters of creamy flowers in late spring or early summer, followed by bright orange-yellow berries, which usually persist all winter. It reaches 10 ft (3 m) high and 6-8 ft (1.8-2.4 m) wide and has narrow leaves that are dark and glossy

Pyracantha coccinea

above but gray and hairy beneath. 'Gnome,' a dwarf cultivar reaches a height of 6 ft (1.8 m) and a spread of 8 ft (2.4 m); it is hardy to zone 6. 'Yukon Belle' is another exceptionally cold-hardy cultivar, overwintering in zone 5. Just 6-10 ft (1.8-3 m) high and wide, it is semievergreen and bears orange berries.

Pyracantha 'Apache' is a disease-resistant, compact cultivar that grows to a height of 5 ft (1.5 m) and a spread of 6 ft (1.8 m). It bears large red fruits.

Pyracantha atalantioides is an upright and fast-growing shrub, 10-15 ft (3-4.5 m) high and wide. This species has large, glossy deep green leaves. Flat clusters of white flowers are borne in late spring or early summer, followed by crimson berries in fall.

Pyracantha coccinea is successful overwintering in zone 6. It grows 10-15 ft (3-4.5 m) high and wide, with narrow, pointed midgreen leaves. In mid- to late spring the shrub bears wide clusters of white flowers, followed by dense clusters of rich red berries. The cultivar 'Kasan' is cold-tolerant.

It grows 10 ft (3 m) tall and wide, and bears orange-red fruits.

Pyracantha 'Fiery Cascade' grows to a height and spread of 10 ft (3 m). It is of upright habit, with small leaves and a profusion of small orange-red berries. It is reliably hardy in zone 6.

Pyracantha 'Mohave' grows up to 10 ft (3 m) high and wide. It is outstanding for its mass of bright red berries but is unfortunately prone to scab.

Pyracantha 'Navajo' is smaller than most firethorns, rarely more than 5 ft (1.5 m) high, but it is wide-spreading. The small orange or orange-red berries appear late in the season; they are borne in heavy clusters.

Pyracantha 'Orange Glow' is dense and vigorous, and grows to 10 ft (3 m) or more high and wide. In fall its branches are weighed down with bright orange, persistent berries.

Pyracantha 'Teton' is a disease-resistant cultivar that grows to a height of 16 ft (4.9 m) with a spread of 9 ft (2.7 m). This is an exceptionally cold-hardy shrub, and it bears yellow-orange fruits.

Pyracantha 'Mohave'

Rhamnus

buckthorn

Pyracantha coccinea, flowers

Cultivation

Plant container-grown specimens in fall or early spring in fertile, well-drained soil; either a moderately acid or an alkaline pH is fine. Firethorns thrive in either full sun or partial shade.

Place hedging plants 15-24 in (38-60 cm) apart and cut the current season's growth back by half. Pinch back the growing tips of young shoots when they reach 6-8 in (15-20 cm), and repeat in late summer to induce bushy growth from the base. Clip established hedges to shape between late spring and midsummer.

Provide trellis or wire support for espaliered pyracanthas; they do well on north- and east-facing walls. Tie in vigorous growth each year between midsummer and early fall. Prune unwanted shoots from late spring to midsummer.

Pruning is not necessary on freestanding shrubs.

Propagation In mid- to late summer take 3-4 in (7.5-10 cm) cuttings of the current year's shoots; root in a propagation unit.

Pests/diseases Aphids and scale insects may infest stems; fireblight and scab are the most common problems.

Rhamnus alaternus 'Argenteovariegata'

❑ Height 1-15 ft (30-450 cm)
❑ Spread 8 ft (2.4 m)
❑ Foliage shrub
❑ Any well-drained soil
❑ Sunny or lightly shaded site
❑ Hardy zones 7-9, depending on species

This large genus of trees and shrubs includes a few evergreen types grown primarily for their attractive foliage and fruits. They are easy to grow in well-drained soils, and they tolerate salt spray, heat, drought, and air pollution.

Popular species

Rhamnus alaternus is hardy only in zones 8-9, but it grows rapidly to a height of 10 ft (3 m) and a spread of 8 ft (2.4 m). The stiff branches are covered with small, lance-shaped, shiny green leaves. In midspring clusters of yellow-green flowers are followed by red berries that ripen to black. In mild gardens, fruiting is often prolific. The cultivar 'Argenteovariegata' has leaves irregularly edged with cream.

Rhamnus californica is a West Coast native that is hardy in zones 7-9. The leaves are large (1-3 in/2.5-7.5 cm long) and dull or glossy green; the large berries ripen from green to red to black. This species may exhibit a low, spreading form, reaching a height of only 3 ft (90 cm), or it may grow to a height of 15 ft (4.5 m). 'Eve Case' is a rounded form that grows to 4-8 ft (1.2-2.4 m) high and wide. 'Seaview' is a spreading cultivar that may be maintained at a height of 1½ ft (45 cm) and a spread of 8 ft (2.4 m).

Cultivation

In fall or spring plant in any well-drained soil in a sunny or lightly shaded spot. Regular pruning is not necessary.

Propagation Increase by layering in spring. Separate from the parent plant 1 to 2 years later.

Pests/diseases Trouble free.

Rhododendron

rhododendron

Rhododendron 'Furnivall's Daughter'

☐ Height 1-40 ft (0.3-12 m)
☐ Spread 1-40 ft (0.3-12 m)
☐ Flowers midwinter to early summer
☐ Moist, rich, acid soil
☐ Lightly shaded site
☐ Hardy zones 4-8, depending on species

The diversity of rhododendrons is depicted by its thousands of species, hybrids, and cultivars — they vary greatly in size, color, performance, and hardiness. The genus includes deciduous and evergreen types, from almost tree-sized shrubs to dwarfs.

There is a vast range of flower shapes, textures, scents, and colors (white, cream, yellow, orange, pink, scarlet, crimson, purple, and lavender). Though normally late-spring bloomers, some species bloom in other seasons.

Many rhododendrons also have beautiful leaves. They may be little larger than those of heathers or up to 2½ ft (75 cm) long.

While experienced gardeners have long distinguished between rhododendrons and azaleas, botanists classify both in the genus *Rhododendron*. This book follows the traditional gardening practice; the two are considered separately, with azaleas following rhododendrons.

Rhododendrons flourish in dappled shade; however, they will grow in a sunny spot. Most perform best on acid soil and in areas of temperate climate and abundant rainfall — conditions typically found in the eastern states and the Pacific Northwest.

Popular species

Rhododendron aberconwayi is hardy to zone 7. The shrub grows 7 ft (2.1 m) high and 5 ft (1.5 m) wide with brittle, leathery leaves. Loose clusters of saucer-shaped whitish-pink flowers spotted with maroon appear in late spring.

Rhododendron arboreum, hardy to zone 8, is 20-40 ft (6-12 m) high and wide. The shiny dark green foliage has silver- or brown-felted undersides. In late winter and early spring the species displays compact clusters of pink, white, or deep red bell-shaped blooms.

Rhododendron augustinii (hardy to zone 7) has an upright habit. It grows 6-10 ft (1.8-3 m) high and

Rhododendron yakusimanum

5-6 ft (1.5-1.8 m) wide. The pointed dark green leaves are scaly beneath. In mid- and late spring it bears clusters of trumpet-shaped flowers. They range in color from mauve to dark blue; the throats are spotted with green.

Rhododendron campylogynum (hardy to zone 7), a dwarf species, reaches only 1½ ft (45 cm) high and wide. The small dark green

Rhododendron lutescens

leaves turn bronze in winter. Its bell-shaped flowers in varying shades of purple appear in late spring and early summer.

Rhododendron carolinianum is hardy to zone 5. A small, rounded shrub, it slowly grows to a height and spread of 3-6 ft (1-1.8 m). It produces narrow, elliptical 2-3 in (5-7.5 cm) long dark green leaves and displays 3 in (7.5 cm) clusters of pure white to rose or lilac-rose flowers in late spring.

Rhododendron catawbiense, native to eastern North America, is hardy to zone 5. It slowly reaches 6-10 ft (1.8-3 m) high and 5-8 ft (1.5-2.4 m) wide. In late spring it bears lilac-purple flowers with green or yellow throat markings.

Rhododendron ciliatum (hardy to zone 8) is of spreading habit, growing 4-5 ft (1.2-1.5 m) high and 6-8 ft (1.8-2.4 m) wide. The dull green leaves are bristly. In midspring it bears clusters of red flower buds, which open into pink bell-shaped blooms. Given a site sheltered from spring frost, the flowers appear in abundance.

Rhododendron cinnabarinum (hardy to zone 8) reaches 6-10 ft (1.8-3 m) high and up to 4-6 ft (1.2-1.8 m) wide. In late spring and early summer large clusters of tubular orange-red blooms open against gray-green leaves.

Rhododendron decorum (hardy to zone 7) grows 6-10 ft (1.8-3 m) high and wide. The smooth leaves are gray-green above and smoky blue beneath. It has fragrant, funnel-shaped pale pink or white flowers with green centers, opening in mid- to late spring.

Rhododendron haematodes is hardy to zone 7. A low-growing

Rhododendron rubiginosum

Rhododendron racemosum

Rhododendron yunnanense

shrub, it is 3-4 ft (1-1.2 m) high and 6 ft (1.8 m) wide. Its leathery mid-green foliage has orange-brown felted undersides; in late spring clusters of brilliant red funnel-shaped flowers appear.

Rhododendron hippophaeoides (hardy to zone 6) is one of the hardiest of the early-flowering species. It throws up suckers and grows 4-5 ft (1.2-1.5 m) high and wide. It has gray-green and scaly leaves, and in early spring to mid-spring it bears funnel-shaped mauve and pink blooms.

Rhododendron lutescens (hardy to zone 7), a 10 ft (3 m) high and 5-7 ft (1.5-2.1 m) wide species, is best grown in woodland shelter. The lance-shaped leaves are glossy bronze to dull green. From midwinter to midspring it bears an abundance of funnel-shaped yellow flowers singly or in pairs.

Rhododendron macabeanum is hardy to zone 8. It reaches tree-like proportions: 25 ft (7.5 m) high and 10-15 ft (3-4.5 m) wide. The 1 ft (30 cm) long, dark green leaves are silvery white and hairy on the undersides. In midspring it bears compact clusters of bell-shaped yellow flowers marked purple at the base of the petals.

Rhododendron maximum (hardy to zone 4) is a vigorous shrub,

growing 4-15 ft (1.2-4.5 m) tall in the northern part of its range and reaching 30 ft (9 m) tall and wide in the South. Its leaves grow up to 10 in (25 cm) long; the late-spring or early-summer flowers are purplish-pink to white, spotted with olive-green to orange.

Rhododendron moupinense, a dwarf shrub, is hardy to zone 8. It reaches 2-5 ft (60-150 cm) high and 3-4 ft (90-120 cm) wide and has midgreen and glossy leaves. Tubular white or pink flowers speckled with red appear in late winter and early spring.

Rhododendron pseudochrysanthum (hardy to zone 8) is slow-growing and compact, reaching 8 ft (2.4 m) high and 6 ft (1.8 m) wide. Its young leaves and shoots are gray-white and covered with fine hairs. The bell-shaped flowers are pink.

Rhododendron racemosum is a free-flowering species, hardy to zone 6. It is 1-6 ft (30-180 cm) high and 3-5 ft (90-150 cm) wide with gray-green leaves. Funnel-shaped flowers in shades of pink appear from early to late spring.

Rhododendron rubiginosum is hardy to zone 6. One of the few species to tolerate alkaline soil, it is 6-10 ft (1.8-3 m) high and 4-8 ft (1.2-2.4 m) wide. Funnel-shaped

lilac-pink blooms appear from early spring to midspring among dull green leaves with scaly and rust-colored undersides.

Rhododendron sutchuenense is hardy to zone 6, growing 12 ft (3.7 m) tall and wide. Its rose-lilac bell-shaped blooms speckled with purple appear in early spring. The leaves are gray-green.

Rhododendron thomsonii (hardy to zone 8) reaches 8 ft (2.4 m) high with a spread of 6 ft (1.8 m), and is clothed with shiny dark green leaves. It bears clusters of blood-red flowers with a waxy texture in mid- to late spring.

Rhododendron yakusimanum (hardy to zone 5) is a dwarf species reaching only 2 ft (60 cm) high and 2-3 ft (60-90 cm) wide. It has dark green leathery leaves that are felted and fawn-colored beneath. Pink buds open into white bell-shaped flowers in late spring and early summer.

Rhododendron yunnanense is a compact shrub reaching 10-12 ft (3-3.7 m) high and wide. It is hardy to zone 7 and may be semideciduous after a cold winter. The brittle dark green leaves are hairy on top. This species bears an abundance of white or pale pink flowers in late spring and early summer.

Rhododendron 'Purple Splendor'

Rhododendron pseudochrysanthum

Rhododendron 'Blue Bird'

Rhododendron 'Nova Zembla'

Rhododendron sutchuenense

Popular hybrids

Most of the huge number of hybrids are free-flowering in late spring and early summer; the blooms are usually funnel-shaped and borne in large clusters. The leaves are glossy and dark green. Hardy through zone 6 unless otherwise noted, they are hardier than the species, tolerating cold and exposure. Hybrids are ideal for large-scale planting, and taller types are popular as screening.

'Anna Rose Whitney' is a vigorous shrub up to 10 ft (3 m) high and 8 ft (2.4 m) or more wide. It bears dense clusters of deep rose-pink flowers spotted with brown.

'Blue Bird' is 3-5 ft (1-1.5 m) high and 3-4 ft (1-1.2 m) wide. It is a small, neat shrub with rich violet-blue blooms in midspring.

'Blue Diamond,' a slow-growing shrub, reaches 3 ft (90 cm) high and wide. It bears tight clusters of small, rich violet-blue flowers.

'Blue Peter' has an abundance of frilled cobalt-violet blooms. It reaches 5-10 ft (1.5-3 m) high and 4-8 ft (1.2-2.4 m) across.

'Blue Tit' has lavender-blue flowers in midspring. It is a compact shrub, 3 ft (90 cm) high and wide.

'Boule de Neige' (hardy to zone 5) has large trusses of white flowers. It is rounded and compact, 5 ft (1.5 m) tall and 8 ft (2.4 m) wide.

'Chikor' has pale yellow flowers. At only 1-2 ft (30-60 cm) high and wide, it is ideal for a rock garden.

'Chink' flowers early in spring with pale yellow-green blooms. It grows to 3-5 ft (1-1.5 m) high and 3-4 ft (1-1.2 m) wide.

'Crest' has primrose-yellow flowers and exceptionally large leaves. It has a height of 5-10 ft (1.5-3 m) and a spread of 4-8 ft (1.2-2.4 m).

'Elizabeth' (hardy to zone 5) grows to 3-5 ft (1-1.5 m) high and 3-4 ft (1-1.2 m) wide. This shrub has large trumpet-shaped scarlet-red flowers.

'Exbury Naomi' has lilac-pink flowers tinged with yellow; it grows 15-20 ft (4.5-6 m) high and 12-17 ft (3.7-5.2 m) wide.

'Fastuosum Flore Pleno' has double mauve flowers. This hardy shrub (to zone 5) grows 15-20 ft (4.5-6 m) high, a little less wide.

'Furnivall's Daughter' (hardy to zone 5) has light pink flowers blotched with crimson. It grows 10-15 ft (3-4.5 m) high and 8-12 ft (2.4-3.7 m) wide.

'Gomer Waterer' bears white flowers flushed with pale mauve; it reaches 10-15 ft (3-4.5 m) high and 8-12 ft (2.4-3.7 m) wide.

'Grumpy,' a dwarf form, is 2-3 ft (60-90 cm) high and wide. It has cream flowers flushed with pink and spotted with orange-yellow.

'Mrs. Charles E. Pearson' has pink-mauve flowers spotted brown. It grows 10-15 ft (3-4.5 m) high and 8-12 ft (2.4-3.7 m) wide.

'Nova Zembla' is extremely resistant to heat and cold; it overwinters reliably in zone 5. It has red flowers on a 6 ft (1.8 m) shrub.

'Pink Pearl' bears rose-pink flowers, which fade to white. One of the taller and more popular hybrids, it is 15-20 ft (4.5-6 m) high and 12-17 ft (3.7-5.2 m) wide.

'P.J.M.' is the name of a group of hybrids. They are hardy to zone 4 and bloom in midspring. Reaching a height and spread of 3-6 ft (1-1.8 m), they bear flowers in shades of bright lavender-pink; their foliage turns purple in fall.

'Purple Splendor' has royal purple flowers with black markings. It grows 5-10 ft (1.5-3 m) high and 4-8 ft (1.2-2.4 m) wide.

'Ramapo' (hardy through zone 5 and into zone 4), a compact form, grows 2-3 ft (60-90 cm) tall and wide. In early spring to midspring it has bright violet-pink flowers.

'Roseum Elegans' is a 6 ft (1.8 m) tall and wide, rounded shrub. It

Rhododendron 'Anna Rose Whitney'

Rhododendron catawbiense

Rhododendron 'Elizabeth'

tolerates summer heat; it is hardy in the warmer parts of zone 4. It has lavender-pink flowers.

'Vulcan' (hardy to zone 5), a compact, mounded shrub, reaches 3-5 ft (1-1.5 m) tall and wide. It has heavy trusses of red flowers.

Cultivation
With the exceptions already noted, rhododendrons will not grow in alkaline soil. They prefer well-drained but moist, acid loam; enrich light soils and lighten heavy soils with sphagnum peat or leaf mold. Select a lightly shaded site sheltered from cold winds.

Plant in fall or spring, choosing a site where spring-flowering types are protected from early-morning sun.

In spring feed the plants with a specially formulated acidic fertilizer. Pruning is not needed, but deadhead shrubs after flowering.

Propagation Layer large-leaved species at any time of year. Sever them after 2 years. Increase small-leaved species and hardy hybrids by taking semimature cuttings in summer.

Pests/diseases Rhododendron stem borer may tunnel into stems and branches; black vine weevils gnaw leaves and roots. Caterpillars, Japanese beetles, and lacebugs may attack foliage; fungal leaf spots, root-rot fungi, and stem dieback can be troublesome.

Rhododendron 'Chink'

Rhododendron (azalea)

azalea

Rhododendron 'Hino-crimson' (Kurume)

- ❏ Height ½-10 ft (15-300 cm)
- ❏ Spread 1-10 ft (30-300 cm)
- ❏ Flowers midspring to midsummer
- ❏ Moist, rich, acid soil
- ❏ Sheltered, partially shaded site
- ❏ Hardy zones 5-9, depending on species

The evergreen azaleas are among the most stunning of the shrubs that flower in spring. Their moderate size makes them more suitable for small gardens than their large-leaved relatives, the rhododendrons. Dwarf types are ideal for rock gardens and raised beds.

Botanically, azaleas belong in the *Rhododendron* genus, but they are popularly regarded as a separate group.

Azaleas thrive in woodland conditions; because of their modest size they are best planted as edgings to clearings, at the front of lightly shaded shrub borders, or along streamside banks.

Azaleas are either deciduous or evergreen. The hardy evergreen azaleas described here are generally low-growing and of a spreading habit. Their funnel-shaped or flat flowers are borne in small clusters at the tips of the shoots. Colors are predominantly pink, red, and mauve, though they also include white and varying shades of cream, yellow, and orange. The small green leaves sometimes change color in fall.

Popular species

Rhododendron indicum, syn. *Azalea indica,* is a small dense shrub growing 3-6 ft (1-1.8 m) high and 3-4 ft (1-1.2 m) wide. It is hardy in zones 6-8. The lance-shaped, glossy dark green leaves and shoots are bristly; they often turn crimson and purple in fall. In early summer wide, funnel-shaped pink or bright red flowers are borne singly or in pairs.

The species is variable in performance, but more reliable cultivars are available, including 'Balsaminiflorum,' a dwarf form that bears double salmon-pink flowers, and 'Macrantha,' a compact form (to 3 ft/90 cm high), with double red flowers.

Rhododendron kaempferi is very hardy (zones 5-9). Reaching 5 ft (1.5 m) high and wide, it is almost deciduous as only a few of the small dark green leaves persist through winter. A free-flowering species, it bears orange, salmon-pink, or brick-red blooms with darker speckles in late spring.

Rhododendron kiusianum, syn. *R. obtusum japonicum,* is sometimes semievergreen or even deciduous and is hardy to zone 7. It grows 3 ft (90 cm) high and 5 ft (1.5 m) wide. Its small oval leaves are glossy dark green. Clusters of funnel-shaped flowers appear in late spring and early summer; they are mostly purple, but may be shades of pink or crimson.

Rhododendron nakaharai is a near-prostrate, creeping species, only 6 in (15 cm) high but 1 ft (30 cm) or more wide. It is hardy

Rhododendron 'Betty' (Kaempferi)

in zones 6-9. The densely hairy shoots are clothed with small dark green leaves that are pale green on the undersides. Clusters of two or three funnel- or bell-shaped, bright red flowers appear in midsummer.

Rhododendron obtusum, from Japan, is also known as Kirishima azalea. Hardy to zone 6, it is a small shrub, about 3 ft (90 cm) high and wide. The hairy branches are set with small glossy green leaves and almost hidden by an abundance of flower clusters in late spring; these flowers are scarlet-crimson. 'Amoenum' has brilliant magenta or rose-purple hose-in-hose flowers (one blossom set within another).

Rhododendron yedoense (Yodogawa azalea), a semievergreen or deciduous shrub hardy to zone 6, is 5 ft (1.5 m) high and wide. In late spring it has purple flowers. The variety *poukhanense* (Korean azalea) is hardy to zone 5 and bears rose to lilac-purple flowers.

Azalea hybrids

A vast number of evergreen azalea hybrids have been raised in the United States, Europe, and Japan. They are arranged in groups according to main parentage and flower size. Those described here are hardy and grow to 2-4 ft (60-120 cm) high and 3-6 ft (1-1.8 m) wide.

Gable hybrids are very cold hardy, overwintering successfully in zone 6. These medium-size shrubs, 3-4 ft (1-1.2 m) tall, bear flowers in colors of red, salmon-pink, white, and rose-pink. 'Herbert' is especially cold hardy and offers purple hose-in-hose flowers marked with a dark blotch; 'Karen,' also very cold hardy, has lavender-pink flowers.

Girard hybrids are a group of evergreen hybrids bred for cold

Rhododendron 'Pink Pearl' (Kurume)

Rhododendron 'Palestrina' (Vuykiana)

Rhododendron 'Hot Shot' (Girard)

climates; generally, they overwinter and flower successfully in the warmer regions of zone 5. These include a number of compact forms that grow to a height of just 2-2½ ft (60-75 cm) but with a somewhat greater spread. The foliage is a rich, glossy green and the large flowers are in shades of white, pink, orange, and red. 'Hot Shot' displays scarlet blossoms 2½-3 in (6.25-7.5 cm) in diameter.

Glen Dale hybrids are free-flowering shrubs that are typically hardy through zone 7. The individual flowers are up to 4 in (10 cm) wide. Popular types include 'Buccaneer' (vivid orange-red) and 'Gaiety' (purple-pink).

Kaempferi hybrids are very hardy and free-flowering, with blooms up to 2 in (5 cm) wide. Some types have hose-in-hose flowers. Cultivars include 'Betty' (bright salmon-pink), 'Blue Danube' (violet-blue), 'Christina' (red; hose-in-hose), 'Fedora' (pink with darker blotch at center), 'Mikado' (late-blooming; apricot-salmon), Royal Pink (purple), and 'Silver Sword' (bright pink to red flowers; leaves edged with white).

Kurume hybrids, the largest of the hybrid groups, originated in Japan. These hybrids are generally hardy to zone 7 if grown in sheltered sites. The low-growing and floriferous shrubs usually have small flowers, rarely more than 1 in (2.5 cm) wide. Popular cultivars include 'Addy Wery' (deep orange-scarlet), 'Apple Blossom' (light pink), 'Azuma Kagami' (bright cyclamen-pink; hose-in-hose), 'Coral Bells' (coral-pink; hose-in-hose), 'Hershey's Red' (large red early flowers; hardy to zone 6), 'Hino-crimson' (crimson-scarlet), 'Hino-degiri' (crimson), 'Hino-mayo' (clear pink), 'Pink Pearl' (dwarf shrub; pink; hose-in-hose), and 'Rosebud' (rose pink; hose-in-hose).

Vuykiana hybrids, originated in Holland, are hardy to zone 7 and the warmer regions of zone 6.

Rhododendron 'Hino-degiri' (Kurume)

They display large flowers that grow up to 3 in (7.5 cm) wide. This group includes 'Beethoven' (orchid-purple; fringed), 'Palestrina' (white with green stripes), and 'Vuyk's Rosy Red' (deep rose-red with dark markings).

Cultivation

Azaleas have the same cultural needs as other rhododendrons: moist, acid soil rich in organic matter. They need shelter from cold winds, and while they will tolerate full sun if the roots can be kept moist, azaleas do better in light shade, especially as the flowers tend to fade in hot sun.

Plant in fall or early spring. Mulch annually with leaf mold to keep the shallow-growing roots cool and moist. A yearly application in spring of an acid fertilizer is often beneficial for established shrubs.

Pruning is unnecessary, but deadhead faded flowers; snap them off by hand, taking care not to damage the new small buds at the base.

Propagation In summer you can take 2-3 in (5-7.5 cm) cuttings from nonflowering side shoots; root in a cold frame or other protected spot.

Pests/diseases Azaleas are affected by the same disorders as rhododendrons (see p.158).

Rhodothamnus
rhodothamnus

Rhodothamnus chamaecistus

- Height 10 in (25 cm)
- Spread 1 ft (30 cm)
- Flowers mid- to late spring
- Moist, rich soil
- Cool, shady site
- Hardy to zone 6

A member of the heath family *(Ericaceae)*, the little *Rhodothamnus chamaecistus* is a dwarf sub-shrub of compact growth, suitable for the rock garden. It rarely grows more than 10 in (25 cm) high, and has bright green leaves arranged in whorls along wiry stems. From midspring onward, the foliage is almost hidden by an abundance of saucer-shaped pale rose-pink flowers.

Like other members of the heath family, this hardy shrub will grow best in peaty, moist soil. But unlike its relatives, rhodothamnus is tolerant of alkaline conditions.

Cultivation
In spring or fall, plant this species in any moist soil rich in organic content. Choose a cool site, with shade over the root area; though the plant grows in dense shade, it produces fewer flowers. Pruning is unnecessary.
Propagation Take heel cuttings from young side shoots in summer or early fall; root in a cold frame or other protected spot.
Pests/diseases Dieback and root-rot fungi can be a problem.

Ribes
ribes

Ribes laurifolium

- Height 3-6 ft (1-1.8 m)
- Spread 4-12 ft (1.2-3.7 m)
- Flowers late winter to spring
- Any well-drained soil
- Sunny or lightly shaded site
- Hardy zones 5-10, depending on species

The *Ribes* genus includes gooseberries, currants, and deciduous spring-flowering shrubs. Ornamental evergreen species are less common, but are well adapted to the West Coast. They are tolerant to drought, and offer aromatic foliage and handsome flowers.

Popular species
Ribes laurifolium is a sparsely branched shrub, 3 ft (90 cm) high and wide, that is hardy to zone 5. The ovate, leathery, and coarsely toothed leaves are dark green above, pale green and lustrous beneath. It blooms from late winter into spring, with male and female flowers on separate plants. Male flowers are borne in long, drooping greenish-yellow sprays.
Ribes speciosum is a native of the southern California coast, reaching a height of 3-6 ft (1-1.8 m). It bears drooping, fuchsialike crimson flowers from midwinter to midspring.
Ribes viburnifolium grows to just 3 ft (90 cm) tall but up to 12 ft

(3.7 m) wide. Arching wine-red stems carry dark green, roundish, pine-scented leaves. It bears light pink to purplish flowers in early spring, followed by red berries.

Cultivation
In fall or spring plant in any good, well-drained soil in sun or light shade. Prune at ground level only to cut out old stems on overgrown shrubs after flowering.
Propagation You can take 3-4 in (7.5-10 cm) long heel cuttings in early fall, and root in a cold frame or other protected spot.
Pests/Diseases Currant aphids, scale insects, and spider mites may be troublesome. Anthracnose may cause defoliation, and cane blight can kill whole stems.

ROCK ROSE — see *Cistus, Helianthemum*

Ribes laurifolium

Rosmarinus

rosemary

Rosmarinus officinalis

❑ Height 2½-4 ft (75-120 cm)
❑ Spread 3-4 ft (90-120 cm)
❑ Flowers late spring
❑ Well-drained to dry soil
❑ Sunny site
❑ Hardy zones 7-8

Rosemary *(Rosmarinus officinalis),* one of the classic culinary herbs, has its place in the ornamental border and in the kitchen garden. As an evergreen, its narrow white-felted leaves, which release their aromatic oils freely, are a source of year-round interest. They are used fresh or dried for flavoring in many dishes. Also attractive are the blue-gray flowers, which open in late spring.

Although it is native on hot limestone hillsides, rosemary will prosper in colder, wetter climates, provided it is in a sheltered and sunny position. It will not withstand severe winters, however; nor will it tolerate excessive summer humidity and heat.

Popular cultivars

Several cultivars have been developed from *Rosmarinus officinalis.* Those with a tall, upright habit can be used for informal hedging; the prostrate forms make excellent ground covers. 'Collingwood Ingram' reaches a height of 2½ ft (75 cm) and a spread of 4 ft (1.2 m) in warm, dry climates. Its gracefully curving branches bear flowers of bright blue-violet.

'Miss Jessop' is a strong-growing, upright cultivar carrying deep blue-green leaves and bearing pale mauve flowers.

'Prostratus' is a mat-forming cultivar with fresh green leaves and lavender-blue flowers; it is hardy only to zone 8.

'Tuscan Blue' bears clear blue flowers and light green, relatively broad leaves on an erect shrub.

Cultivation

Plant in spring in ordinary well-drained soil in a sunny spot. At the northern edge of its range, protect in winter with a straw mulch over the roots.

Cut out dead shoots in early spring and shorten long, straggly shoots by up to half. Lightly trim hedging plants after flowering.

Propagation Take 4 in (10 cm) cuttings of semimature shoots in mid- to late summer, and root them in a cold frame or other protected spot. Grow on in pots indoors over the winter, and plant out in spring.

Pests/diseases Trouble free.

RUE — see *Ruta*

Ruscus

butcher's broom

Ruscus aculeatus

❑ Height 2-3 ft (60-90 cm)
❑ Spread 2-3 ft (60-90 cm)
❑ Primarily berrying shrub
❑ Ordinary well-drained soil
❑ Sunny or shady site
❑ Hardy zones 8-9

The handsome butcher's broom *(Ruscus aculeatus)* is a useful plant. It spreads 2-3 ft (60-90 cm) high shoots through corners of deep shade where little else survives; yet it tolerates sun if given sufficient moisture. What appear to be leaves, pointed ovals of glossy green, are really modified stems; in early spring to mid-spring they bear small white flowers. Male and female flowers are mostly borne on separate plants, but bisexual forms are available.

If plants of both sexes are grown together, the female flowers will be followed by marble-sized berries. These ripen to a handsome display of cherry-red in late summer or early fall, and may persist until spring. The branches are often cut and dried for Christmas decorations.

Cultivation

Plant in spring in ordinary well-drained soil in shade; butcher's broom will also grow in sun, except in the Southwest. It does not mind competition from tree roots. Grow in groups of three to five containing both sexes.

Remove any deadwood in early spring to midspring.

Propagation Lift, divide, and replant large clumps in spring.

Pests/diseases Trouble free.

Ruta

rue

Ruta graveolens 'Jackman's Blue'

❑ Height 2-3 ft (60-90 cm)
❑ Spread 1½ ft (45 cm)
❑ Primarily foliage shrub
❑ Ordinary well-drained soil
❑ Sunny site
❑ Hardy zones 4-10

Ruta graveolens, a hardy evergreen subshrub, was once widely used as a medicinal and disinfectant herb but is now mainly grown for its decorative value. Reaching 2-3 ft (60-90 cm) high and 1½ ft (45 cm) wide, it is distinguished by the filigreelike, bitterly aromatic blue-green foliage that clothes the plant.

Above the leaves, clusters of flowers are borne in early summer to midsummer or later. They are sulfur-yellow with cupped, fringed petals. Most gardeners remove the flowers as they appear.

'Jackman's Blue,' a compact form that seldom flowers and has almost metallic blue leaves, is a striking cultivar.

Cultivation

Plant in fall or early spring in ordinary well-drained soil in a sunny spot. Trim the plants back to old wood in midspring.
Propagation Take cuttings of lateral shoots 3-4 in (7.5-10 cm) long in midsummer.
Pests/diseases Trouble free.

ST.-JOHN'S-WORT — see *Hypericum*

Santolina

lavender cotton

Santolina pinnata neapolitana

❑ Height 1½-2½ ft (45-75 cm)
❑ Spread 1½-4 ft (45-120 cm)
❑ Flowers midsummer
❑ Ordinary well-drained soil
❑ Sunny site
❑ Hardy zones 6-9, depending on species

These dwarf shrubs with silver-gray feathery leaves are ideal for the front of a shrub border. They release a strong aromatic scent whenever brushed in passing by. They are also suitable in rock gardens or as low informal hedges.

Popular species

Santolina chamaecyparissus, syn. *S. incana,* a dense plant, reaches 1½-2 ft (45-60 cm) high and wide. It has silver-gray feathery leaves and bright lemon-yellow flowers. *Santolina pinnata neapolitana* is hardy to zone 7. It grows into a dome 2-2½ ft (60-75 cm) high with long, feathery gray leaves. It bears bright yellow blooms. *Santolina rosmarinifolia,* syn. *S. virens,* hardy to zone 7, has vivid green threadlike leaves and yellow flowers. It is 2 ft (60 cm) high and 3-4 ft (90-120 cm) wide.

Cultivation

Plant in fall or spring in ordinary well-drained soil in a sunny site.

Remove dead flower stems. Cut back untidy specimens into old wood in midspring or after flowering. Do not allow plants grown as hedges to flower.
Propagation Take cuttings of half-hardened side shoots, 2-3 in (5-7.5 cm) long, in midsummer.
Pests/diseases Trouble free.

Santolina chamaecyparissus

Sarcococca

sweet box

Sarcococca hookerana

❑ Height 2-4 ft (60-120 cm)
❑ Spread 2-4 ft (60-120 cm)
❑ Flowers early spring
❑ Any good soil
❑ Sunny or shaded site
❑ Hardy zones 6-8

Sarcococcas are grown for their handsome foliage and tiny, but fragrant, white flowers in early spring. Their dwarf, suckering habit makes them ideal ground cover for shady sites, as well as for sunny ones in areas with cool summers. Glossy black berries may follow the flowers.

Popular species
Sarcococca confusa (hardy only to zone 7) is a dense, dome-shaped shrub. It grows 3 ft (90 cm) high and 4 ft (1.2 m) wide and carries dark green leathery leaves.
Sarcococca hookerana is of upright habit. Hardy in zones 6-8, it grows 4 ft (1.2 m) high and 2 ft (60 cm) wide with narrow light green leaves. The variety *humilis* is a dwarf, about 2 ft (60 cm) high and 3 ft (90 cm) wide; its leaves are glossy dark green. It is more cold-hardy than the species.

Cultivation
Plant in fall or spring in any good soil. Sarcococca thrives on alkaline soil in shade or sun. Pruning is not necessary.
Propagation Remove and replant rooted suckers.
Pests/diseases Trouble free.

Senecio

senecio

Senecio laxifolius

❑ Height 2-6 ft (60-180 cm)
❑ Spread 2-8 ft (60-240 cm)
❑ Flowers early summer to midsummer
❑ Any well-drained soil
❑ Sunny site
❑ Hardy zones 8-10

Senecio is a large genus of shrubs, climbers, and perennials that has long been familiar to knowledgeable gardeners in warm, dry regions. Originally comprised of more than 1,500 species, a number of plants have been reclassified by botanists in recent years; as a result, many senecios have been assigned to other genera. Because the reclassified plants are still referred to as senecios by the nurseries that grow them, they are listed as senecios here; however, the new botanical name is given in parentheses.

The evergreen shrubby senecios are native to New Zealand, and they are best adapted to cultivation in a similar climate, such as found in Pacific Coast gardens.

Ever-gray rather than evergreen, these senecios will tolerate sub-freezing temperatures for the most part, so long as the cold period is not too intense or prolonged. Most of these plants will shrug off a night of moderate frost (28°F/-2°C, for example), but won't survive a week of such cold or even a single night where the thermometer drops to the single digits. These plants thrive in full sun and are exceptionally wind resistant; they are useful as informal hedges in seaside gardens.

Senecios are valuable in mixed and herbaceous borders, where their foliage introduces pockets of calm. Long-stalked, loose clusters of daisylike flowers are borne in summer; many gardeners find that the blooms detract from the beauty of the foliage and snip off the flower stems.

Popular species and hybrids
Senecio compactus (now *Brachyglottis compacta*) is a dense and

Senecio greyi hybrid, in flower

Senecio greyi hybrid

compact shrub about 3½ ft (1.1 m) in height and with a spread of 6 ft (1.8 m). The oval, wavy-edged leaves are dark green above and covered with a white felt on the undersides; the young shoots and flower stalks are also white. Bright yellow flower clusters are borne throughout summer.

Senecio greyi (now *Brachyglottis greyi*) is a distinct species, but most plants offered by nurseries as *S. greyi* or *S. laxifolius* are really hybrids between this species, *S. compactus,* and *S. laxifolius.* The hybrids are generally hardier than the species; these shrubs grow to a height of 4 ft (1.2 m) with a spread up to 8 ft (2.4 m). The oval leaves and the shoots are covered with a soft white felt. Yellow flower heads are displayed in summer.

Senecio laxifolius (now *Brachyglottis laxifolia*) is rare in cultivation, having been superseded by hybrids. It is a spreading shrub, 3 ft (90 cm) high and twice as wide, with thin, oval gray-white leaves that age to dark green. Large, loose clusters of golden yellow flowers appear in summer.

Senecio monroi (now *Brachyglottis monroi*) grows as a hardy, dense, and domed shrub, 4-6 ft (1.2-1.8 m) high with a spread of 2-4 ft (60-120 cm). The oblong leaves differ from those of other senecios in having prominent wavy edges; they are thickly covered with fine white hairs on the undersides and are midgreen to deep green above. This species is one of the best in flower, with large and bright yellow clusters in midsummer.

Senecio reinoldii (now *Brachyglottis rotundifolia*) is a robust shrub tolerant of strong seaside winds. It grows 3 ft (90 cm) or more high and wide and bears rounded, thick and leathery, glossy dark green leaves. Insignificant yellow flowers are borne in midsummer.

Cultivation

Plant in fall or spring in any well-drained soil. Select a site that is in full sun. All the species and cultivars featured will do particularly well in coastal gardens; while they are highly tolerant of exposure to strong winds, they rarely survive prolonged spells of hard frost.

For hedges, space young shrubs 1½ ft (45 cm) apart; during the first growing season, pinch out the growing tips of leading shoots several times to induce bushy growth from low down.

Remove faded flower stems and cut out any straggly shoots that spoil the rounded shape of the shrubs. Hedges should not be clipped, but cut faded flower stems back to healthy leafy shoots in fall.

Propagation In late summer to early fall take 3-4 in (7.5-10 cm) cuttings of semimature lateral shoots, and root in a cold frame or other protected spot over winter.

Transfer the rooted cuttings to an outdoor nursery bed in mid-spring; let them grow on until you move them to their permanent positions in fall.

Pests/diseases Trouble free.

SILK-TASSEL BUSH — see
Garrya
SILVERBUSH — see
Convovulus

Skimmia

skimmia

Skimmia japonica, berries

- ❏ Height 2-5 ft (60-150 cm)
- ❏ Spread 3-6 ft (1-1.8 m)
- ❏ Flowers mid- to late spring
- ❏ Ordinary well-drained soil
- ❏ Lightly shaded or sunny site
- ❏ Hardy zones 7-8

These easy to grow bright-berried shrubs thrive in light shade, as ground cover beneath trees, or in a sunny site if they are shaded from strong midday sun. Skimmias do well in seaside gardens and, because of their tolerance for polluted air, in urban settings. Late-spring frosts can damage emerging new growth; ideally, set these shrubs in a sheltered spot.

Small, sometimes fragrant cream-white flowers are borne in rounded clusters in spring. Most skimmias are unisexual, bearing female and male flowers on separate plants. For the females to produce their splendid fall display of brilliant berries, it is essential to grow a male specimen nearby.

Popular species

Skimmia japonica is a spreading shrub that is usually 3 ft (90 cm), but occasionally up to 5 ft (1.5 m), high and 5-6 ft (1.5-1.8 m) wide. Its oval lance-shaped leaves are pale green and leathery. The male shrubs have the largest and most fragrant flowers, but the female shrubs produce the round bright red berries. Outstanding cultivars include 'Bronze Knight' (male; pointed, lustrous dark green leaves; red winter flower buds; shiny bronze-red stalks), 'Foremanii' (syn. 'Veitchii'; female; large flowers; brilliant red fruit clusters), 'Nymans' (female;

Skimmia japonica, male flowers

particularly large and profuse scarlet berries), and 'Rubella' (male; large clusters of deep red winter buds that open in early spring to white flowers; leaves are usually edged with crimson in cold winters).

Skimmia laureola reaches 3 ft (90 cm) high and spreads to 5 ft (1.5 m). It carries aromatic, oblong, pointed leaves clustered together at the tips of the shoots. This is the best species for flowering, bearing large scented clusters of cream-white flowers in spring. Most plants are male, but 'Isabella,' a female, produces bright red berries.

Skimmia reevesiana is now regarded by most authorities as a subspecies of *S. japonica.* It is a compact, spreading shrub, 2-3 ft (60-90 cm) high and 3-4 ft (90-120 cm) wide; it is hardier than the ordinary *S. japonica.* It carries narrow, lance-shaped midgreen to dark green leaves that often have paler margins. The white flowers, in late spring, are bisexual; they are followed by oval crimson berries that persist through winter.

Cultivation

Plant in early fall to midfall or early spring to midspring in ordinary well-drained soil. Set the shrubs in a lightly shaded site or in sun. At the northern edge of their range, use a winter mulch to cover the roots of young plants.

Pruning is generally unnecessary, except for cutting back any frost-damaged shoots. Berrying stems can be cut for indoor decoration in winter.

Propagation Take 3 in (7.5 cm) heel cuttings of half-hardened side shoots, and root in a cold frame or other protected spot. The following spring transfer the rooted cuttings to an outdoor nursery bed, and grow them on for 2 or 3 years before planting them out in their permanent positions in fall or spring.

Pests/diseases Few pests trouble skimmias; other disorders are due to adverse growing conditions. Frost will cause whitened leaves; in spring cut back any damaged shoots to healthy wood. Yellowing leaves and dieback of the shoots are common symptoms of alkaline soils; apply an acid fertilizer to rectify the problem.

Skimmia japonica 'Rubella'

Solanum

potato vine

Solanum jasminoides

❏ Height 10-20 ft (3-6 m)
❏ Climber
❏ Flowers early summer to midfall
❏ Any well-drained soil
❏ Sunny, sheltered site
❏ Hardy zones 8-10

When these splendid climbers are in full bloom it is hard to believe they belong to the same genus as the potato. From early summer to fall the dark green foliage is hung with great clusters of slightly fragrant, purple or white starry flowers with prominent stamens.

Popular species

Solanum crispum has dark green leaves and grows up to 15-20 ft (4.5-6 m) high. 'Glassnevin,' the most popular cultivar, has purple-blue star-shaped flowers.
Solanum jasminoides (jasmine nightshade) has twining stems up to 10-15 ft (3-4.5 m) high. Hardy only to zone 9, it bears glossy pale green leaves and white flowers, or white flowers tinged with blue.

Cultivation

Plant in any well-drained soil against a sheltered south- or west-facing wall in spring. Tie the stems to wires or a trellis.

In spring thin out weak growth and cut back any stems damaged by frost. To control *S. crispum*, cut the previous season's shoots back to 6 in (15 cm) in spring.
Propagation In summer take 3-4 in (7.5-10 cm) cuttings of side shoots; root in a propagation unit.
Pests/diseases Aphids may infest stems and shoots, creating secretions that foster sooty mold.

Solanum crispum 'Glassnevin'

Sophora

sophora

Sophora tetraptera

❏ Height 12 ft (3.7 m)
❏ Spread 6 ft (1.8 m)
❏ Flowers mid- to late spring
❏ Fertile, well-drained soil
❏ Sunny, sheltered site
❏ Hardy to zone 8

Sophora tetraptera is the national flower of New Zealand. This is a cold-sensitive shrub growing some 12 ft (3.7 m) high and half as wide. It bears elegant foliage: long, narrow leaves made up of a dozen or so pairs of leaflets. Most of the old leaves fall in midspring as bunches of golden waxy pea flowers open.

After flowering, the current year's leaves unfold from furry new shoots and seedpods develop, hanging like strings of four-winged beads.

Cultivation

Plant sophora in early spring to midspring in fertile, well-drained soil in a sunny spot against a south- or west-facing wall sheltered from cold winds. Pruning is not necessary.
Propagation Seed is the usual means of increase.
Pests/diseases Trouble free.

SPIKE DRACAENA — see
Cordyline

Stranvaesia

stranvaesia

Stranvaesia davidiana

- ❏ Height 12-18 ft (3.7-5.5 m)
- ❏ Spread 12-18 ft (3.7-5.5 m)
- ❏ Flowers early summer
- ❏ Fertile, well-drained soil
- ❏ Sunny or partially shaded site
- ❏ Hardy zones 8-9

Looking something like its relative the cotoneaster, *Stranvaesia davidiana* offers a good show in all seasons. In spring there is the reddish color of new growth, and in late spring or early summer there are the 4 in (10 cm) clusters of white flowers. The foliage turns purplish or bronze in fall, and the berries ripen to brilliant scarlet, hanging in clusters along the branches until spring.

Cultivation
In midfall or spring plant in any fertile, well-drained soil in sun or partial shade. Give this shrub plenty of room; in hot inland sites protect it from drying winds and provide ample irrigation.
Propagation Take heel cuttings, 3-4 in (7.5-10 cm) long, of half-hardened side shoots, and root in a propagation unit.
Pests/diseases Fire blight may attack this shrub.

STRAWBERRY TREE — see *Arbutus*
SUN ROSE — see *Helianthemum*
SWEET BAY — see *Laurus*

Taxus

yew

Taxus baccata 'Fastigiata'

- ❏ Height 1-12 ft (30-370 cm)
- ❏ Spread 1-10 ft (30-300 cm)
- ❏ Coniferous shrub
- ❏ Any well-drained soil
- ❏ Sunny or shaded site
- ❏ Hardy zones 5-7

Yews are extremely long-lived, and many types eventually develop into magnificent specimen trees, too tall for garden planting (see p.49). But these fine conifers grow slowly and respond well to clipping and topiary work, so they can easily be kept at a manageable size. In addition, there are a number of naturally dwarf cultivars. *Taxus baccata* is hardy to zones 6-7; the other yews cited here are hardy in zones 5-7.

Popular species and cultivars
Taxus baccata 'Aurea' (golden English yew) is a compact conifer, 8 ft (2.4 m) high and 6 ft (1.8 m) wide. It has luminous golden yellow foliage.
Taxus baccata 'Fastigiata' (Irish yew), a columnar cultivar, naturally grows to 30 ft (9 m) high but may be maintained by clipping at 12 ft (3.7 m) high and 2 ft (60 cm) wide. The leaves are dark green.
Taxus cuspidata 'Aurescens,' a compact form of the Japanese yew, grows only 1 ft (30 cm) high and 3 ft (90 cm) wide. New needles are deep yellow; as they mature, they turn green.
Taxus cuspidata 'Nana,' a slow-growing form of the Japanese

Teucrium

germander

Taxus × media 'Densiformis'

Teucrium chamaedrys

yew, may grow to a height of 10 ft (3 m) or more if unchecked, but it is easily contained at a smaller size. Typically twice as wide as high, it is a rich green color.

Taxus × media 'Densiformis,' a compact shrub, grows to 3-4 ft (1-1.2 m) high and about 4-6 ft (1.2-1.8 m) wide. Its bright green needles turn darker in winter.

Taxus × media 'Hatfieldii' is a broad, pyramidal shrub with dark green needles. It may reach a height of 12 ft (3.7 m) and a width of 10 ft (3 m) if left unpruned.

Cultivation

Yews thrive in any type of soil and any site except a wet, boggy one. Plant in fall or spring.

Pruning is unnecessary, but the shrubs can be clipped to shape at any time of year.

Propagation In early fall to mid-fall, take 3-4 in (7.5-10 cm) heel cuttings of lateral shoots. Root them in a cold frame or other protected spot.

Pests/diseases Scale insects and taxus mealybugs may attack stems and foliage; black vine weevils may attack needles and roots; twig blight may cause dieback.

TEA TREE — see *Leptospermum*

- ❏ Height 8-60 in (20-150 cm)
- ❏ Spread 1-4 ft (30-120 cm)
- ❏ Flowers early summer to early fall
- ❏ Any well-drained soil
- ❏ Sunny, sheltered site
- ❏ Hardy zones 5-10, depending on species

Germanders vary from creeping subshrubs to medium-size evergreen shrubs. They are valued for their year-round small-leaved foliage and their abundant flower spikes throughout summer. Low-growing types are suitable for rock gardens and ground covers; the taller germanders are good for shrub borders and walls.

Popular species

Teucrium chamaedrys (wall germander) is hardy in zones 5-10. This subshrub is only 8 in (20 cm) high but it can spread downy branches to 12 in (30 cm) or more from a creeping rootstock. The small, aromatic toothed leaves are ovate, bright green above and gray beneath. It bears purple-pink flower spikes from midsummer until fall. Wall germander is suitable for a rock garden or as ground cover; in the wild it inhabits old walls and ruins.

Teucrium fruticans (shrubby germander), hardy in zones 8-10, is a tall species, 5 ft (1.5 m) or more high and almost as wide. It is a splendid specimen shrub, especially by the sea. The gray-green leaves provide a pleasant aroma when bruised. It displays pale lavender flowers from early summer until early fall. 'Azureum' is an attractive deep blue cultivar, but more tender than the species.

Cultivation

Plant *T. chamaedrys* in fall or spring, *T. fruticans* in mid- to late spring. Both species thrive in any well-drained soil, but *T. chamaedrys* does best on poor soil. Both need a site in full sun; in all but virtually frost-free gardens, grow *T. fruticans* against a sheltered south- or west-facing wall.

It is rarely necessary to prune; for *T. fruticans,* cut shoots damaged by frost back to healthy wood in spring; trim the shrub to shape after flowering.

Propagation You can increase *T. chamaedrys* in late spring by taking 2-3 in (5-7.5 cm) cuttings of basal shoots; root them in a cold frame or other protected spot. For *T. fruticans,* take 4-10 in (10-25 cm) heel cuttings of side shoots in mid- or late summer; root in a propagation unit.

Pests/diseases Trouble free.

Thuja
arborvitae

Thuja occidentalis 'Rheingold'

Thuja plicata 'Stoneham Gold'

Thuja occidentalis 'Danica'

- ❏ Height 1-12 ft (30-370 cm)
- ❏ Spread 1-5 ft (30-150 cm)
- ❏ Coniferous shrub
- ❏ Any moist soil
- ❏ Sheltered, sunny site
- ❏ Hardy zones 2-9, depending on species

Thuja, a genus of coniferous trees (see also pp.49-50), includes a few slow-growing dwarf species and cultivars. They make handsome specimen shrubs for small gardens and are well adapted for use in the East and Midwest. The aromatic foliage is borne in flat sprays; their various shades of green and golden yellow often change hue in fall and winter.

Popular species and cultivars
Thuja occidentalis (American arborvitae) is parent to several slow-growing shrubby cultivars. These are hardy in zones 2-8.
'Danica' is 20 in (50 cm) high and 15 in (38 cm) wide. It is rounded, and has dark green leaves.
'Golden Globe' grows 3 ft (90 cm) high and wide; it is of rounded habit, with golden foliage.
'Hetz Midget' grows extremely slowly to 1 ft (30 cm) high and wide; the foliage is dark green.
'Lutea' is a conical shrub 2½-3 ft (75-90 cm) high. The foliage is golden yellow on top and light yellowish-green beneath.
'Rheingold' has a conical shape; it grows to 3 ft (90 cm) high and 2½ ft (75 cm) wide, with copper-gold leaves. Winter-flowering heathers are ideal plant partners.
'Smaragd' is a conical conifer, 6 ft (1.8 m) high and 3 ft (90 cm) wide; it has emerald-green leaves.
'Sunkist,' a pyramidal-shaped cultivar with golden foliage, gradually reaches 6 ft (1.8 m) high.
'Wansdyke Silver' grows slowly to 5 ft (1.5 m) high; it is conical in habit, and carries conspicuously variegated cream-white foliage.
Thuja orientalis, syn. *Platycladus orientalis*, bears foliage in frond-like vertical sprays. Its foliage is less aromatic than that of *T. occidentalis*, and its growth habit is more erect. *T. orientalis* is less hardy, thriving only in zones 6-9.

A number of dwarf cultivars can be found in this species.
'Aura Nana' is a rounded shrub, 2-2½ ft (60-75 cm) high; it has golden-green leaves.
'Juniperoides,' a slow-growing, bushy, conical shrub, eventually reaches a height of 6 ft (1.8 m) and a spread of 3 ft (90 cm). The foliage is blue-gray in summer, plum-purple in winter.
'Rosedalis' grows slowly to a rounded shrub, 2 ft (60 cm) high and 1½ ft (45 cm) wide. The soft juvenile foliage is canary-yellow in spring, sea-green in summer, and plum-purple in winter.
Thuja plicata, hardy in zones 6-7, has pineapple-scented foliage. Slow-growing cultivars include:
'Cuprea' has a broad pyramid shape, growing to 3 ft (90 cm) high and wide, with yellow-tipped dark green foliage.
'Rogersii,' small and rounded, is 1-1½ ft (30-45 cm) high and wide, with golden-bronze leaves.
'Stoneham Gold' has a squat conical habit; it is 2-3 ft (60-90 cm) high and 2 ft (60 cm) wide. The green foliage is tipped with gold.

Cultivation
Though easily grown in ordinary soil, thujas thrive in deep, moist conditions. Plant between late fall and early spring in a sheltered site in full sun. Pruning is unnecessary.
Propagation In fall take 2-4 in (5-10 cm) tip cuttings; root in a cold frame or protected spot.
Pests/diseases Bagworms, leaf miners, and canker sometimes infest thujas.

Trachelospermum

star jasmine

Trachelospermum jasminoides

❏ Height 10-15 ft (3-4.5 m)
❏ Climber
❏ Flowers spring to early summer
❏ Fertile, well-drained soil
❏ Sheltered, sunny wall
❏ Hardy zones 8-10

Star jasmine is a self-clinging climber grown for its fragrant flowers and oval, glossy dark green leaves; it also makes an excellent ground cover. The blooms appear in spring or early summer.

Popular species
Trachelospermum asiaticum can grow 15 ft (4.5 m) high. It is of dense habit, with branching and hairy stems covered with a curtain of foliage. Hardy to zone 8, it bears creamy white to yellow flowers in mid- to late spring.
Trachelospermum jasminoides reaches 10-12 ft (3-3.7 m) high. After a slow start, it becomes a fast grower. It has outstanding foliage. The white flowers, borne in late spring or early summer, release a wonderful fragrance.

Cultivation
Plant in fall or spring against a sheltered, sunny wall. These climbers thrive in well-drained soil enriched with organic matter. Thin out overvigorous shoots in early spring to midspring.
Propagation Layer stems in fall and sever a year later.
Pests/diseases Mealybugs, scale insects, and spider mites may infest foliage and stems.

Tsuga

hemlock

Tsuga canadensis 'Pendula'

❏ Height 1-3 ft (30-90 cm)
❏ Spread 2½-5 ft (75-150 cm)
❏ Coniferous shrub
❏ Moist, well-drained soil
❏ Partially shaded site
❏ Hardy zones 3-7

Most hemlocks are tall, graceful trees (see p.51), but a few dwarf cultivars have been developed from *Tsuga canadensis*. They are suitable for small gardens, where their attractive weeping branches and graceful outlines make them ideal as specimen shrubs. They are also good focal points in large rock gardens.

Popular cultivars
'Bennett' is a slow-growing, spreading shrub, 1 ft (30 cm) high and 2½ ft (75 cm) wide. The dense foliage is midgreen.
'Jeddeloh' forms a low mound, 1 ft (30 cm) high and 2 ft (60 cm) wide, of pale green foliage.
'Pendula' is 3 ft (90 cm) high and 5 ft (1.5 m) wide. It forms a dense mound of weeping branches, covered with rich green foliage.

Cultivation
Plant in midfall or spring in any deep, well-drained but moisture-retentive soil. Choose a partially shaded site, sheltered from east winds. Pruning is not necessary.
Propagation In early fall, take 1-3 in (2.5-7.5 cm) long heel cuttings; root in a cold frame or other protected spot.
Pests/diseases Hemlock woolly adelgid has become a major problem in the Northeast; scale insects and spider mites may also attack hemlocks.

Ulex

gorse

Ulex europaeus

❏ Height 5-6 ft (1.5-1.8 m)
❏ Spread 5-6 ft (1.5-1.8 m)
❏ Flowers spring through fall
❏ Any well-drained soil
❏ Sunny site
❏ Hardy to zone 6

This European native has become naturalized in some regions of the Middle Atlantic and the Pacific Northwest. Although the main crop of fragrant, pealike yellow flowers arrives in spring, gorses *(Ulex europaeus)* bloom intermittently until early winter. This dark green shrub, reaching 5-6 ft (1.5-1.8 m) high and across, is too wild in appearance and too spiny to fit into highly cultivated areas; however, its ability to thrive on poor soil makes it useful as a ground cover for dry banks. It is also an ideal choice for exposed seaside gardens.

Cultivation
Plant out container-grown specimens between midfall and early spring in any well-drained soil in full sun. Keep the soil ball intact to avoid root disturbance. Cut back tall, leggy plants to within 6 in (15 cm) of the ground in early spring to encourage new growth from the base.
Propagation Take 3 in (7.5 cm) cuttings of the current year's side shoots in late summer; root in a cold frame or protected spot.
Pests/diseases Trouble free.

Viburnum

viburnum

Viburnum tinus

Viburnum davidii

- ❏ Height 2-15 ft (60-450 cm)
- ❏ Spread 4-15 ft (1.2-4.5 m)
- ❏ Flowers early winter to early summer
- ❏ Good, moist soil
- ❏ Sunny or partially shaded site
- ❏ Hardy zones 5-10, depending on species

The evergreen viburnums are highly valued in the shrub border, supplying attractive year-round foliage, clusters of often fragrant flowers, and decorative berries. For the finest display of berries, plant viburnums in groups of three to ensure cross-pollination.

These shrubs thrive in woodland conditions; in the garden they need cool, moist but well-drained soil. They flourish in the temperate climate of the Pacific Northwest but also perform reasonably well in the eastern states, especially in coastal regions.

Popular species

Viburnum × burkwoodii, hardy in zones 5-8, grows 8 ft (2.4 m) high and 9-12 ft (2.7-3.7 m) wide. The waxy, sweetly scented white flowers (pink in bud) are borne in flat, wide heads between early and late spring. The leaves are glossy

dark green, with brown felt on the undersides. This is the best species for midwestern gardens.

Viburnum davidii is hardy in zones 7-9. It has a low, spreading habit, reaching 2-3 ft (60-90 cm) high and 4-5 ft (1.2-1.5 m) wide. The glossy dark green leaves are prominently veined. Small clusters of white flowers appear in early spring to midspring, but the shrub is grown mainly for its decorative turquoise berry clusters that persist well into winter.

Viburnum rhytidophyllum is a fast-growing, handsome species that is hardy in zones 6-8. It has horizontal branches and grows up to 10-15 ft (3-4.5 m) high and 10-12 ft (3-3.7 m) wide. Flat, wide heads of white flowers open in mid- to late spring, followed by red berries that eventually turn black. The large leaves are lance-shaped and corrugated. The species thrives on alkaline soil.

Viburnum tinus grows into a large, domed shrub about 7-10 ft (2.1-3 m) high and 7 ft (2.1 m) wide; hardy in zones 8-10. This is one of the most popular winter-flowering shrubs, closely set with lance-shaped midgreen to deep

green leaves. The white flowers (pink in bud) are carried in flat heads at the end of shoots intermittently from early winter to late spring. The berries are black.

Cultivation

All viburnums do best in good, moist but well-drained soil and in light shade or sun. Shelter early-flowering plants in a site sheltered from cold winter winds and where morning sun cannot damage flower buds frozen during the night. Plant in fall or spring.

Thin out old overgrown shoots in late spring.

Propagation In summer or early fall, take 3-4 in (7.5-10 cm) heel cuttings of side shoots; root in a cold frame or other protected spot.

Pests/diseases Bacterial and fungal leaf spots may attack foliage; powdery mildew and scale insects may also occur. These problems are rarely serious.

Viburnum davidii, berries

Vinca

periwinkle, vinca

Vinca major

Vinca minor 'Gertrude Jekyll'

- Height 2-12 in (5-30 cm)
- Spread 3-4 ft (1-1.2 m)
- Flowers early spring through fall
- Any well-drained soil
- Partially shaded or sunny site
- Hardy zones 5-8, depending on species

Hardy and invasive, periwinkles are popular low-growing ground-cover plants, trailing and creeping to form extensive carpets of evergreen foliage. They are useful beneath deciduous trees and shrubs and for covering steep banks, growing equally well in sun and light shade. Flowering is most profuse in sun, but the shrubs make dense weedproof cover in shade.

The five-petaled blue, purple, or white flowers are borne singly from the leaf axils from early spring through summer and intermittently until fall.

Popular species

Vinca major (greater periwinkle), hardy to zone 7, reaches a height of 6-12 in (15-30 cm) and a spread of 3-4 ft (1-1.2 m). It is a rampant species with erect shoots that will later trail and root where the tips touch the ground. The small heart-shaped leaves are glossy and midgreen to dark green. Bright blue flowers appear from midspring to early summer, often with a second flush of bloom in fall. This is an excellent plant to let cascade out of window boxes and containers. The cultivar 'Variegata' has leaves blotched and margined with cream-white; the flowers are lavender-blue.

Vinca minor (lesser periwinkle) is the hardier species, thriving in zones 5-8. It has smaller leaves and flowers than *V. major*. As it grows only 2-4 in (5-10 cm) high and 3-4 ft (1-1.2 m) wide, it makes a dense and neat ground cover. The oval, glossy deep green leaves grow on wiry stems. The flowers, approximately 1 in (2.5 cm) wide, are bright blue in the species. Several cultivars are available with flowers in different colors: 'Argenteo-variegata' (blue flowers; leaves variegated cream-white), 'Atropurpureum' (deep plum-purple flowers), 'Azurea Flore Pleno' (double sky-blue flowers), 'Bowles Variety' (small light blue flowers), 'Burgundy' (plum-purple flowers), 'Gertrude Jekyll' (small, glistening white flowers), 'Rosea' (violet-pink flowers; smaller leaves), and 'Shademaster' (purple flowers).

Cultivation

Plant in fall or spring in ordinary well-drained garden soil in a partially shaded or sunny spot. The plants tolerate hard clipping and benefit from annual trimming in early spring, when old shoots can be pruned out.

Propagation The trailing stems of these plants root from every node that is in contact with the soil; if necessary, dig them up, divide, and replant between fall and spring. Alternatively, take 6 in (15 cm) long stem sections in early fall or spring, and insert them obliquely where they are to grow; they root easily.

Pests/diseases Fungal blight and canker may cause dieback; fungal leaf spots may also attack the foliage.

Yucca
yucca

Yucca gloriosa 'Variegata'

Yucca filamentosa 'Variegata'

- ❏ Height 2-6 ft (60-180 cm)
- ❏ Spread 3-6 ft (1-1.8 m)
- ❏ Flowers midsummer to late fall
- ❏ Any well-drained soil
- ❏ Sunny site
- ❏ Hardy zones 3-10, depending on species

Yuccas are excellent shrubs for bringing an exotic air to a garden. Despite their subtropical appearance, there are several types that are reasonably cold hardy, and though yuccas are drought tolerant, many flourish in moist climates. They can be included in mixed borders, but are better as focal points and specimen plants placed where their architectural qualities can be appreciated.

These are long-lived shrubs that flower annually once mature, carrying their huge spikes well above the foliage.

Popular species
Yucca filamentosa (Adam's needle), hardy in zones 4-10, grows to 2-2½ ft (60-75 cm) tall and 3-4 ft (1-1.2 m) wide. The narrow blue-green foliage has margins covered with curly white hairs. After plants mature in 2 or 3 years, cream-white bell-shaped flowers appear in plumelike spikes 3-6 ft (1-1.8 m) high from late spring to midsummer. 'Variegata' bears cream- or yellow-edged leaves.
Yucca glauca (small soapweed) is hardy in zones 3-10. It has a low,

often prostrate stem that carries a hemispherical burst of foliage 3-4 ft (1-1.2 m) wide. Individual leaves grow up to 2½ ft (75 cm) long and ¾ in (19 mm) wide. The spikes of greenish-white flowers, borne in mid- to late summer, grow up to 4½ ft (1.4 m) tall.
Yucca gloriosa (Spanish dagger), hardy in zones 7-10, bears dense rosettes of stiff green leaves at the top of a slow-growing woody trunk. Its bell-shaped cream-white flowers are tinged red on the outside; they appear in dense upright spikes, 3-6 ft (1-1.8 m) above the foliage, between late summer and late fall. This species does not flower until it is at least 5 years old. 'Variegata' has leaves striped yellow.

Cultivation
Plant in spring or fall in any well-drained soil — including poor, sandy soil — in full sun. Pruning is not necessary.
Propagation In early spring to midspring remove rooted suckers; replant in permanent sites.
Pests/diseases Brown spots with gray centers on the leaves are due to leaf spot.

Plant Hardiness Zone Map

Selecting plants suitable for your climate is half the secret to successful gardening. The U. S. Department of Agriculture (USDA) has created a plant hardiness zone map as a guide. Each zone is based on an average minimum winter temperature. Most nurseries and mail-order companies have adopted this map and indicate zones for their plants. Once you identify the zone you live in, buy only plants that are recommended for that zone. Local conditions, such as a garden near a pond or in a higher mountainous elevation, can affect the climate and the zone. In such cases, contact your local Cooperative Extension Service for assistance in adapting the map to your garden.

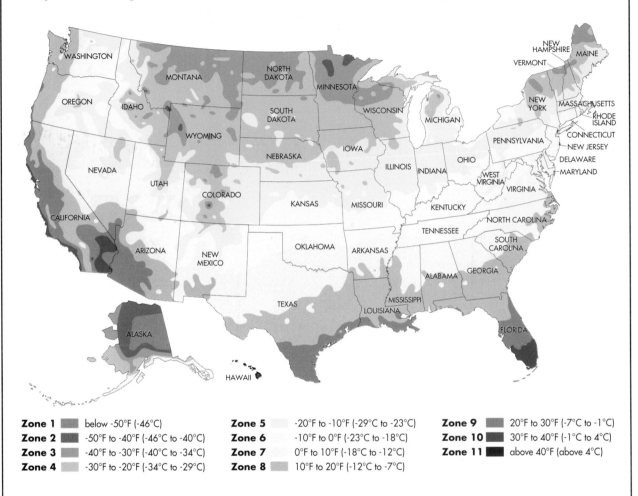

Zone 1	below -50°F (-46°C)	**Zone 5**	-20°F to -10°F (-29°C to -23°C)	**Zone 9**	20°F to 30°F (-7°C to -1°C)
Zone 2	-50°F to -40°F (-46°C to -40°C)	**Zone 6**	-10°F to 0°F (-23°C to -18°C)	**Zone 10**	30°F to 40°F (-1°C to 4°C)
Zone 3	-40°F to -30°F (-40°C to -34°C)	**Zone 7**	0°F to 10°F (-18°C to -12°C)	**Zone 11**	above 40°F (above 4°C)
Zone 4	-30°F to -20°F (-34°C to -29°C)	**Zone 8**	10°F to 20°F (-12°C to -7°C)		

ACKNOWLEDGMENTS

Photo Credits
A-Z Botanical Collection 34(tc), 46(tr), 50(b), 74(tl), 97(r), 106(b); Heather Angel 61(tc), 62(tl), 112(b), 115(tr), 118(b), 133(tr), 142(l); Gillian Beckett 22, 110(tr,b), 113(b), 115(tl,b); Brian Carter 68(b); Walter Chandoha 151(l); Eric Crichton 13(t), 24(t), 26(tr), 31(tl,b), 37(r), 38(tl), 41(bl), 43(cr), 44(cl), 60, 61(bl), 64(l), 67(l), 70(tl), 78(bl), 79(tc,b), 80(tl), 81(tr,b), 85(tl,b), 86-88, 94, 75(b), 96(b), 98(b), 99(r), 106(tr), 119(b), 121-122, 123(tr), 125, 127(l), 128, 132, 133(tl,b), 136(l,c), 137(l), 138(tl), 128, 132, 133(tl, b), 136(l,v), 138(tl), 139(l), 146(tl), 147(r), 152, 153(b), 154, 155(t), 158(b), 163(r), 164(t), 165(l), 168, 171(tl), 172(tl,tr), 173(tr); Thomas E. Eltzroth 31(tc), 32(r), 71(l), 79(tl), 84(c), 91(l), 127(c), 140(tl); Derek Fell 117(b); Philippe Ferret 11(b), 12(t), 13(b), 172(tc); Garden Picture Library (David Askham) 135(tl), (Brian Carter) 49(tl,tr), 66(t), 148(tr), (C. Fairweather) 162(b), (John Glover), 2-3, 15(t), 28(tr), 33(t), 69(bc), 135(tc), 148(tc), 167(tr), (Neil Holmes), 31(b), 62(tc), 157, 161(b), (Lamontagne) 130(tl), (J.S. Sira) 59(b), 82(r), (Brigitt Thomas) 15(br), (John Wright) 18(b); Bob Gibbons 28(b), 47(b), 148(tl); John Glover 6-8, 14(l), 25(l), 42(l),

45(b), 50(tr), 62(tr), 68(tr), 73(b), 76(r), 78(br), 84(r), 103(r), 120, 126, 129(bl), 136(r), 143(cr, tr), 149(l); David Gould 79(tr), 93(c), 95(t), 96(t), 98(t); Jerry Harper 17(t), 18(tr); Pamela Harper 49(c), 65(r), 66(b), 68(tl), 69(br), 70(b), 71(r), 72, 73(r), 74(tr,b), 77(r), 99(l), 114(tr), 119(t), 146(b), 147(l), 158(l), 159, 161(tl); Saxon Holt 149(r); Lamontagne 18(tl), 18-19(b), 19(t), 21(b), 26(cr), 27(tl), 40(l), 42(tr), 44(br), 48(l), 50(tl), 83(l), 167(b); Andrew Lawson 150; S. & O. Mathews 21(t), 27(tr), 35(cr), 113(t), 153(tl), 155(bl), 158(tr); James McInnis 170(l); Tania Midgley 14(r), 17(b), 20, 26(tl), 27(cr), 34(tl), 39(c), 56(t), 57(b), 63(l), 65(l), 78(t), 80(tr), 89(b), 90, 97(tl), 100(tr), 102(t), 103(l), 138(tr), 153(tr), 155(br), 156(r), 160(t), 161(tr), 166(tl), 171(b); Natural Image (R. Fletcher) 51(r), 55(t), 59(t), (P. Wilson) 34(tr); Clive Nichols front cover, 4-5, 33(b), 69(t), 83(r), 92(r), 100(tl), 109(r), 144; Photo/Nats (Liz Ball) 35(tl), Betsy Fuchs 156(l), (Robert E. Lyons) 23, (Ann Reily) 118(tr), (Laura C. Scheibel) 47(tr), (Virginia Twinan-Smith) 160(b); Photos Horticultural back cover, 1, 10, 11(t), 12(b), 15(bl), 16, 24(b), 25(c), 28(tl), 29, 32(l), 35(tr), 36, 37(l), 38(tr,b), 39(r), 41(t,br), 42(cl), 43(t), 44(t), 45(t), 46(l), 47(tl), 48(r), 52, 54, 55(b), 56(b), 57(b), 58(b), 61(tr), 74(tc), 75, 82(l), 85(tr), 89(tr), 91(tr),

92(l), 93(l), 101, 104, 105(t), 107, 108, 109(l), 110(tl), 111, 112(tl), 114(tl,b), 116, 117(tl), 123(tl,b), 124(tr,b), 127(r), 129(t), 130(b), 134, 135(tr,b), 137(r), 138(b), 140(tr), 141(r), 142(c,r), 143(tl), 146(tr), 148(b), 151(r), 165(r), 169(l), 170(r), 173(b); Harry Smith Collection 25(r), 30, 31(tr), 34(b), 39(l), 40(r), 51(l), 58(t), 61(tl), 63(r), 64(r), 67(r), 69(bl), 70(tr), 73(tl), 76(l), 77(l), 81(tl), 84(l), 89(tl), 93(r),97(b), 100(b), 102(b), 105(b), 106(tl), 112(tr), 117(tr), 118(r), 124(tl), 129(br), 130(r), 131, 139(r), 140(b), 141(l), 145, 162(t), 163(l), 164(b), 166(r), 167(tl), 169(r), 171(tr), 173(tl), 174, 175

Illustrator

Elisabeth Dowle 14; Graphic Chart & Map Co., Inc. 176

Reader's Digest Production
Assistant Production Supervisor: Mike Gallo
Electronic Prepress Support: Karen Goldsmith
Quality Control Manager: Ann Kennedy Harris
Assistant Production Manager: Dexter Street
Book Production Director: Ken Gillet
Prepress Manager: Garry Hansen
Book Production Manager: Joe Leeker
U.S. Prepress Manager: Mark P. Merritt